Crime & Corruption

From Satan to Saint

Attention Authors

'We Convert Fighters into Writers'. It has been the motto of Manas Publications for more than four decades. Our message to the world is that India can win the battle not only by the bullet but also by the pen. There is no dearth of intellectuals in our country, but their knowledge is confined to them only. No sincere effort has been made by any other publisher to channelise their knowledge in national interest. That is why the talent of a large number of intellectuals remains latent. An author transforms his knowledge into a manuscript, and it is our job to spread his/her knowledge by converting it into a beautiful book. For over four decades, Manas has been motivating the intellectuals by publishing their manuscripts and would like to publish your manuscript too. If you or your colleagues have any manuscript ready for publication or are working on it, kindly contact us with detailed synopsis and list of contents. We will transform your work into a valuable publication. If you wish, we can also suggest you the suitable subjects for writing the books related to your area of expertise. Manas is known for its publishing quality and commitments. We take utmost care in production and give wide publicity to the book as well as its author through our national and international distribution network.

Crime & Corruption

From Satan to Saint

Thakur Shailendra Nath

Manas Publications
(We Convert Fighters into Writers)
New Delhi-110002 (INDIA)

MANAS PUBLICATIONS
(We Convert Fighters into Writers)
(Publishers, Library Suppliers, Importers & Exporters)
4402/5-A, Ansari Road (Opp. HDFC Bank)
Darya Ganj, New Delhi-110 002 (India)
Off. 23260783, 23265523, Fax: 011-23272766
E-mail: manaspublications@gmail.com
manaspublications@yahoo.com

ISBN 978-81-7049-481-2
₹ 995/-

Designed at
Manas Publications

Printed in India at
Rajdhani Printers, Delhi
and Published by Mrs Suman Lata for
Manas Publications, 4402/5-A, Ansari Road
(Opp HDFC Bank),
Darya Ganj, New Delhi-110 002 (INDIA)

CONTENTS

	Preface	07-09
1.	Introduction	11-60
2.	Occupy Wall Street Agitation	61-72
3.	Combating Corruption	73-163
4.	Crime Control	164-189
5.	Purification of Mind	190-223
6.	Dissolving Mental Impurity	224-245
7.	Conclusion	246-303
	Index	305

PREFACE

I am pleased to present my book "Crime and Corruption"- before the readers. This book is all about the transformation of human beings, about converting their negative traits into positive qualities to achieve creativity. There are two aspects of looking at things in life. Most people would consider cheating as one of the worst crimes since it affects the victim. There is, however, another way of looking at the same problem. Some may draw inspiration from it, to begin a new life.

India is a developing nation. Presently, reforms have stalled in democratic India, with its freedom of representation and speech, may be because its capacity for consensus building has not caught up with the complexity of its reforms agenda. Taking unpopular decisions while effectively communicating the rationale and winning popular consent is the need of the hour.

People who have contributed to the nation's growth should be commended by all, though most may not require any treatment. We require to cure only those persons who were born in India but have not proved their worth and are the liabilities on the society.

Their mental status should be uplifted. Such persons are hardened criminals, terrorists, smugglers, tax evaders, and are indulged in fraud and corruption. They should be called modern 'Sinners'. Their negative energy is urgently required to be converted to positive one and utilized for creative work. Their irrational thought may be converted to rational thinking. We have a great epic *The Ramayana* written by Rishi Valmiki who was once a robber transformed by the Rishi Narad to be a great poet. The result of transformation of King Ashoka to Boddh Bhikshu is still seen by his everlasting welfare work. Raja Rammohun Roy did not leave any stone unturned in eradicating the `Sati Pratha' by his great social reform. Likewise, corruption in our society can also be uprooted by social awakening backed by strong law.

Neurobiological scientists have made a discovery that may make the reduction of traumatic memories a reality. War veterans, rape victims and other people who have witnessed horrific crime that haunt them may someday have such memories weakened in their brains and trauma reduced to some extent. This has been eliminated during experiment in small snail called Aplysia and neurons in a Petri dish. They discovered that the long term memory for sensitisation in the marine snail can be erased by inhibiting the activity of a specific protein Kinase—a class of molecules that modify proteins by chemically adding phosphate to them.

These days youngsters from nuclear families feel emotionally deprived and seek inner peace through new age methods. Havans, chanting, spiritual cooking, yoga practice and even feeding dogs are in vogue. Night clubs, cafes, social networks, games and gadgets don't provide spiritual satisfaction. Youth find spirituality to be enjoyable, practical and value-adding. They also realize that they need lots of energy, clarity, confidence and concentration of mind not when they are old but right now in their present age. A lot of young people want to make a difference. They want to be rebels with a cause and meditation and spiritual practices help them channellise those thoughts into action. Spirituality tends to give them a sense of comfort and peace. It is the time we live in that are to blame, constant change is creating havoc in personal and work lives. Competition is intense, materialism on the rise. Whether at work or in society people are constantly being judged. In such a scenario, instructions get amplified and weapons in the personal arsenal are never enough. Some try hard in hope of constantly improving themselves by unlocking their limitless potential.

Simply watching the rising sun daily in the morning with pure mind and clear heart, gives wonderful results in the development of one's personality. While watching the sun, one should feel that all the impurities like lies, cheating, fraud, corruption, jealousy, hatred, enmity and other negative thoughts are gradually coming out and all good and positive energy is going inside along with the rays of the sun. The rapid change in behaviour and thinking, one can feel after constant practice for some time. Men have tremendous power; only thing required is to systematically awaken those powers. It all depends on one's capacity, intelligence and sincerity. If we do any work with pure mind and clean heart it always yields fruitful results.

I am indebted to my department and senior officers and colleagues who have provided me necessary help and guidance in writing this book. I am also thankful to Manas Publications, who has agreed to publish this book. The help extended by M/s Gupta Services, Gwalior, in typing of this book cannot be forgotten.

I am indebted to my family members—my wife Prabha, my eldest daughter Anzulica and son-in-law Anunay, and younger daughters Shrutica and Jaishika for their very positive attitude. I would not have found a congenial environment at home for undertaking the onerous task of writing this book under trying times, covering a wide range of complex issues of crime and corruption.

I welcome criticism and suggestions for improving the quality of this book from my readers.

Thakur Shailendra Nath

Chapter 1

INTRODUCTION

Heroes are born or created even at the moment of defeat. Because the meaning of winning is based on a series of defeats. Paradoxical though it may seem, countries are not ruined solely by thieves and criminals. Instead, it is equally ruined by the cowards, lazy men, and women. Having said that, we now move onto today's India and look at what ails the youth and the young India.

What Ails the Youth

Today, India's youths are desperate and are ready to do anything; they will fast unto death, shout slogans, keep vigil for important causes with candle lights, take to the streets, vandalize public facilities, some even lay down their lives too, if somebody gives them hope, arouses their sentiments and convinces them to believe that change is in their hands.

It is this very naiveté of the youth that unscrupulous *netas* seize upon to exploit, to the maximum. But none of these leaders possesses any ideals unlike Mahatma Gandhi or Swami Vivekananda. Corruption and crime go hand in hand. Every concerned citizen should ask themselves. Are we frittering away all the gains that we have made in the past few years? It is a cause of huge worry that our much-hyped reforms are hardly sustainable and the reason behind it should be found out immediately. India can ignore only at its own peril.

There is no one single cause to crime. While we are all responsible for our own actions, it is wrong to hold an individual solely responsible for his misdeeds. There are several factors such as culture, family values, educational, political and economical system, etc, that contribute to the criminal behaviour of an individual. We, as a society, should assume at least partial responsibility on ourselves to remedy the situation, in which criminal minds may breed or thrive.

The underlying cause of crime may be tackled through preventive measures, such as rehabilitating the offenders and offering them an attractive alternative to wean them away from crime. Punishment deals with symptoms of crime, whereas prevention deals with its root cause.

A new solution to contain crimes may be to offer a triple-action formula, just like those much-touted tablets that purportedly attack the disease on three fronts. In a similar way, a triple-action formula for crime would work on three fronts of the social disorder: the source, the symptoms and the malady. Where policy makers and scientists are short of a fix, people should come forward to offer efficient resolution—the crime cure. This cure may be a part of a therapy programme and must be available over the wealth counter (because it offers an attractive alternative, wealth, to stem crimes).

Before thinking up a crime solution that actually works, we need to dig deeper into the root cause of crime. Only then can we find the right solutions that directly attack the source, rather than limiting ourselves to deal with the symptoms through punitive measures. If we want to know the exact cause of crime, it would be necessary to narrow it down to a specific geographic location or region.

People are not bad by nature, but sometimes they are simply too weak to resist the demons that play on their weaknesses. Not everyone is made of steel to defend oneself against the demonic forces like fear, ignorance, hatred, revenge, envy, greed, lust, prejudice, arrogance, ambition and so on.

Though some of us may succeed in resisting them, it is easy to fall prey to such emotions. It takes great courage to overcome these negative forces that dominate us.

There are two important reasons why they rule us completely. Lack of faith and self-confidence in oneself. We lack in courage, tolerance, understanding, forgiveness, honesty, integrity, modesty, generosity, love, compassion and so on. As a result, there is not enough motivation to develop and use them.

Most criminals are physically strong, while they pump up their body muscles, failing to strengthen their mental and emotional muscles. The reason why their strength becomes a weakness is because they are not balanced.

We may do well to learn from the story of the greatest Samurai warrior, Musashi Miyamoto, his journey from being just a tough warrior to a true hero, equally strong on all three fronts: physical, mental and emotional. Underneath all the weaknesses lies a genuine human desire to do well. When we detach ourselves from our source (Inner Power), we find ourselves either in wrong place at wrong time, or in a wrong state of mind, causing us to do the wrong things.

The modern world has just acquired seven deadly sins of our times. They are: Racism, terrorism, drinking, domestic violence, tax evasion, bullying, and bigotry. According to a poll carried out by *CBS Reality*, racism has topped even terrorism. The poll has branded the original sins of wrath, envy, greed, gluttony, sloth, lust and pride as outdated. Today, we are witnessing a `tsunami' of corruption in India.

Lack of proper education causes many to fail to distinguish between right and wrong. Often times the offenders don't think they are doing anything wrong. It seems right from their point of view. Poor judgment is also manifested by them, while thinking they could get away with it.

Being raised in a dysfunctional family, or coming from a disadvantaged background, are not necessarily the only factors that lead one to commit crime. There are millions of people living in a similar situations that don't resort to crime.

Poverty is often blamed for crime. But we are bombarded everyday with materialism. We want more and more material things in our life. Some are willing to do anything, even indulge in crime, to get them. Unemployment is another factor that contributes to crime.

Economically deprived neighbourhoods may breed criminals. Some are sucked into it by the events beyond their control. Poor parenting skills, harsh discipline, lack of parental control, dysfunctional family and alcoholic parents and so on also contribute to breeding of criminals.

Studies have shown that 85 per cent of all children that exhibit behavioural disorders come from homes where they had no fathers. Ninety per cent of all homeless and runaway children and eighty per cent of rapists come from such homes. Seventy per cent of juveniles in state-run institutions come from fatherless homes. Eighty five per cent of all youths in jails grew up in a fatherless homes.

Cold winter nights keep criminals off the streets, leading to a decrease in crime. Crime researchers aver that one of the hidden consequences of global warming will be an increase in street crimes during mild winters. Studies have suggested that warmer climates boost aggression hormones such as epinephrine and testosterone.

Miscarriage of Justice also Leads to Crimes.

According to Federal Bureau of Investigation (FBI) of the USA, the following factors which contribute to crime are:

1. Population density and degree of urbanization.
2. Variations in the composition of population, particularly youth concentration.
3. Stability of population with respect to resident's mobility, commuting patterns and transient factors.
4. Modes of transportation and highway systems.
5. Economic conditions, including median income, poverty level and job availability.
6. Cultural factors and educational, recreational and religious characteristics.
7. Family conditions with respect to divorce and family cohesiveness.
8. Effective strength of law enforcement agencies.
9. Administrative and investigative emphasis of law enforcement.

However, the factors listed above provide no insight into the variables that mould crime across the globe. Many variables, while having significant impact on crime, are not readily measurable or applicable in all locations. In order to make valid assessments of crime, one needs to take into considerations geographic and demographic factors specific to each jurisdiction. The transience of the population, its racial and ethnic makeup, its composition by age and gender, educational levels, and prevalent family structures are all key factors in assessing and comprehending the crime issue.

Playing on their fear of punishment may deter most people, but it is not enough for some criminals. Social welfare is one of the greatest counter measures to keep the unemployed youth from resorting to desperate means. Sports provide an outlet for young men to keep themselves out of trouble.

Mind therapy—spirituality—provides a sense of the higher Truth, a journey from the stressful reality to the splendours of the transcendental world. It helps us to negotiate life's contradictions and paradoxes, inspiring us to find something powerful to overcome our pessimism, distrust and lack of meaning in life, etc.

Yin and Yang

In Chinese philosophy, the concept of yin-yang (which means 'shadow and light'), is used to describe how polar opposites or seemingly contrary forces are interdependent on each other. Yin-Yang forms the basis of many branches of classical Chinese philosophy and science. It also provides an important guideline on which traditional Chinese medicine is largely based, being a central principle in different forms of Chinese martial arts such as *baguazhang, taijiquan* (T'ai chi), and *qigong* (Chi Kung) and of I Ching. Many natural dualties—eg, dark and light, female and male, low and high, cold and hot, water and fire, earth and air—are thought of as manifestations of yin and yang.

You simply can't appreciate a bi-polar condition without understanding the polarity since one defines the other. How can we experience a yin without a yang, white without black or, in the case of heaven, the good without the bad? Pure bliss proffered by religious texts may sound great but without comparison, even bliss becomes blasé.

There is a perception that yin and yang correspond to evil and good. However, in Daoist metaphysics, good/bad distinctions and other dichotomous moral judgments are perceptual and not real and yin-yang is an indivisible whole. In the ethics of Confucianism most notably in the philosophy of Dong Zhongshu, (c. 2nd century BCE), a moral dimension is attached to the idea of yin and yang.

Yin and yang are not opposing forces (dualities), but complementary forces, unseen (hidden, feminine) and seen (manifest, masculine), that interact to form a greater whole, as part of a dynamic system. Everything has both yin and yang aspects as light could not be seen if darkness didn't exist, and shadow cannot exist without light. Either of these aspects may manifest more strongly in a particular object depending on the criterion of the observation. The concept of yin and yang is often symbolized by various forms of the Taijitu symbol, for which it is probably best known in the West.

In Daoist philosophy, yin and yang, arrive in the dàodéjīng in Chapter 42. It becomes sensible from an initial quiescence or emptiness (wuji, sometimes symbolized by an empty circle), and continues moving until quiescence is reached again. For instance, dropping a stone in a calm pool of water will simultaneously raise waves and lower troughs between them, and this alternation of high and low points in the water will radiate outward until the movement dissipates and the pool is calm once more. Yin and yang thus are always opposite and equal qualities. Further, whenever one quality reaches its peak, it will naturally begin to transform into the opposite quality: for example, grain that grows to its full height in summer (fully yang) will produce seeds and die back in winter (fully yin) in an endless cycle.

Yang is the white side with the black dot on it, and yin is the black side with the white dot on it. The relationship between yin and yang is often described in terms of sunlight playing over a mountain and a valley. Yin (literally the 'shady place' or 'north slope') is the dark area occluded by the mountain's bulk, while yang (literally the 'sunny place' or 'south slope') is the brightly lit portion. As the sun moves across the sky, yin and yang gradually trade places with each other, revealing what was obscured and obscuring what was revealed. Yang, by contrast, is fast, hard, solid, focused, hot, dry and aggressive; and is associated with fire, sky, the sun, masculinity and daytime.

Yin-Yang Balance and You

Yin and yang are two sides of dualism. It is the tail and the head of a coin. They exist alongside one another. The head cannot exist without the tail, and vice versa. Everything in this world is a dualism. In it, you can always find yin and yang. The earth we live on is yin, and the sun that brings us warmth is yang. A woman is yin, and a man is yang. Sadness is yin, while joyfulness is yang. Generally, yin is passive, oppressed and feminine. Yang, on the other hand, is active, bright and masculine. Managing yin-yang is something that we have to do all the time. Knowing how the yin and the yang energies can be altered helps us to have a better control of reality. By altering the yin-yang relationship, you can make the energy towards your advantage, or strike a new balance that is are often helpful to all parties involved. Let's look at an example. Imagine that you are in a heated argument. In most cases, we tend to become agitated when the other party begins to argue. This is quite natural. Unfortunately, the heated energy is yang. When you respond with agitation, it is also yang, and the whole situation will get off-balance. Try doing something to avert the 'yang-yang' imbalance, and achieve the 'yin-yang' balance. Instead of rebuttal, stay silent for a moment. See what happens! You are now introducing to the energy field a noticeable level of yin energy. In other words, you are now altering the state of the energy field by lowering the yang energy. If probably managed, a result can be an amicable yin and yang balance, which is beneficial to both parties.

Will O' Wisp

On July 23, 2007, two criminals murdered a woman and her two daughters after entering her home in Cheshire, Connecticut. Both of them were condemned to death. In 2009, however, the Connecticut General Assembly sent legislation to the Governor to abolish the death penalty. The Governor vetoed the proposal citing the jury's recommendation in the case that "there are certain crimes so heinous, so depraved, that society is best served by imposing the ultimate punishment on the criminal."

In *Free Will*, the neuroscientist-philosopher Sam Harris raises a caveat. "Whatever their conscious motives, these criminals cannot know why they are as they are," he writes. "Nor can we account for why we are not like them." Then he performs a thought experiment, "as sickening as I find their behaviour, I have to admit that if I were to trade places with one of these men, atom for atom, I would be him." In other words, if you had the same genes, same environment, and the same life experiences, you too would have acted exactly as (they) did, Harris reiterates. But what if you find that they had brain tumours that accounted for their violent acts? Our moral intuitions would shift dramatically. But isn't a disorder only a special case of physical events giving rise to thoughts and actions?

So "how can we make sense of our lives, and hold people accountable for their choices, given the unconscious origins of our conscious mind?"

To convert a criminal into a honourable citizen it takes more than the fear of punishment. Arts can do wonders in transforming any individual, including criminals. Triple action transition formula uses the power of inspiration to persuade criminals to make a jump to the right side.

Remodelling the system--educational, economic, jurisdiction—is a core necessity. There is a saying that if you want to change others, start by changing yourself. Everything is related and we all are in a way responsible for the way our world is. By transforming the causes (one of which is the system) we can both prevent and reduce crime and corruption and make people from `Satan' to `Saint.'

No doubt, every criminal should be punished, but he also needs to be rehabilitated so that crime may not be repeated. Punishment is good for two reasons: it shows the offender that one cannot commit crimes and get away with it. As a form of prevention—fear of severe punishment is often (but not often enough) the main reason for law-abiding citizens not to end up on the wrong side of the law. However, the question is how severe the punishment should be. Any sentence that is longer than two years can have adverse effect on the convict, apart from the cost for our, taxpayers. Being incarcerated in prison for longer periods of time may prove more difficult to resume normal life for the convict. He might as well resort back to crime. Investing in improving the system instead of accommodating prisoners seems more effective in the long-term.

Both criminals and those on the fringes, can be reformed by being given life solutions for inspiration as alternatives to crime. Providing therapy as psychotherapy, using various art-forms as means to alter human condition and possibly convert a criminal into a honourable citizen. Mind therapy affects positive change and growth in all areas of criminals' life: health, wealth and relationships. It is mainly used to increase insight and judgment, restore balance, release stress, relieve traumatic experiences, boost intellectual, intuitive and perceptual abilities, build better relationships in both private and business life, as well as to find comfort and pleasure.

Indulging in or practising arts can keep individuals out of trouble and provide a good outlet for people expressing emotions and develop creativity that can be channelled into business performance, and monetized. However, there are some cases of art-forms that are counter-productive and induce crime instead, such as certain high-beat music, aggressive films and literature promoting heroes that use violence or other criminal activities to solve problems.

The *Puranas*, which are said to be commentaries on the *Vedas*, list a total of 28 *narakas*, or hells, where sinners are sent to after death by *Yamadharma,* strictly according to the nature and seriousness of their sins. Of these, two are of rather special interest. *Vaitarani,* for instance, is the *naraka* for kings who have violated the edicts of the Sastras. It is actually a river filled with human excreta, urine, blood, hair, bones, nails, flesh, fat and other kinds of unclean substances. There are also said to be various kinds of ferocious beasts in it, so that those who are cast into it are constantly attacked and mauled by them. Additionally, sinners have to serve out the terms of their punishment by feeding themselves upon the contents of this river.

Sarameyasanam, on the other hand, is reserved for those found guilty of acts like inflammatory speech and actions, poisoning of food, mass slaughter and ruining the country. In this *naraka*, nothing but the flesh of dogs is available as food. In addition, there are 700 extra dogs which are as ferocious as leopards that attack the sinners from all sides and tear their flesh from their bodies. In contrast, the 26 other *narakas* reserved for murderers, rapists, unfaithful partners, people indulging in unnatural sex and those who insult Brahmins or partake of meals without worshipping gods or honouring guests, almost pale in comparison. Such offenders are usually only beaten, burnt or flogged.

French scientist Luc Montagnier, the 2008 Nobel prize winner for discovery of the HIV virus, has shown that it is possible to replicate and transfer DNA strands from one test tube to another by passing a low level electromagnetic (EM) radiation of 7 Hz.

This is almost like teleportation of life and, if proved correct, could be one of the most revolutionary discoveries of modern times.

Body is repaired, rejuvenated and kept healthy by production and replication of good DNA. Also, in deep meditation, the brain produces EM waves called *theta* and *alpha* waves ranging from 4-12 Hz but mostly in the range of 7-8 Hz. Possibly, deep and regular meditation helps in rejuvenation of the body by helping replicate good DNA.

Patanjali Yoga says: "By *sanyam* or deep meditation on the elements, a yogi gets a perfect body of beauty; grace, strength and hardness of a thunderbolt." Meditation is like an elixir of life. Deep meditation is basically focussing the mind on a single thought for a long time. Patanjali describes it as *sanyam* or a combination of contemplation, meditation and *samadhi* and when all these three things are achieved, it's a complete mastery.

More scientific studies have shown the direct effect of meditation on DNA and gene expression, that meditation helps in delaying the process of ageing by increasing telomerase activity. Telomerase is an enzyme which repairs the DNA. Chromosomes have caps of repetitive DNA called telomerase at their ends. Every time cells divide, their telomerase shorten, which eventually prompt them to stop dividing and die. This results in the ageing process. However, telomerase enzyme stops the shortening and meditation helps in increasing the activity of this enzyme.

Another Harvard University study showed that meditation directly affects genes by switching them on and off to combat the bad effects of free radicals, which are produced when we are emotionally and physically stressed out. All these have proved the positive effect of meditation at the cellular level in the human body, though the exact mechanism is still unknown. Montagnier's work may hold the key to this puzzle.

Similarly, during dreaming process the brain produces 4-7 Hz *theta* waves. Research has shown that deep sleep and dreaming is essential for our well-being and helps us in consolidating our daytime memories by removing some of the frivolous ones. However, it is quite possible that besides the memory consolidation, 4-7 Hz EM waves may also help in rejuvenating the body and mind by enhancing the replication of DNA.

The DNA teleportation experiment has also showed that DNA template was teleported to another test tube containing only water; that low level radiation of 7 Hz produced a memory in water which matched the DNA molecule. Water with its unique weak hydrogen bond can form almost infinite number of structures and it seems the low level radiation simply helped in this process. The ability of water to form `memory structures' under external influence could also be the basis of *achaman*—a ritual of sipping water after reciting Vedic mantras that is believed to have therapeutic effect on its practitioner. Chanting creates a `memory structure' in water, somewhat like homoeopathic medicine where high potencies don't have original medicine in it but the `memory structure' of the medicine persists in water.

Islam

Islam lays great emphasis on learning, for it is learning that leads to intellectual and spiritual development. However, by virtue of our limited lifespan, it is well-nigh impossible for an individual to know everything there is to know. Therefore, taking lessons from not only what one encounters in one's life but also from the experiences of others is crucial to one's growth. Learning may be acquired for its own sake, but it also causes one to lead a life that is meaningful and fulfilling, one that brings satisfaction and peace. Individuals learn from other individuals. We learn from nature, as we must. However, that is not all. We can learn lessons from Satan, too. Satan, according to Islam, is like one of us, that is, another of God's creations and Satan was created even before human beings were created. After having created man, God asked Satan to bow to Adam.

The *Quran* gives an account of this first encounter with Adam, the first man as well as the first Prophet, and Satan: "When we said to the angels, 'Bow down before Adam', they all bowed except Satan." (2:34). In refusing to obey God's command, Satan yielded to his ego and became arrogant. Ego, which has been at the root of most problems faced by human beings, is considered an evil. But we should appreciate that ego, a part of nature, is not all that bad.

Ego has its positive and negative points. From ego comes determination, the ability to make decisions. And without determination we accomplish little. Conversely, a negative point of ego is that it can lead one to act with arrogance. This prevents us from thinking objectively and so we could become victims of our own failings. Such a fate can be avoided by effectively managing the ego. We should not only learn the art of ego management, but must also refrain from hurting the egos of others. More often than not, one's ego is dormant. It is better to leave it in that state, for provocation of the ego can cause undesirable results.

It is this ability to manage potentially explosive situations which maintains normalcy, thus leaving our peace of mind undisturbed. It enables us to work towards higher goals, without having our attention diverted towards unproductive activities.

Two Birds

The famous twin birds' verse from the Rig Veda. "Two birds, close companions, beautiful of wing, cling to one common tree," says the Vedic seer (*Dwa suparna sayuja sakhaya samanam vrikshyam*). The birds in the verse are probably orioles, writes KN Dave in his *Birds in Sanskrit Literature,* considering the epithet '*suparna*' and the fact that one of the birds eats figs from the branch while the other is merely content to watch on. In contrast, the great Vedic commentator Sayana looked upon the two birds as a metaphor for the vital and the supreme spirit, both dwelling in the same body. The vital spirit enjoys the fruit or rewards of actions while the Supreme Spirit is supposed to be a passive spectator. Other scholars have interpreted the term two fair-winged birds (*dwa* suparna) fancifully as "two species of soul; day and night; the Sun and Moon and even as stars or as sacred metres." The Vedic verse itself, however, clarifies that the bird that eats is the individual immersed (*nimagno*) in the world and, hence, has sorrow. When it sees the other golden-winged detached companion sitting poised upon the branch, its sorrow passes as well. Shaking off from its wings both sin and virtue, the golden bird reaches its own supreme identity. As Rabindranath Tagore said, both birds are within us: the objective one with its business of life; the subjective one with its disinterested joy of vision. Their merger results into a Unified Whole.

Moreover, from this one event in the history of creation—Satan's refusal to bow to Adam, there is more to be learnt. What does it show? It reveals that Satan had become ungrateful. That is, he paid attention only to what he did not have and not to what he had. For example, when God created Satan, He bestowed upon him many powers, yet it was not appreciated. Satan, therefore, not only failed to manage his ego, but also became ungrateful to God. He forgot that though he did not have one per cent of all that he wanted, he still had ninety-nine per cent ingratitude which is the result of an unawareness of many blessings that God has bestowed on us. It is only when we focus on what we have not been granted that we grow negative and begin to complain incessantly. It is at such moments that we need to stop and rediscover the blessings that have been bestowed upon us. This alone will help us to cope with life's challenges.

For a nation with a glorious past, India's mood is unbecoming of her. For at least a year, we have berated ourselves and behaved as if we had forgotten our purpose. Little wonder, then, that industrial growth has slumped, investor confidence has evaporated, the stock markets have fallen and inflation has risen alarmingly. As growth has slowed, the fiscal situation has worsened. The Indian economy, it seems, is caught in a downward spiral. The government has been plagued by corruption, scams and exacerbated by the anti-graft crusade launched by Anna Hazare.

To make matters worse are the sovereign debt crisis in Europe and faltering economy of the US. For the *aam admi,* an under performing economy and a sluggish government spells more economic troubles. Professionals fear they may not be able to afford a better lifestyle despite their hard work. Millions of rural and urban poor, hit hard by runaway prices and job losses, face a bleak future, if the conditions don't improve. For corporate India, gloomy economic situation hinders its ability to tap fully into India's market potential and compete meaningfully on the global stage. No doubt we are passing through an uncertain phase, but time and again we have shown a remarkable ability to surprise ourselves and the rest of the world. This is because, for all our apparent differences, we are bound together by the harmony of Indianness. When we rise up together, we are a sight to behold.

The Sam Pitroda-led National Innovation Council has published a report on its one-year achievements. There's a lot to be said for its efforts. It plans to support, with technology, innovators and finance, skill clusters like the auto components belt at Faridabad or Agartala's bamboo industry. It plans to map local cultures, histories and ecologies, give fellowships and promote new thinking in schools and colleges. Connecting India's 2,50,000 *panchayats* with high-speed fibre optic and a broadband network is a good idea, as is the plan to allow India's nearly 800 MPs to use part of their area development funds to reward local innovators.

An India Inclusive Innovation Fund (IIIF), with an ultimate corpus of ₹5,000 crores, will promote innovators in areas like health, education, farming and handicrafts. There's a lurking suspicion that even if some of these measures work, others will choke under the dead weight of government. After all, the administration hasn't managed to figure out a relatively easy problem like devising a secure and efficient internet operation to be used within central government offices. The biggest problem dogging Indian innovators is the difficulty of getting funds to finance research, development and products.

Our universities don't foster enough cutting edge research. Entrepreneurs and researchers with bright ideas find themselves starved for finance and give up after a while, or find personal sources of funds to sustain their work. India doesn't have the hierarchy of investors from early-stage angels to late stage private equity players who are willing to take risks on start-ups, unlike Silicon Valley that has in large enough numbers. Banks look for multi-year sales or profit records and strong balance sheets before lending. They make money lending to established businesses, leaving innovators empty handed. The IIIF might bring some welcome funds and fill some gaps, but to support long term innovation, the financial sector needs to develop in size, articulation and variety.

Formula 1 Grand Prix in India was controversial in a country that still struggles with some of the worst poverty in the world. But it did point to the dynamism and potential that still waits to be unlocked in the country, if it can be done equitably and with vision. Many outside observers were startled by the way the anti-corruption movement derailed the government's own agenda. But the distance between the Formula 1 race and the reality for India's poorest in part explain it. What is India's finish line, and who gets to cross it? It is a debate that is not unique to India, but the Indian experience is, as ever, unique. The accountability of the haves to the have-nots is a global question, integral in many ways to the debate about globalization itself. In a nation that is home to a third of the world's poor living below $1.25 a day, the disparities are visible and obvious. High-profile cases such as the sale of 2G telecom spectrum are a reminder that governments must always prove it beyond doubt that they are acting fully in the interest of its citizens. Fall in that, and the risk is that the public wish a plague on the houses of both politics and business.

Amongst businesses—Indian and foreign alike—there is a concern that the momentum of the last decade may be faltering. A slow-moving bureaucracy and big business are both at odds with dynamic entrepreneurship. There is a concern that the exceptional growth of the last decade is in spite of, rather than because of, government policies. But this does not have to be the case. The Cabinet recently approved India's National Manufacturing Policy, aimed at developing manufacturing from sixteen per cent to twenty five per cent of GDP. Given India's somewhat unique development pattern, with a move to services without the transition through manufacturing, it is vital for future productivity that this strategy is implemented. Incorporating the vast informal economy, creating skilled jobs and lifting people out of poverty are all drivers which point to the need for decisive leadership and quicker policy action. With some nine million new job seekers entering workforce every year, India can ill-afford ignore it. The right strategy focused on areas where the government can act as a facilitator to business—investing in skills and education, science and research base, and infrastructure is precisely the role for government. Building an economy's capabilities rather than owning or running business is the better role for the state in the 21st century.

Hand-in-hand with domestic industrial development, India needs to assert its international trade agenda. The two are mutually reinforcing: both require openness, both benefit from greater collaboration and the free flow of ideas and investment. This has to be right, not only with Pakistan, but with Bangladesh, Sri Lanka, and into south-east and central Asia. Levels of trade openness and integration are surprisingly low in the region and it will take strong economic and political leadership to promote a free, inclusive trade agenda.

The V-shaped flight formation of migratory birds such as geese serves a purpose: all the birds fly in the upward from the wing-tip vortices of the bird ahead. This helps each bird in supporting its own weight in flight by achieving a reduction of induced drag by up to 65 per cent that can increase their range by 71 per cent more, if they fly on their own. If a bird strays, it suddenly feels the increased air resistance and quickly gets back in again. However, the lead bird of the flock, along with those at, the extreme trailing ends, does not benefit from the aerodynamics of the formation and, thus, tends to tire faster. In order to spread the fatigue evenly; these birds deliberately fall away from the formation at regular intervals and get into selective mid-sections while other birds take up their original point and pole positions. The V-formation also has another advantage. It allows all the birds to remain in constant visual contact with one another and communicate among themselves. For example, if one bird becomes sick or injured and drops out, two other birds immediately peel away to help. They usually remain with it till the bird recovers or dies before rejoining the flock or getting into another one. There are big lessons to be learnt in this about leadership, unity of purpose, communal existence, sharing responsibilities and the importance of teamwork which are way too obvious. In reality, only the combat air forces of the world have successfully assimilated them. Their strike aircraft almost invariably fly in V-formations.

Salt on Poverty's Wounds

There are three ways in which a person gets a headline right: deep thought, instinct, and good luck. Of the three, instinct might prove to be the most reliable, since it does not permit space for doubt. The favourite word used to describe the cessation of hostilities between two at a particularly volatile moment in their war, was `truce'. The Oxford dictionary defines `truce' with its usual pithy perfection: "An agreement between enemies or opponents to stop fighting for an agreed period of time." A truce does not signify the end of war, and it isn't.

The artillery of Delhi's intra-party wars is disinformation; the battlefield is mostly newsprint; the first casualties are bureaucrats, particularly those under consideration for some choice posting. There is an old Indian saying from the feudal days: when you want to destroy a king, first kill his parrot. That is the fate of officials close to ministers; they get trapped in poison weeds planted by the opposition. As in any war, the circumference of damage is inevitably far larger than the circle of target. Institutions get battered, as much as individuals. When critical ministries like Finance and Home are involved, government becomes dysfunctional. This is not sniper fire, this is civil war, symptom of a much more serious malaise.

Stability in power is not merely an attribute of numbers, and levels of support in the legislature. An American President does not need a majority in the Senate, but Barack Obama's mooring has come unhinged. There is no threat to present government tenure yet, but its coalition has lost its centre of gravity. Its majority is sustained by the compulsion to postpone accountability, although in a democracy this cannot be an indefinite luxury. Survival may be certain, but governance becomes uncertain. When a government loses discipline and direction, it can inflict self-damage in the most curious, if revealing, ways.

The Planning Commission, to offer the most recent instance, has poured salt upon poverty's wounds with a fervour that the electorate will remember long after feuds fade into the subconscious. His economists must have done the math: calculated the minimal calorie requirements for survival, costed it and emerged with the now infamous ₹32 definition of daily urban need. Statistics are a trap in an insensitive mind. They may be necessary for policy, but they must be refurbished by the human touch in politics. Here is a statistics that Planning Commission might consider worth a thought or two. Its officials live in the most exclusive residential zone of India, or perhaps Asia, in one of the strings of multi-acre palaces built for the elite of the ruling class in Lutyen's Delhi. If the Government had ever thought of selling its officers bungalow, it would fetch ₹400 crores or more. Economists in the Planning Commission have computers which can count and divide. They would calculate that every blade of grass in officer expansive, grace-and-favour residence is worth more than ₹32.

General Jack Jacob, our living hero of the Bangladesh war, has said cockney ditty British soldiers under his command would sing during the Second World War. It's the rich who get the pleasure, it's the poor who take the blame, It's the same the whole world over, isn't it a bloody shame? Within months of victory in this great world war, these impoverished cockneys threw out Winston Churchill, the genius who saved his nation, in an election that became an avalanche, because they were tired of taking the blame while the nabobs drank champagne. Democracy hath no fury like the poor scorned.

The popular outrage over the official definition of poverty at abysmally low levels of daily income, of ₹26 in rural areas and ₹32 in urban areas, assumes the state will deny basic services to a household whose income is above the figure. This appears to be totally erroneous. There is no mechanism in the hands of the government to ascertain income or expenditure to identify the 'poor' on the ground. The poverty data generated at aggregate level is only useful for intergovernmental transfers or allocations under anti-poverty programmes and it is well known that these are determined also by several other socio-political considerations. The state governments would identify the poor on the ground based on indicators proposed by committees for rural and urban areas respectively. In case the total number thus generated is higher than that obtained through the Tendulkar formula, the former must be accepted. This does not mean that there should be no cap on the number of targeted beneficiaries in heavily-subsidized anti-poverty programmes. It is a tragedy that 400 million people in the country do not have even the income defining the official poverty line when the government promises a dream of inclusive growth. Tendulkar Committee does not dispute that, despite decline in the percentage of the poor over the past decades, the number of persons not having the normative calorie intake of 2,400 and 2,100 calories in rural and urban areas respectively, has not gone down, Scholars like Sukhatme, Minhas, Deaton, etc, have, nonetheless, criticized 'calorie fundamentalism' noting that people on their own are opting for lower calorie intake due to changed consumption habit, without jeopardizing their health. However, even if the revised norm of 1,800 calories of the Food and Agriculture Organization (FAO) is accepted, hunger and malnutrition in the country would remain a matter of anxiety.

The decline in infant mortality rate (IMR) has had a setback in recent years. Reporting of ailments tends to be less in low expenditure categories and among scheduled caste and tribes, particularly in rural areas, due to their lack of affordability of treatment. What adds to their misery is that only 20 per cent of their ailments are treated in government hospitals and the hospitalisation in public institutions has gone down from 60 per cent to 38 per cent over the period of last one and a half decade. The decline in enrolment at school starts at the age of 11 and at 14, about 45 per cent of the children are out of the educational system. Despite the calorific basis scaffolding the poverty line being dismantled by the Planning Commission as also several eminent economists, the relationship of calories deficiency below 2,000 calories per day with malnutrition, IMR and education of the mother is well established with the data from National Health and Family Survey. Given this scenario, there is an urgent need to compel the government to address the problems of these 400 millions by strengthening the public delivery of food, healthcare and education.

The figure of ₹32 is hardly adequate to meet the necessities of life but the same was not there in early 1970s. The real problem is not that the government in the past addressed the problems of only those below this line but actually did not address them adequately. And, most certainly did not succeed, if it did. The myth that a researcher, administrator or activist, who supports, anti poverty programmes with a larger canvass and claims a higher percentage of people to be poor is more progressive than one who is focused on a well-identified smaller group, needs to be dismissed. The government must focus on households that do not get enough food, cannot send and retain their children in school, leave their ailments untreated, as their first priority. Acceptance of the proposition that it is impossible to identify the destitute and poor from the others and therefore cannot be targeted with differential levels of subsidy due to rampant corruption implies defeat of the system of governance. Similarly, the argument made by some, under supposedly human right framework, that the public policy must only create institutional and legal framework to guarantee everyone the basic needs and do away with targeted programmes, is rooted in the interest of the middle class who have been pressuring the state to open the doors of anti-poverty programmes for them. There have been failures in 'managing negative perceptions' of the people regarding the functioning of the government, as admitted at the highest level but there have been real failures as well. All these have led to distrust and suspicion in public mind for the state apparatus. This explains why the figure of poverty line, which has gone not only unchallenged but almost unnoticed for the last four decades, is being used to question the intent and seriousness of the government in addressing the needs of the poor.

The Suresh Tendulkar Committee actually raised the number of people under the poverty line from 22 per cent (the Planning Commission estimate) to 32 per cent. Thus, another 120 million people were considered poor. Another major improvement that it had discarded the below poverty line (BPL)/above poverty line (APL) system of assessment in which the poorest of the poor (BPL) were earning ₹10 per day and the not-so-poor (APL) were earning above it, but below ₹14. Thus, millions of poor souls were hovering between poverty lines.

The system now accepted by the Planning Commission, with adverse media and civil society reactions, is actually a major improvement. Irrespective of where you fix the poverty line, the government will need to create additional funding to the tune of about 2 per cent of GDP just for food, drinking water and sanitation. Another 2 per cent of GDP is required for increased spending on health, without which we will only be perpetuating existing poverty. So, an additional 4 lakh crores needs to be generated. There is absolutely no way the government can raise or spend that sort of money without getting into a debt trap unless it raises taxes and recovers revenue foregone to corporate. But will the government muster the requisite political will to do this? Corporate and HNIs will have to do their bit, a la Warren Buffett, if we have to eradicate poverty.

In a country like India, with vast inequalities and disparities, subsidies cannot be wished away. However, the costs of subsidies have to be clearly and transparently borne upfront. Subsidies cannot be administered by sleight of hand. The present forms of subsidies have created disparities not only across sectors but between segments of the same sector. They create vast opportunities for arbitrage and rents, and have made some grow at the cost of others. More dangerously, by completely distorting price signals, they are now severely limiting long-term access to fuel supplies. The administration of subsidies through price controls does little to solve far more pressing problems that have to do with issues of access and entitlements to energy resources. Therefore, even where we recognize the need for subsidies, we need to overhaul them to address issues of access directly. Today, in the face of global recession, we face a double jeopardy. The impact of the slowdown threatens our export markets. It puts a big question mark on how far our service sector-led growth will take us down the road to employment generation for the millions entering our workforce each year.

If recovery is a longer haul, the only solution will be to stimulate the domestic economy by higher spending on infrastructure. This only can sustain growth in employment and mitigate the effects of slowdown across the world. Let us recognize that in the coming time, our efforts to sustain even a decent modicum of growth is going to be severely hampered by our ability to access energy.

Who Cares for the Poor

The poor in India have two enemies greater than even abject poverty: the Government and anti-poverty activists. Neither is focused on genuinely eradicating poverty. In Government, The Planning Commission has the task of counting India's poor. They also have the task of monitoring the efficacy of the Government's anti-poverty programmes. At the controversial poverty line estimated at a per capita daily expenditure of ₹32 in urban areas (and ₹26 in rural areas), around 32 per cent of Indians live below the poverty line. In 2006, the number below the poverty line estimated using the same methodology, but different cut-offs, was 37 per cent. Planning Commission has a vested interest in showing that poverty has declined in the last five years, even if that requires counting out millions of poor households. Any other conclusion would be a damning indictment of a Government that deliberately fashions itself as pro-poor.

But beware of the outraged crusaders. The loudest noises of

protest at the ₹32 estimate came from civil society activists some of who also double up as members of the quasi-Government National Advisory Council. That intervention has ensured that the poverty bar will be raised. Anti-poverty crusaders in a civil society have a vested interest in high poverty numbers. It gives them a *raison d'etre*, and generous funding, for the pro-poor NGOs they run. Those on the NAC have an additional vested interest. With a little help they can use the excuse of high poverty to exercise enormous political clout and pressurize the Government into committing more funds for dubious and ineffective anti-poverty schemes. For band of cynical left-of-centre advisors, the poor are an important vote bank which they believe can be easily captured by generous handouts from the state coffers, whether loan waivers or employment guarantees.

The ardent liberalizers believe that economic growth will eventually lift everyone out of poverty. It hasn't. The NAC believe that 100 days of work and cheap food are sufficient. They are not. In fact, populist handouts have lulled the Government into believing that they have done enough for the poor. The reality is that NREGA is not a job's programme. It's merely a social safety net, and a very thin one, at that.

Countries like South Korea and Taiwan eradicated poverty in a single generation. It requires economic growth. India has achieved that. It also requires people to have proper, productive jobs. That in turn requires investment in human capital: education and skills. A largely uneducated population living off farming is never going to escape poverty. But nobody is outraged by this reality. No one, either in Government or in the quasi-Government has put his political weight behind long-term solutions to poverty. Mandarins and activists can fight all they want over where to draw the poverty line but India will remain poor until it invests in its people.

But it is entirely stupid to wonder whether, irrespective of how it plays out, the 2G controversy has produced some positive results. The main worry is that the 2G controversy is creating instabilities. But instability by itself is not a negative concept in a political economic context. There can be positive instabilities. 2G has produced some, and it's not an unimpressive list. The now-famous 2G note has been widely seen as having brought to public domain some dissonances in the party's and the government's top-rung leadership. But politics doesn't need to look pretty. The party may well benefit from instability at the top if that produces some sort of leadership test: who can best lead the government into the next election. 2G has also strengthened the competitive characteristics of the leaders' market that's a question the Opposition party may have to answer sooner rather than later. The elaborate but unconvincing fudge created by the opposition on the leadership question, will be tested most severely by brighter prospects of political advantage. There's certainly a case to be made that some of the 2G-engendered judicial interventions/ innovations need to be carefully assessed. Is the Supreme Court too actively involved, is court monitoring of a CBI investigation really desirable, is the trial court too harsh on its bail-or-jail calls—these are better questions to ask than those provoked by judicial in-activism. Even the fact that there are legally-informed doubts over the strength of the prosecution's case in 2G proceedings, is a good outcome. The 2G case will likely set useful precedents, not just legally, but in terms of official investigative procedure as well, in a country that will almost certainly witness more high-profile corruption cases. A similar argument, about setting useful markers for future, can be made about the complicated subset of 2G that involves the relationship between government policy and government revenue. The alleged 2G scam is the manner in which the ex-telecom minister allocated licences. The 2G licence policy, one that did not aim to maximize revenue, should be a separate issue. Many think they are not but they should be. No one, minimally informed of the multi-disciplinary nature of governance, can argue that getting the maximum price for 'natural' and 'national' resources always ensures the greatest good.

It can be, and has been, argued that keeping entry costs in telecom low increases customer base and, by giving, government a healthy revenue share, it's not responsible either.

It is vital that we keep making the distinction between policy and revenue and do not accept that revenue maximization is the only government goal whenever policy and revenue are on the table. The 2G controversy, especially the legal side of it, may well end up sharpening this debate and bring clarity to the distinction. Future policy decisions on a wide range of sectors may benefit from that. Those sceptical of the above positive instabilities will probably laugh at this one, the 2G controversy has also made the argument for good economic governance stronger. True, that sounds funny when set against loud complaints about what everyone is calling the Centre's policy paralysis. Ever since its May 2014 election victory and much before the 2G story became big, seemed to have decided that fiscally-backed social-economic engineering could all but replace supposedly metropolitan, big-ticket policy initiatives. Nothing has shown up the hollowness and the danger of that argument more than the 2G controversy.

Bribe giver should not Get Amnesty

Civil society movements against corruption are playing a hypocritical game by targeting alleged bribe takers, while it is well known that bribe givers have also greatly prospered by paying money. The high-pitched tone of the anti-corruption movement has effectively ensured that very little attention is paid to the elitist manner in which the problem of corruption has been framed. The elitism is perhaps best seen in the effective distinction that is sought to be made between the bribe giver and the bribe taker. While the bribe taker is painted in the darkest of colours, the bribe giver is treated as the victim of the exercise. Participants in the agitation have no compunction about admitting that they have been bribe givers. The fact that they have gained some benefit by paying the bribe is conveniently ignored. Indeed, this distinction has even led to a demand that the bribe giver be granted amnesty so that he can expose the bribe taker.

There are two types of bribe givers in India: out of compulsion and a nexus between two parties for mutual benefit. Such a law will mostly protect the first type, but will not clean up the nexus. What we need is heavy punishment for both the giver and the taker.

If a person gains just his due, a bribe giver is a victim and doesn't deserve punishment. If a person/company pays a bribe for personal gain, it is a graver crime. Here, a bribe giver is to be punished and the quantum decided by harm done to another person/company or the nation.

The protection of the bribe giver that is implicit in the movement is also reflected in its choice of the types of corruption it is willing to target. It is now widely believed that there is a section of India's business community that has benefited substantially by its willingness to bribe its way to the top.

The movement does not find it necessary to target this group. It also does not hesitate to flaunt its stars without putting them under any pressure to speak of the black money that is widely believed to rule their industry. The issue, then, is not a corruption per se, but a battle that has been effectively defined as one between a section of the elite and the political class. And this battle is rooted in a longer-lasting conflict that has emerged in Indian political economy; a conflict between the policy-making elite and the elected politician.

This conflict arises from a fundamental dualism in the nature of Indian governance. In choosing to go in for a democracy in a largely illiterate population at the time of Independence, the then political leadership could not rely on the elected representatives to understand the nuances of policy making. This task was handed over to a new elite that was at one time westernized but has become less so over the years. Political Party sought to address the conflict between elected representatives and policymakers by creating a new institutional device. The anti-defection law ensured that elected representatives had to vote for the policies the leadership chose or face losing their seats. The elected representatives were forced to vote for policies even if it went against the interests of those in their constituencies who voted them to power.

Government recognized the inherent instability of, such an arrangement and sought to defuse the situation by creating MP's Local Area Development Fund. This fund did help MPs support specific causes in their constituencies, but it was not large enough to guarantee re-election. The additional funds were, then to be augmented through means that were not always legal. While the leadership did not openly approve of this corruption, it did little to suggest strong disapproval. The elected representatives were expected to be comfortable in their corrupt ways without bothering about policy making.

This arrangement began to break down with the coming of coalition politics at the Centre. Regional parties claimed important ministries. And then they did the unthinkable of actually making policy, without the permission of the policy making elite. A minister went so far as to actually defy the policy making elite and come up with a telecom policy that made mobile telephony in India among the cheapest in the world. It created a mobile revolution that ensured that ordinary workers even in rural areas could be accessible to potential employers.

This revolutionary change could not be tolerated by the policy-making elite without losing control of policy making. The fact that corruption had now become the main form of political financing came in handy. The magnitude of corruption was then further exaggerated by getting the CAG to effectively define the government as a profit making body. Any sale for less than the highest price was then treated as corruption, even if the benefits of a lower price were passed on to consumers.

The policy-making elite may have won this round, but the elected representatives are not going to simply go away. As the policy-making elite fights to keep in place a system where they have the power while the elected representatives are accountable, it will not hesitate to use the brush of corruption to tar every political institution. It is, after all, their last stand against India's democratization.

The Right to Reject

Ordinarily, the Right to Vote is exercised by the citizens to elect a representative who will represent the needs and aspirations of the people. It is, therefore, rather ironical to debate whether the voters should have the right to reject all the contesting candidates in the form of protest votes.

The right to recall and the right to reject would have a telling effect on our polity. The former would effectively wipe out the false illusion of immunity that our elected representatives currently flaunt, unmindful of their dismal performance during their tenures. However, the right to reject `all candidates' in a particular constituency will not have the desired effect. Indian voters generally vote for a specific party and not necessarily the candidate. Often the party may be the right choice, if not the candidate fielded. The right to reject should clearly identify the object of the rejection-party or candidate. Compilation of such information will provide crucial data to any political party about how many votes it has effectively lost by fielding an unworthy candidate.

Electoral reforms of several strands and layers have to be

considered and reviewed. The electorate needs to have a system that can clearly reflect its choice of a representative. Presently, the electorate does not fully participate in exercising its franchise; many among them feel the list of candidates offered, by political parties or the independents does not adequately meet with their aspirations. In this background, the right to reject—presumably, all candidates in the ballot paper—is suggested as a means to weed out 'unworthy' candidates. This is a simple and easy suggestion, no doubt attractive too. But it raises questions about its effectiveness in a system where, as it is, a substantial number of voters stay away. Therefore, does this, by implication, call for compulsory voting? Otherwise, how do we get to know the choice of those who, having come to know of the available candidates, make up their minds and stay away from voting? Hence, in the age of electronic voting machines (EVMs), in the absence of compulsory voting and in order to capture those not approving of available candidates, we need a 'none of the above' button. Even this may not guarantee the participation of those in the 'staying away' list. The successful implementation of compulsory voting too is yet to be fully tested.

Experts feel that online voting may be a useful idea. Confidence and faith in the use of technology in electoral matters is still in the nascent stage, the worldover faith in the EVMs as a fool-proof method for election purposes is yet to be completely established, all though the EVMs are widely being used. Therefore, the online idea, shall remain only so for some more time.

It may be useful to note that while rejection can be a powerful tool of disapproval, it is not the same as recall. In a multi-party parliamentary democracy, even recall will have to be fine tuned, so that the objective is not defeated. Cynicism cannot drive reforms. Building pressure on political parties to keep away from unworthy candidates is painfully slow. However, it shall be positive and more suitable for a sustainable reformatory action.

Most of the emerging representative democracies seem to

suffer from having elected representatives who do not seem to fulfil the criterion of representing the people's needs and aspirations. This is partly because the party system "in these democracies is often distorted. Many of them function on feudal basis without internal democracy. In many political parties, the office bearers hold the position not by virtue of their popularity within the party, determined on the basis of free internal party elections, but owe their positions to a coterie of leaders having a stranglehold of the party. Another reason for the poor quality of electoral candidates is due to faulty electoral system such as the First Post. The Post system adopted as a colonial legacy.

The need for electing good and competent representatives in a democracy is too obvious, especially in the context of varied economic and social challenges in modern governance. The failure to have competent representatives in the legislatures has resulted in many suggestions being made to improve the quality of representatives. One of the suggestions considered by many countries is the 'Right to Reject' the contesting candidates by the voters if they are not acceptable.

In India, due to the faulty functioning of political parties and defective electoral system with votes being split, there is a justifiable and immediate demand to introduce the Right to Reject—known as Negative Vote—as a method to compel the parties to nominate better candidates in view of delays in other electoral reforms. Public interest litigation on this demand is pending before the Supreme Court. While the government has reservations citing implementation difficulties, the Election Commission, earlier supported this proposal before the court in the larger interests of electoral democracy as the implementation difficulties can be easily overcome.

The Election Commission has signalled thumbs down to Team Anna's proposal for the inclusion of 'Right to Reject' and 'Right to Recall' clauses in election rules. Chief Election

Commissioner SY Quraishi said the proposal could destabilize the political process. The CEC's views was shared by several other experts, who saw the proposal as unworkable in a multi-party democracy. In a multi-cornered contest, not many candidates get more than 50% votes. A decision to treat anything less as a rejection of the electorate would be impractical. The CEC said the Right to Reject, in this context, will lead to frequent elections, something that the country can ill afford. "Our main fear is that if we start rejecting all candidates, we will have another election and people already complain of election fatigue," Quraishi said. Anna Hazare has been demanding annual performance audits of MPs, Right to Recall elected representatives and Right to Reject candidates contesting elections. In a letter to the PM, Anna had sought his views on these demands. "There should be an option 'none of the above' in the electronic voting machine and if this option gets the maximum votes, then a re-election should be ordered," Anna had said in his letter to the PM. The PM had said that political consensus was required to act on these suggestions. "Our government is actively considering various proposals related to electoral reforms. Among the proposals being considered is the 'Right to Reject' which you have mentioned. In a democratic society, politic consensus is necessary on some issues. We want to discuss several proposals on electoral reforms with all political parties and act on proposals on which there is broad agreement."

Coalgate

The political debate on 'Coalgate' is likely to be a zero-sum game unless it includes discussion on a rational policy. The warring political parties share a proportion of blame in the scam. Cancelling all coal block allotments will be disastrous for our already critical power situation. Corruption in allotment of coal blocks should not go unpunished, but there is some merit in the argument that the objective of allotment of coal blocks to corporate bodies, especially for power stations, should be to boost generation at a lower price rather than earn more revenue for the government that the proponents of the auction route the CAG and Supreme Court included (in spectrum allotment case)—suggest. This is imperative as electricity tariffs in India are already high.

A process of allotments made on recommendations of individuals, state governments and even committees is a recipe for corruption. A better approach could be allotment of coal blocks by global competitive bidding to qualified companies who would commit to supply coal efficiently at the lowest price. Power-generating companies wanting to develop captive mines would also need to commit the lowest coal price to be included in the power tariff structure as a variable component. For monitoring implementation of the allotment terms, including regulation of coal prices, an independent regulator on the lines of CERC/SERC could be set up since the Ministry of Coal failed in this role. A similar policy; *mutatis mutandis* could be formulated for steel and cement plants.

An investigation published in the newspaper exposed how a West Bengal-based company has quietly emerged as the second largest private coal mine owner by exploiting loopholes in policy. Though private miners can mine coal only for captive cement, metal or power plants. It shows that it is possible to do none of the above but still operate coal mines. This is done by forming joint ventures with state power companies and then creating corporate structures to make sure that profits are pocketed largely by itself, and not by the state entities. Clearly, this implies that its state-owned partners are complicit in this arrangement; such complicity can only occur if such companies enjoy political/heft. Political discretion is rife in the allocation and operation of coal, mines, which were nationalized in 1973, and where private participation is allowed under a set of rules and guidelines that give enormous powers to State and Central governments to allocate mines as they see fit. This policy of coal nationalization has reached the end of its utility. It has to change, quickly. The government's response to allegations about graft in coal mining has been mixed. It has denied deliberate wrongdoing, blamed existing policy for any lapses and launched probes to investigate a clutch of mine-owning companies. These are knee-jerk responses to events, not deliberate policy action. What it really needs to do is to scrap the Coal Nationalization Act and the policy of captive mining. The government then has to auction the right to mine coal in a fair and transparent way to qualified mining companies from all over the world. The auction should ask all interested miners to bid for the highest amount of revenues that it is willing to share with the state where the mine is located. These auctions should be designed well, to ensure that they attract the maximum number of participants. This kind of purposeful policy action will attract investors, boost growth and get the economy back on the rails again.

India's coal sector is governed by opaque rules that promote discretion and graft. Coalgate and CAG report apart, we need to get away from government intervention and discretion. We need to roll back nationalization. Initially, coal mining was private and goes back to 1774. At first, this was concentrated in the Raniganj belt in West Bengal and then spread to the Jharia belt in Jharkhand. The quality of Raniganj coal was very good in addition to some parts of Chhattisgarh.

Planning led to National Coal Development Corporation (NCDC) in 1956. Until the Second Five-Year Plan (1956-61), NCDC's role was limited to running 11 collieries that had been owned by the Railways. During Second, Third (1961-66) and Fourth (1969-74) Five-Year Plans, NCDC was given the task of diversifying beyond the Raniganj-Jharia belt. There was a perception that there was market failure in the sense that the private sector would not possess financial resources required for capital investments. Therefore, it wouldn't also be able to access modern technology, such as collaborations NCDC brought with Poland, the former Soviet Union, Japan, the former West

Germany and France. Subsequently, in 1975, NCDC became Central Coalfields Limited (CCL). Nationalization of coal mines was not only because of perceptions of market failure, or because of the view that the coal sector would have to be 'planned' in some sense. There was also the perception that coal mines were not safe and workers were exploited. For example, there were several films based on coal mine disasters around that time. As everyone knows, nationalization was in two phases.

When coal mines were nationalized, there continued to be captive mining by private enterprises that produced iron and steel and sub-leasing of these mines was also allowed. These were terminated in 1976. However, after the reforms of 1991, there was again an amendment, allowing for captive coal mining in the private sector for power generation, washing of coal obtained from a mine and other notified end uses, cement production being one. An amendment to the Nationalization Act, permitting private participation in non-captive mining, has been pending from at least 1997.

Therefore, those who are eligible to mine coal is predetermined. Other than CIL and Singareni Collieries Co, coal mining in the non-captive domain is only done by Bihar State Mineral Development Corporation and Jammu & Kashmir Minerals. The Mines and Minerals Development and Regulation Act of 1957, or MMDR Act, is another relevant piece of legislation. This covers all mining, not just coal.

However, because MMDR Act also covers coal, mining companies have to obtain mining leases from state governments under MMDR Act, if coal-bearing land needs to be acquired under the Land Acquisition Act. These leases, for 20-30 years, with a further extension period of 20 years, are granted by state governments after approval has been obtained from the Centre. When it is said that pricing and distribution of all grades of coal have been deregulated from January 2000, it is with this circumscribed context in mind.

The policy on coal is inordinately complicated. Under the Constitution, coal is a Union subject, under Central control. However, coal resources are distributed across states. After nationalization, coal is completely controlled by the government, with the exception of captive mines. To complicate matters, there are two completely separate processes.

First, there is the process of setting up a coal mine, with attendant land, forest and environmental clearances. Secondly, there is the process of allocating the coal that has been produced. On approved end-uses for which captive blocks can be allocated, applications are directed to a screening committee. The present guidelines say, "Preference will be accorded to the power and the steel sectors. Within the power sector also, priority shall be accorded to projects with more than 500 MW capacity. Similarly, in steel sector, priority shall be given to steel plants with more than one million tonne per annum capacity."

This is fair enough. However, other than power and steel, they also say, "Inter-se priority for allocation of a block among competing applicants for a captive block may be decided as per the following guidelines: status (stage) level of progress and state of preparedness of the projects net worth of the applicant company (or in the case of a new SP/JV; the net worth of their principals); production capacity as proposed in the application; maximum recoverable reserve as proposed in the application; date of commissioning of captive mine as proposed in the application; date of completion of detailed exploration (in respect of unexplored blocks only) as proposed in the application; technical experience (in terms of existing capacities in coal/lignite mining and specified end-use); recommendation of the administrative ministry concerned; recommendation of the state government concerned (i.e., where the captive block is located); track record and financial strength of the company."

The point is simple. These criteria are objective and transparent enough, there is too much discretion in the system, leading to the possibility of inevitable abuse. Blocks allocated to state companies do not even go through a screening committee process. The list is circulated internally to Central ministries and state governments and on the basis of the interest shown, allocations are done by the Ministry of Coal. Some blocks are directly given to the Ministry of Power. At least for these, allocation is through tariff-based competitive bidding. There is, thus, a case for moving to competitive bidding for all captive blocks.

Are Creative People more Dishonest?

The Evil Genius is a familiar trope. It's everywhere from Mephistopheles in Goethe's *Faust* to Ernst Stavro Blofeld, the James Bond villain known as 'Number I.' Recent research indicates that a psychological truth may underlie the stereotype. Studies conducted by Francesca Gino of Harvard Business School and Dan, Ariely of Duke University suggest that creativity fuels dishonesty and that dishonest behaviour triggers creativity. It may be a cycle that reinforces itself.

You could have a situation in which creativity initially pushes you across the line and then dishonesty heightens creativity, which might make it easier to cheat again. It's a downward spiral. Gino and Ariely's paper, "The Dark Side of Creativity: Original Thinkers Can Be More Dishonest" focuses on the first part of the equation: how creativity affects dishonesty.

The first study featured in the paper uses survey data compiled from 99 employees across 17 departments at an unnamed US advertising agency in the South. The employees were asked to indicate how likely they'd be to engage in various ethically questionable behaviours—everything from stealing office supplies to inflating business expense reports. They also rated the level of creativity required for their specific jobs: (Their answers were cross-checked by evaluations from three top managers, who also rated the creativity of each department). They found a positive correlation. The more creativity required on the job, the more unethical behaviour was self-reported. Subsequent studies seem to indicate that these findings weren't simply a result of more honest reporting on the part of creative employees.

This isn't to say that graphic designers are necessarily more dishonest than, say, accountants. Creative types are simply at a higher risk for behaving unethically because they can more easily find reasons why their behaviour is not problematic. In other words, original thinkers aren't more ethically depraved than the rest of us; they're just better equipped to find ways of being dishonest without compromising their own self-regard.

Other studies compared cheating in people who'd been primed for innovative thinking vs. those who hadn't. Half the test subjects were asked to unscramble sentences that specifically addressed creativity a technique proven to trigger original thinking. The other half unscrambled neutral sentences with no mention of creativity. Next, the test subjects were placed in various situations in which cheating was given an incentive in the prospect of earning small amounts of money. Subjects encouraged to think creatively were consistently more likely to cheat.

The link between creativity and dishonesty may even extend to situations in which the distinction between right and wrong is quite clear, making creative justification more difficult. To test this asked 159 primed and non-primed subjects to roll dice once and then self-report their results, from one to six. They were given monetary rewards for each roll proportional to the number displayed by their dice: $1 for a one; $2 for a two; $3 for a three, so on and so forth. Those primed for creativity reported an average roll score of five, compared with an average roll score of 31/2 reported by neutral subjects. Gino and Ariely didn't know for sure whether lying came into play, but the results are certainly suspicious. Now dishonest behaviour influences creativity;

preliminary findings from a study indicate that cheating itself may inspire and enable creative thinking. What's happening is that after you've cheated, you're trying to justify cheating and if you're asked to perform a task, you'll probably going to be more creative. Dishonest behaviour is after all, also influenced by the environment. Research shows that when you teach people to do cost-benefit analysis they'll give, more weight to their own self interest. Often [business students] apply that framework to contexts where maybe they shouldn't.

Political Nexus Crumbling

Even a year ago, many Indian businessmen believed a combustible combination of derring-do and political connections could be a heady mix for creation of wealth in India. In a recent open letter, the second in nine months, drafted by senior business leaders such as Deepak Parekh, Chairman of HDFC, and N Vaghul, who built institutions such as ICICI Bank from ground up, expressed concern over what they describe as a growing nexus between corporates and politicians. That nexus, the 14 signatories fear, "is one of the greatest threats for the Indian economy." A combination of a vigilant judiciary, activists wielding tools such as the Right to Information Act and public interest litigation; frenetic, and some argue, over-the-top media coverage; and investors wreaking retribution in the stock markets have abruptly halted their dream run. "The system got so saturated with corruption that the system itself became a whistle-blower. Somebody who did not get a project started rattling on the one that did," says Santosh Hegde, the former Lokayukta of Karnataka, whose investigations exposed mining barons, the Reddy brothers, in Karnataka, who have become symbols of an allegedly corrupt business-politics nexus. Years ago, before the current backlash against corruption, the real estate arm of a listed firm boasted of winning projects much before the government awarded them to his group. This was at an international road-show, where investors were from different parts of the world and not used to such chutzpah from an entrepreneur.

For sure and much to their amazement, they later found out that the industrialist was on the ball and the projects were eventually won by his group. But the real estate baron as well as several other politicians and businessmen are now cooling their heels in Tihar jail, accused of one scam or the other. Several influential and ambitious industrialists with dreams of turning their businesses into global enterprises now find themselves hitting a wall, having broken some law of the land.

"Because of all the recent arrests and incarceration of politicians and businessmen, it appears that the politician-businessmen nexus is breaking down," said veteran journalist and political analyst Paranjoy Guha Thakurta. "One of the critical links that need to be broken is around the issue of election funding. If corrupt businessmen are funding the election of politicians of dubious record, they are going to expect returns on that investment," said Thakurta, who is one of the petitioners in the PIL filed in the Supreme Court in connection with the 2G scam. The market is taking notice of the troubles of politically well-connected companies. "Investors are increasingly realizing that factors like political connections can have significant impact on the earnings of the companies they invest in," says Gaurav Mehta of Ambit Capital. Increasingly, brokerages such as Ambit Capital are giving significant weightage to risks arising from political connections, poor corporate governance and suspect accounting policies while issuing investment recommendation on stocks.

According to an April 2011 report from Ambit Capital 'A New Dawn in India', businesses with strong political connections have underperformed the broader market by 14 per cent in the year to April 2011, when the study was undertaken. Presumably, the under-performance could have only aggravated. "Whilst the recent spate of corruption scandals has soured investor sentiment regarding India, it has had a salutary effect in forcing investors to focus on fundamentally high quality companies," noted Saurabh Mukherjea and Gaurav Mehta of Ambit Capital. "For the first time in five years, we now have a situation where politically well-connected companies are no longer outperforming the market." Concurring with Mukherjea and Mehta is Shriram Subramanian, founder and managing director of In Government Research, a firm tracking corporate governance and advising institutional investors. "Promoters and management of companies have very little to gain in the long term by indulging in shenanigans—political favours, corruption, accounting gimmicks, evading taxes, etc. In the longer run, it all catches up and wipes out their wealth and reputation built assiduously over the years."

According to Subramanian, "the low PE multiples of many companies that have perceived "political risks are symptomatic of the way investors treat these stocks. Returns for investors could be higher—purely due to PE multiple expansion—if these companies focused on mitigating political and governance risks." Both the analysts from Ambit Capital and Subramanian were reluctant to name individual companies. However, Ambit's research has identified firms in sectors such as power, capital goods, infrastructure and construction, real estate, technology, metals and mining, as well as telecom and media as having strong to medium political connections. The market has already delivered its verdict. It is now for the corporates concerned to decide if they want to change or not. "Till around 2007 or so, factors like corporations using political connections for competitive advantage or using creative accounting to fudge numbers did not catch investors' attention. However, the crisis, subsequent recovery and series of events still unfolding in India have made these issues hard to dismiss," says Mehta of Ambit Capital.

The Maran brothers are another case in point where being members of the ruling coalition at the Centre and in their southern fiefdom alleged to have brought them advantages. It is now haunting them, as they face a CBI investigation. The brothers deny any wrongdoing. According to the head of a policy think tank, the rampant trend of politicians turning businessmen need to be investigated. "These are the very people who are privy to insider information, and take advantage of this exclusive information. A key difference that has happened this time around, is that the attitude of judiciary has changed. If earlier, accused businessmen were easily able to get bail or even anticipatory bail, now they are finding it harder and harder to secure bail," News agency PTI reported "bail is the rule, jail is an exception" in reference to several businessmen and politicians languishing in jail. He went on to further ask, "if you lock up top businessmen, will investment come?" Maybe because of such comments, activists like Hegde hope the media plays a critical role in sustaining the change that is underway by keeping the discussion alive.

In a democracy, the government must be seen to respond to overwhelming public sentiment if only in order to retain power what we are seeing now with some politicians and businessmen in jail is not the emergence of a new dynamic between the state and the corporation, but short-term appeasement. It is not law alone that is catching up with the miscreants. Retribution is also at hand from an unforgiving.

Fiscal deficits aren't expressed in absolute numbers. They are expressed as shares of GDP and, therefore, budget targets are also of that nature. There is a numerator and a denominator in the deficit target. The budget expected nominal GDP growth of 14.5 per cent this fiscal, broken up into 9 per cent real growth and 5.5 per cent inflation. What measure of inflation? The GDP deflator is used for this calculation, not the wholesale or consumer price index. Cynics may say government got something right. It got the 9 per cent number bang on, but it applied to inflation, not growth.

Inflation is raging at around 9 per cent. Government spokespersons have assured us, at several points in time, inflation will decline—beyond September, beyond March, beyond August, beyond every conceivable month you can think of. These have all been proved hopelessly wrong. An astrologer would have done better. No wonder, when asked about the price rise, a UPA minister lamented he was not an astrologer. The FM has again assured us inflation will decline to 7 per cent by March 2012. If it does, no credit will be due to government. At the level of policy formulation, government has no idea about handling any of the three components of inflation—food, petroleum and manufactured products. What is inflation based on the GDP deflator likely to be? Probably around 7 per cent and real growth will be around 7.5 per cent. That's an aggregate of 14.5 per cent and we are fine on the denominator, so to speak. The problem is with the numerator: the difference between government receipts and government expenditure. Tax receipts are relatively fine. The problem is with non-tax revenue. Disinvestment has disappeared and there is no windfall gain through spectrum likely. Nor can expenditure be contained. Consequently, we may end the year with a fiscal deficit/GDP ratio of 5.5 per cent , almost a full percentage point above the official target. Doubtless some government spokespersons will say 5.6 per cent is close enough to 4.6 per cent .

What's wrong with a deficit? We all borrow and live beyond our means at some point in time. It all depends on why we borrow. If we borrow to purchase assets or increase our future productivity, there will be less of complaint. But the government isn't borrowing for this. It isn't borrowing for capital expenditure. It is borrowing for consumption expenditure. Wages and salaries, pensions, interest payments, subsidies, and even NREG work -all this is unproductive. There's no need to make a fetish of the fiscal deficit. But revenue deficit-the difference between the government's running expenditure and recurring income-is the real problem. The revenue deficit would seem to be under serious pressure. This means the government is increasingly unable to finance its functioning from its regular income. In these conditions, GoI's borrowing from the market goes up and that drives up interest rates and squeezes out private borrowing, both for consumption expenditure and for 'investment. If it borrows from RBI, RBI pumps liquidity into the system, contributing to inflation. All of us collectively bear costs of government's profligacy. And the government is a huge entity, so all these effects are substantial. That's the reason deficits are dangerous. The question, therefore, is whether the government can course -correct. Recent history does not hold out much hope. The big increase in government expenditure was justified in the name of the 2008 global financial crisis and the recession that followed. But UPA I's increase in public consumption expenditure pre-dated the global financial crisis. After the initial shock of the crisis was over, we should have encouraged the switch from public consumption expenditure to private investment and consumption expenditure. Instead, we did the reverse. In the name of inclusive growth, we effectively reduced and shackled growth. The high growth phase of 2003-07 was driven by low interest rates and public savings. This government, despite its considerable economic expertise in-house, failed to appreciate this and all of us are bearing the costs.

The Dark Side of Leadership

Many leaders get to the top by imposing their will on others, even destroying people on their way. When they reach the top, they may be paranoid that others are trying to knock them off their pedestal. Sometimes they develop an impostor complex, caused by deep insecurities that they aren't good enough and may be unmasked. To prove they aren't impostors, they drive so hard for perfection that they are incapable of acknowledging their failures. When confronted by them, they convince themselves and others that these problems are neither their fault nor irresponsibility. Or they look for scapegoats to blame for their problems. Using their power, charisma and communications skills, they force people to accept these distortions, causing entire organizations to lose touch with reality. At this stage, leaders are vulnerable to make big mistakes, such as violating the law or putting their organizations' existence at risk. Their distortions convince them they are doing nothing wrong, or they rationalize that their deviations are acceptable to achieve a greater good. It's lonely at the top, because leaders know they are ultimately responsible for the lives and fortunes of people. If they fail, many get deeply hurt. They often deny the burdens and loneliness, becoming incapable of facing reality. They shut down their inner voice, because it is too painful to confront or even acknowledge.

Plan Your Approach

It is well known that for any work to be done effectively and successfully, proper planning, approach and willingness to change, when necessary, are necessary. Right thinking, perceptions, resilience, assertiveness, focus, 'flow' such virtues are integral to this fulfilment. Indeed, for one's spiritual progress too, a similar strategy and vision are vital! There are as many paths as there are seekers and, therefore, each has to divine that which would suit him well. He should also ponder intelligently his own life (past and present). Dwelling also on the needed changes, he could commence the process by asking himself certain simple, yet probing, questions as stated below :

(1) Quo Vadis? - Whither goest thou? This would be with regard to one's material, creative and spiritual needs.

(2) In which way, different approaches or attitudes in the past (concerning relationships, opinions, instincts, habits or transactions) could have yielded better results? How to ensure needed changes, at least from now on?;

(3) How to implement practically Oscar Wilde's concept, "Experience is the name which wise men give to their mistakes," also ensuring such 'mistakes' are not repeated?

(4) Can you learn from constructive criticism, also being assertive, not being deterred by 'sneers of selfish men' or foolish persons around?

Prayerful contemplation on such 'goings on' enables one to divine one's own 'truths' for evolving into *karmasu koushalam*. This is brought about, finally, by rightly planning one's approach.

Social and Spiritual Impact

We're all striving to improve the quality of our lives. However, very few attempts to bring about institutional reforms have helped leverage people power to co-create 'overall impact'. When things come to a boil, we do rise up and question the Establishment and sometimes things do change for the better. But how to ensure that the changes whether brought about by people power or good governance get sustained? The freedom movement that liberated India from colonial rule continues to inspire us. Hence we look up to those who provided creative and motivating leadership like Gandhiji. There are many reasons, however, why such leaders are not rare now. First, Gandhiji's leadership was at all times at its zenith, deeply rooted in personal experimentation and interpretation of principles like *ahimsa* and *swaraj*. The concept of 'Be the Change' or to begin with oneself helped awaken so many people, instilling a sense of personal ownership for action that often involved immense sacrifice. Secondly; Gandhi believed in *poorna swaraj*, complete Independence, as did Lokmanya Tilak—to deal with an issue in totality. While regulation and institutional solutions are important, much more emphasis is placed on public behaviour and restraint. Gandhiji constantly inspired people to believe in what they were doing and to patiently demonstrate it in some form. For him, social change evolved out of a shared vision. Development work is not seen as something that ought to deliver 'outcomes' as if an issue is just about fulfilling some sort of a 'resource gap' say a missing piece of legislation, institutional mechanism, monetary or technological provisions. Regulatory and other ways of administration are only the means, for lasting change for the better begins with you and me. Thirdly, Gandhiji saw in us enormous humane and social potential and the huge possibility of its committed and purposeful engagement. This would also steer one away from divisive tendencies like caste, creed, class and language. Gandhiji then set out a strategy to involve people constructively, as a noted author and journalist observed:

1. For pious people there were *satsangs* with multi-faith prayers;
2. To ensure livelihoods there was spinning work and the whole enterprise-solution of *swadeshi* and *khadigram*;
3. For activists it was satyagraha, the principle centred on peaceful non-cooperation;
4. For journalists and others, there were a variety of engagements where their views were aired with a sense of immense personal and collective responsibility.

All of these summed up the message to those in power: 'Quit India'.

Do we see the need for a leadership that can mobilize people into action, beyond demanding systemic provisions? Are we aware of the need for deep, useful engagement, for people to support mechanisms of justice to bring the corrupt to book? How can we help alleviate terrorism instead of getting involved only in scientific explanation of the composition and intensity of a just-exploded bomb that destroyed lives? How many businesses will engage the poorest of the poor through their supply chains to help them take the first step of the economic ladder? Would our actions save or destroy flora and fauna? Can we ensure the safety and nurturing of women and children? Why can't a bit of what moved Gandhi, and through him others, rub off on us so we can take that small step forward? Perhaps then we could be the change we wish to see in the world.

Notes

Chapter 2

OCCUPY WALL STREET AGITATION

A year ago thousands of people from every walk of life converged on Wall Street, New York, triggering a wave of global anti-capitalist protest. Today the movement lies in tatters. Several hundred who regrouped near the NYSE to mark the anniversary not withstanding with its provisional leaders remaining provisional and romance stubbornly refusing to yield to reality. The movement had grown too large too quickly and no one knows what it stands for today. Without leaders or specific demands, what started off as a protest against economic inequality turned into a protest against everything that is wrong with the world.

The protest was first dreamt up by Kalle Lasn and Micath White, the close collaborators behind *Ad Busters*, a slickly-produced, high art magazine that uses the tools of commercial culture to make the case against Capitalism.

The people are now aware of every issue. They are not going to tolerate wrongdoings any more. Slowly, they are coming on to the streets in revolt. It's happening in every part of the world. It shows that there is a desire for change everywhere. People want to lead a happy and peaceful life, and for that, they need a good government. But they also want the freedom of speech and expression. Very soon, there will be a huge change, and the whole world is going to witness it. The people on the streets will create a very beautiful world in the coming days.

People with bumper stickers waving in the air at the Occupy Phoenix protest which is a symbol of the movement itself—a mélange of disparate causes, all of which prompted his blood to boil. Protesters have taken to the streets and parks in cities across the US, and in foreign capitals to boot, all under the banner of the OWS movement. But not every group that has embraced the name, nor every individual who answers its call, necessarily marches in the same contentious lockstep. While the protesters seem united in feeling that the system is stacked against them, with the rules written to benefit the rich and the connected, they are also just as often angry about issues closer to home, like education and the local environment. Each gathering bubbles up from its own particular city's stew of circumstances and grievances, and the protesters bring along their pantheons of saints and villains.

If only real-life Wall Street had redeemed itself following the crash of 2008. America's `Occupy Wall Street' protesters are the latest to hit the streets in a world witnessing people power from Cairo to Manhattan. And they're calling to account all those venal bankers and brokers who—as one demonstrator puts it—"profited on the backs of hard-working people." A 'movement' against 'corporate greed', in a country that's long equated pursuit of happiness with no-apologies pursuit of wealth! Students, unions, community organizations all now castigate the presumed degeneration of the American Dream into a disastrous money chase. It is, as they say, America's Tahrir Square moment. Only, the Arab Spring's about toppling authoritarianism. The American Fall' is about questioning too much freedom. Why, after all, did nobody stop investment banks and hedge funds financing subprime mortgage lenders, and then turning bad debts into deadly repackaged instruments? Why did the authorities blink at lenders and loan underwriters defying safety standards? Why did taxpayer-funded bailouts not chasten the bankers and brokers, who still get bloated paychecks while middle-class Americans struggle to put their kids through college and potential university wits seek jobs in sweatshops? They must be questioned. There are limits to greed, and they lie in making financial systems transparent and accountable. The thing is, which other economic system is as open to bloodless self correction as the now-maligned capitalist system? Must market busts triggered by human recklessness that behavioural economists highlight become an excuse to turn `Big Business' into a cuss word?

The foil to profitable business of any size is usually Big Brother Government. Now, the market can hurt you on occasion. But for the most part it gives huge opportunities for self-advancement to free economic agents. The bounty-hunting dysfunctionality of some can't cancel out the enlightened—because socially attuned self-interest of all others. If the market brings about income disparity; the statist alternative is the 'equality' of low incomes for all save the dacha-dwellers who conflate pittance with per capita. Yes, market rules of fair competition can be manipulated by the corrupt. But command-and-control utopia can't but be corrupt: it demands blind faith in the monopoly of a few over resource disbursal for all. That means, the cake's for the ruling elites. The rest eat mouldy bread.

The world has fallen on bad times, thanks to speculative misadventurism. What a chance for the exhumers of Marx and the factotums of inherited or forcibly wrested privilege to crucify the rich for being rich! Wealth bashers don't distinguish between predatory rich and productive rich. Instead, they brandish 'research' suggesting the wealthy are a soulless tribe lacking in empathy, the kind Scott Fitzgerald portrayed in his book, *The Great Gatsby* (1925). Aren't we missing something here? Such as the rich who're thinkers, producers, job creators, wealth distributors? Not just the big names—America's Bill Gates, 'Tax the rich" Warren Buffett and late Steve Jobs or our very own Tatas and Murthys—but the entire entrepreneurship-driven ecosystem on which we live? Someone should present the facts on how millions of us across the planet feed off the financial and intellectual capital of private business. Maybe then we'll be able to take on the real problem—politically blessed corporate greed—without faddishly feigning there's no corporate good. As anti-hero realizes, money can be the means to good ends; it's not an end in itself. Of course, pulpiteering politicians and activists will miss the point and decry money as the root of all evil. It's so handy to want to make the rich poor when you can't make the poor less poor, let alone rich.

Occupy Wall Street protests across the world have revived interest in sifting 'good Capitalism' from 'bad Capitalism'. Ever since the financial meltdown of 2008, proponents of market capitalism have sought ways to legitimize their greed. Now they fear that a wave of global discontent might overwhelm the only economic system that really works. Even those who concede that Wall Street's operations need to be reformed tend to consider any challenge to 'the market' as blasphemous. Besides, they add, it's easy enough to grumble about the failings of markets but where's the alternative?

This view is both ill-informed and desperately lacking in imagination. Notice that the protesters rallying call is occupy not demolish. Their claim to represent the 99 per cent is not just about severe disparity of incomes and assets. It's a metaphor for society struggling to reclaim both markets and governance. That's why the mere idea of occupying Wall Street evokes a visceral response in a wide range of people in far-flung corners of the world. Instinctively they know that markets are older than capitalism. From weekly moving bazaars in tribal hamlets, to urban department stores and stock markets—we all relish the joys of open exchange. Capitalism is currently the dominant mode of market economy but it is not final. Occupy Wall Street protests are drawing attention to many different ways in which the interface of society, markets and capital is now sought to be reconfigured. Some votaries of change are thought leaders at the heart of the mainstream. Raghuram Rajan and Luigi Zingales made a powerful case against regulatory capture in their book *Saving Capitalism from the Capitalists*. Jeffery Sachs' has just released a book, *The Prize of Civilization*, which critiques the current state of capitalism in the US.

Noble Laureate Joseph Stiglitz's recent essay Of the 1%, by the 1%, for the 1%, is being cited as an inspiration for the protesters. When Stiglitz visited the protesters on Wall Street he once again said that the socialization of losses and privatization of gains is neither capitalism nor a proper market economy. 'That's a distorted economy.'

A network called Real-World Economics is unravelling many of the fallacies that underlie the free-market orthodoxy. For instance, the classical idea of 'economic man' as a narrow self-aggrandizing being has been thoroughly discredited. Research at the interface of neurosciences and economics is reconfirming what most people know in everyday life: that our decisions are determined by a wide range of motivations and not limited to raw selfishness. The George Soros-funded Institute for New Economic Thinking (INET) has created a platform for economists who challenge orthodox assumptions, for example that markets tend to cohere towards equilibrium.

New Economics Foundation in London is another important source for substantial work on the mechanics and principles of economics and markets as if people and environment mattered. If the work of think-and-do tanks seems unimpressive, consider the potential of Socially Responsible Investing (SRI). It is true that much of the over $3-trillion SRI industry is motivated by an expanded definition of risk management.

However, some companies have adopted the triple bottom line—of planet, people and profit—truly out of a commitment to generate value in all three dimensions and thus retain their social-licence to operate. Others have done so because there is increasing social pressure not to grow profits flagrantly at the cost of planet and people. On another grid entirely, the free software/open source phenomenon has celebrated the freedom to cooperate. It has, thus, overturned the assumption that the win-lose variety of competition is the only reliable driver of innovation. It is estimated that over 90 per cent of the world's servers, the backbone of the Internet, are running on open source software. Richard Stallman, the founding *guru* of the free software movement, has tirelessly said that free software developers can and should earn profits. Linus Torvalds, who created Linux, has famously said that he makes enough money to put petrol in his BMW. It is important to acknowledge that there is no single thread narrative which leads us to a coherent alternative to Wall Street's version of the market. Passionate street protests may not, in themselves, offer alternatives or even coherent demands.

But definitive manifestos would be out of place in the 21st century. What our times call for is a dispersed articulation of civilizational values. That means a focus on the kind of society we want to live in and a reconfiguration of the relationship between state, markets and capital. Sifting good from bad capitalism can only be a small part of this endeavour. If you believe that market capitalism, with its greed to fear spectrum, is a given that can be tweaked but not altered, the future seems closed and unpromising.

But if you recognize markets as a social construct, where behaviour is in constant flux depending on how well we tap into the many dimensions of human motivation, then there is great promise of radical innovation and transformation. The orthodoxy will naturally denounce the protesters for threatening to disrupt the only game in town that works. But what if these are instead the harbingers of creative destruction and renewal that creates a new game which could work better?

Occupy Wall Street seems to be an extension of Anna Hazare's crusade against corruption. The rich seem to be getting richer and the poor, poorer. The fault lies in governmental policies across the globe. Food, clothing and shelter seem to be only an election stunt while, in reality; all these are becoming too expensive for the common man. Hunger and want of affordable basic necessities are driving millions to protest, their anger now bursting into an uncontrollable tsunami. Political leaders should clearly see the writing on the wall and amend their ways.

Buoyed by the longevity of the Occupy Wall Street encampment in New York City, a wave of protests swept across Asia, the Americas and Europe, with hundreds and in some cases thousands of people expressing discontent with the economic tides in marches, rallies and occasional clashes with police. In Rome, a rally thick with tension spread over several miles. Small groups of restive young people turned a largely peaceful protest into a riot, setting fire to at least one building and a police van and clashing with police officers, who responded with water cannons and tear gas. The police estimated that dozens of protesters had been injured, along with 26 law enforcement officials; 12 people were arrested.

At least 88 people were arrested in New York, including 24 accused of trespassing in a Greenwich Village branch of Citibank and 45 during a raucous rally of thousands of people in and around Times Square. More than 1,000 people filled Washington Square Park at night, but almost all of them left after dozens of police officers with batons and helmets streamed in and warned that they would be enforcing a midnight curfew. Fourteen were arrested for remaining in the park. Other than Rome's, the demonstrations across Europe largely peaceful, with thousands of people marching past ancient monuments and gathering in front of capitalist symbols such as the European Central Bank in Frankfurt, Germany. Similar scenes unfolded across several continents, including in Sydney, Tokyo, Hong Kong, Toronto, Chicago and Los Angeles, where thousands marched to City Hall as drivers honked their support.

Caste proponents say the census must include question on caste to establish true caste ratios. Opponents say questions on caste are socially divisive. They also raise a behavioural objection: the very announcement of a caste census could encourage people to claim, fraudulently, that they belong to a caste entitled to reservations. This behavioural objection applies as forcefully to surveys for determining poverty. The National Sample Survey Organization conducts periodic surveys on consumption, and data from these surveys are used to determine the official poverty head count. The government assumes that people tell NSS surveyors the truth about themselves. NGO workers in rural areas feel that if a villager talks to fellow villagers, he will probably exaggerate his living standards to get local prestige. But if a villager is talking to outsiders who may influence the giving of subsidies or other benefits, the villager will vehemently claim to be poor and deserving of any benefits available. He has no reason to admit any improvement in living standards. Any psychologist will tell that such duplicity is both inevitable and universal. People respond to incentives and disincentives. So, a necessary condition for an honest survey is that no benefits or penalties should flow from people's replies. That is true for surveys on caste, poverty or anything else.

But governments have long been promising ever more subsidies and entitlements targeted at the poor. This is a strong, growing incentive to under-report consumption. The evidence suggests that this has long been happening. In the

1970s, consumption measured by NSS surveys was 87 per cent of consumption measured by national income statistics. This divergence was bearable. But the divergence has steadily increased over decades. In 2004-05, consumption reported by the NSS was just 48.7 per cent of that reported by national income statistics.

Left economists claim that rich people are progressively under-reporting their consumption to the NSS, but poor ones are not. This is implausible. In the 1970s, in-come tax of 97.75 per cent and wealth tax of 3.5 per cent caused a flight to black money, which nobody reported to the NSS. Consumer imports were illegal and provided by smugglers. Obviously richer people under-reported such consumption. Yet in the 1970s, the two measures of consumption were not far apart.

But over the next three decades, income tax has fallen to 30 per cent, wealth tax is virtually abolished, imports of consumer goods are legal and lightly taxed, and the share of white money transactions has clearly risen, even in real estate. So, the rich have much less reason to hide their consumption than in the bad old days. However, poorer folks have been given increasing incentives to under-report living standards. In the 1970s, most freebies were universal, not targeted at the poorest subsidized food, power, canal water, fertilizer, bank credit and employment schemes were open to all rural folk, not just the poor. Targeting came later. The IRDP scheme provided subsidized microcredit to the poor. The Indira Awas Yojana provided housing subsidies to the poorest. BPL (below poverty line) ration cards provided a higher food subsidy than APL (above poverty line) cards. Rural employment in some cases was targeted at the poor, and so was the farm loan write-off in 2008. The DMK in Tamil Nadu provided coloured TV sets to those below the poverty line. Many such schemes were poorly implemented, and often little money reached the poor. Yet villagers realized that some benefits could flow from fraudulently claiming poverty, while no profit at all flowed from honestly reporting improved living standards. This must have affected the honesty of reporting in NSS surveys. This seems at least a partial explanation of the growing gap between NSS estimates and national income estimates.

Officials continue to treat NSS data as sacred. But companies selling cellphones, shampoo, TVs and other consumer goods view NSS estimates as rubbish. NSS data suggests high poverty and little improvement in rural demand. In fact companies find rural demand is booming, producing record sales. Thanks to rural penetration, cellphone connections are increasing by 19 million per month.

Economist Surjit Bhalla has long denounced official poverty estimates as fiction. By making adjustments consistent with national income data, he reckons that, actual poverty is less than one-third of the official figure. Other adjustments can be made by looking at independent data on rural consumer goods sales. The government has recently raised the poverty line. Around 37 per cent of people are below this higher line. Such upward adjustments are appropriate as living standards rise. But this should not distract from the terrible flaws of NSS data. Government policies have made it profitable for rural folk to exaggerate their poverty.

Protestors Unite in Frustration

But just as the rallies in New York have represented a variety of messages—signs have been held in opposition too. President Barack Obama yards away from signs in support of him—so did protests contain a grab bag of sentiments, opposing nuclear power, political corruption and the privatization of water. Yet, despite the difference in language, landscape and scale, the protests were united in frustration over the yawning gap between the rich and the poor. The protestors have no problem with capitalism per se, but they find the financial system deeply unethical. We shouldn't bail out the banks. We should bail out the people. In New York where the occupation of Zuccotti Park in Lower Manhattan was moving into its second month, a large crowd marched north to Washington Square Park, where it was joined by several hundred college students who decried student debt and unemployment. The crowds marched up Avenue of the Americas towards a heavily-barricaded Times Square, where they joined thousands of other protestors and caught tourists unaware. Some tourists pumped their fists and whooped from atop double-decker sightseeing buses as the protestors cheered back. For the protestors, marching on Times Square held almost as much significance as did protesting against Wall Street. Times Square represents business as usual—buy, buy, buy in this economic climate, watch the latest show. The protest moved back to Washington Square Park, where people listened to speeches and debated whether to stay while police officers marched into the square. Virtually everyone chose to leave, and it was unclear if anyone was arrested. Many headed back to Zuccotti Park, where there is no curfew. Earlier, about a dozen protestors entered a Chase branch in Lower Manhattan and withdrew their money from the bank while 300 other people circled the block, some shouting chants and beating on drums. The former Chase customers, who declined to reveal how much they had in their accounts though a few acknowledged it was not much, said they planned to put their money into smaller banks or credit unions.

The more resources we give to small institutions, the more they'll be able to provide conveniences such as free ATMs and streamlined online banking so they can compete with the larger banks. In Washington, several hundred people marched through downtown, beginning in the early morning, passing by several banks. Escorted by the police, the marchers also demonstrated in front of the White House and the Treasury Department before moving on to a rally on the National Mall, where they were joined by representatives of unions and other supporters. People are beholden to corporate interests no matter how hard you might have worked to get them elected. There is a disconnect. Protests sprang not only from the 'Occupy Wall Street' movement that began in New York, but also from demonstrations in Spain. The global protest effort came as finance ministers and central bankers from the Group of 20 industrialized nations met in Paris to discuss economic issues, including ways to tackle debt crisis.

Chapter 3

COMBATING CORRUPTION

Corruption is a shameful and deplorable act punishable under law. The first casualty of corruption is governance. Corruption cannot be stopped by making better and harsher laws. Laws need to be implemented efficiently and this can happen only with good governance. A better way to reduce corruption is for each of us to reduce our greed. With reduced greed and better implementation of existing laws, corruption can be effectively capped. Besides fuelling corruption, greed for resources and material objects is also creating an unsustainable lifestyle. An emotionally satisfying and decent lifestyle is possible with much less energy consumption than that of the US. This will put much less pressure on the earth's resources and reduce pollution. Simply follow the maxim of "simple living and high thinking."

The basis of greed is desire. Desire manifests itself in different forms like lust, aim, ambition, control and goal. However, the driving force is the same—power, fame, money and control. The brain develops right from birth and fast expanding neuron numbers from memory pathways. This process is accomplished by sensory perception with inputs from the senses helping from memory. We are hardwired to increase our experience and memories and this is the basis of desire.

Corruption is widespread in the society. Even people offer to God bargains like "If you do this favour for me, I will donate ₹ 500 *prasad*" kind of prayer that many of us instinctively think up in our mind. Such a prayer is nothing but a sort of bribe. However, true prayer is to have a conversation—pray to Him, talk to Him, ask Him, but finally leave it to Him to consent your wishes. Trust Him, for He alone knows what is best for you. Thank, praise, love and want God and then leave the rest to Him. Swami Vivekananda says, "He who desires a comfortable and nice life and at the same time wants to realize the self is like the fool, who wanting to cross the river, caught hold of a crocodile mistaking it for a log of wood. "

An outcome of desire is possession. We feel a need to possess whatever we desire—whether it is a person, object or idea. Possession helps in maximization of experience. As we absorb experience through our senses, the brain processes this information. It is during this process that we `decide' whether our desires are fulfilled or not. Fulfillment of desires therefore helps us in releasing the `possessions.' Unfulfilled desires lead to frustration and this makes us want more. This leads eventually to more control and greed, the major causes of corruption.

When concentration on a single thought is carried out regularly and continuously for a longtime, it helps produce a powerful mind and this is the essence of yoga. This allows us to think deeply and concentrate whereby we can get `lost' in processing that information. Such a mind also makes us sensitive and humble, changes our priorities in life and helps us focus on getting personal happiness through mental peace rather than satisfaction of material needs. Besides, it reduces our insecurities and hence gives us a feeling of calmness, well-being and happiness.

A powerful and sensitive mind becomes empathetic to its surroundings and gives rise to the desire to give back something to society and help the less fortunate fellow human beings. Creation of a powerful mind should start from childhood when brainpower is at its peak. When we focus on reading, thinking and contemplation, we can grow to be better human beings and form a gentler and more sustainable society. A small individual step towards a corruption-free society should therefore start from school. With their resources and wealth, captains of the corporate world can create conditions for job generation and for improving the quality of life. For this they need to reduce their greed and not get caught in keeping up with the Joneses by acquiring bigger jets, higher turnover, greater profit—the wish list goes on. Only when all of us become internally secure and reduce our greed would we be able to give something back to society and lay the foundation for a sustainable and corruption-free India.

Corruption is eating into our vitals. There is no doubt about it. Only a strong Lokpal can remove or reduce corruption. In a democratic country such as ours, the common man in about 95 per cent of the cases has to deal with corruption by state government officials. There has to be a comprehensive strategy to contain corruption and punish the corrupt. We have to have decentralized governance, transparency in governance laws, rules which don't give discretionary powers to the establishment and universal declaration of the assets of politicians, bureaucrats, judges and the media, the four pillars of democracy. The bureaucracy, judiciary, media and now the new czars of modern India, the advocates, should declare their assets. We have to bring in reforms in taxation, the judiciary; business rules for bureaucracy, governance (empowerment of elected representatives of rural and urban local bodies) and electoral rules.

The Right to Information Act drafted by the National Advisory Council (NAC) has exposed most of the scams. The stringent amendment to the Money Laundering Act by the government is responsible for some of the ministers still being in jail. Because of the amendment, it is possible to confiscate even a *benami* property. Senior ministers, members of Parliament, bureaucrats and senior officials of powerful corporates are in jail because of this. Agitation is a signal to all politicians and all political parties reform or democracy is in danger. In the age of information technology and 24×7 media coverage, politicians are permanently in the public eye. They have to behave inside Parliament and Assemblies and outside them as well, or perish. The time has now come for all politicians to put their heads together to draft a strong, viable Lokpal Bill and also bring in electoral reforms. Only by doing this will we be able to regain the confidence of the common man.

Corruption in India: An Empirical Study

Over five thousand people were interviewed in a house-to-house survey carried out to assess the citizens' perceptions on corruption prevalent in ten sectors—Education, Health, Police (Law and Order), Power, Telephone (Communication), Railways (Transport), Land and Building Administration, Judiciary, Taxation and Ration (Public distribution system).

An estimated ₹ 26,768 crores were extracted from citizens who interact with these ten sectors. Lower strata with lower earnings are the hardest hit due to corruption. As per perception of the people, Police is the most corrupt sector. However, the impact of corruption is on a much larger scale in the Health and Education Sectors involving far greater number of population. Corruption in Health and Education deprives people of these basic facilities and affects the people. These are co-relates of Human Development. Cross country data of 102 countries show that there is a high rank correlation (0.788) as well as coefficient of correlation (0.766) between Human Development Index (HDI) and Corruption Perception Index (CPI). Countries with low scores in CPI have low HDI.

Many avenues of corruption cannot be dealt with under the Prevention of Corruption Act,1988. In many cases the citizen is not even aware that the practices can be classified as corrupt (e.g., when patients are directed to specific pathological laboratories for conduct of tests). Citizens are resentful of the existence of corruption and are willing to talk about it openly. Formation of interest groups of citizens interacting with various departments can channel the resentment of the citizens constructively. Pressure groups so formed can take up matters with concerned authorities and seek remedy.

In such areas Civil Society organizations can raise awareness among the populace and act as catalysts. Cause for corruption is certainly containing not 'low salary' of those indulging in corruption. It is the lack of effective deterrence in the form of punishment to the corrupt and the lack of adequate supervision.

The fact that money is being demanded directly and openly by the corrupt is a clear indication that the corrupt persons are confident that no worthwhile action can be taken against them. This reflects the fact that those guilty of corruption do not expect to be hauled up. The existing systems for identifying the corrupt and punishing them appear ineffective and provide no deterrence to those indulging in corrupt practices.

Perceptions at best are indicative of the existing malaise in the systems. However, for prioritizing issues, formulations of policies and planning strategies hard data is a requirement. Policies and programmes should not be based on perceptions alone.

Follow up

A survey is not an end in itself. Results of surveys need to be published to raise public awareness, focus debates and promote institutional reform. To this end, TI India proposes to undertake the following steps:

1) Disseminate the results of the survey to legislators,

Central and State Governments, Sectoral Departments and Institutions, NGOs, and the public through print and electronic media.

2) Act as a catalyst to promote Citizens Interest groups and support their actions.

3) Press for the formulation and effective implementation of Citizens Charters in all government departments and allied institutions.

4) Press for Service Charters from private business and institutions involved in delivery of services to the citizens.

5) Press for augmenting the use of Information Technology to enable quick and easy access, and prompt disposal of cases by the government.

6) Press for transparency in actions of the government agencies in the discharge of their functions.

7) Strongly bid for accountability of all functionaries.

8) Continue the programmes already in hand for Moral and Ethical education, introducing Lok Pal (Ombudsman), and e-readiness and judicial reforms.

9) Lobby for immediate legislation of the Right to Information Act.

Perspectives on Corruption—Global Scenario

The Transparency International's (TI) Corruption Perception Index (CPI), 2002 ranks 102 countries in terms of the degree to which corruption is perceived to exist among public officials and politicians. It is a composite index derived from 15 different polls and surveys from 9 independent institutions carried out among business people and country analysts. CPI defines corruption as the abuse of public office for private gains. The index provides an annual snap shot of the views of business people and analysts like bribing of public officials, kickbacks in public procurement or embezzlement of public funds. Of the 102 countries surveyed, seventy countries—including many of the world's most poverty stricken—score less than five out of a clean score of ten. Corruption is perceived to be rampant in Indonesia, Kenya, Angola, Madagascar, Paraguay, Nigeria, and Bangladesh, countries with a score of less than two. Countries with a score of higher than 9, with very low levels of perceived corruption, are predominantly rich countries, namely, Finland, Denmark, New Zealand, Iceland, Singapore, and Sweden.

Consequences of Corruption

Corruption is one of the most damaging consequences of poor governance characterized by lack of both transparency and accountability. Corruption hinders investment and economic growth, and human development by limiting access to basic social services as well as increasing the cost of their delivery. It also increases poverty, subverts the financial system, and undermines the legitimacy of the state. Thus, corruption is anti-poor, anti-development, anti-investment, and inequitable. The cost of corruption to a nation is very high.

Adverse effects of corruption on growth have been statistically corroborated from cross-country data. Based on the corruption rankings data assembled from the business and international communities in seventy countries find a significant negative association between the Corruption Index and the rates of investment and economic growth. A one standard deviation improvement in the Corruption Index is estimated to be associated with an increase in the investment rate by about 3 per cent of the Gross Domestic Product. (Bardhan: "Corruption and Development", *Journal of Economic Literature*, September 1997.)

International Perspective on India

India is amongst the most corrupt countries of the world with a score of only 2.7 out of 10 and ranks 71st amongst 102 countries in 2002. India's score has declined from 2.9 in 1999 to 2.7 in 2002. TI's survey of international business perceptions ranks India worse than China. *World Competitiveness Yearbook 2000* also ranks India amongst those countries where bribing and corruption is very high.

CPI as the name indicates is a study based on perception of business people and risk analysts. It neither reveals the level and extent of corruption nor identifies sectors where corruption is prevalent. It is not based on hard data.

Hence CPI though relevant and gives an overall view, falls short, if its data is to be utilized for identifying areas that need to be tackled, planning activities and conducting programmes for the specific sectors. Hence the need for national and state level assessments of the actual experiences of the common man who is the legitimate recipient of the public services delivered by the government, and bears the brunt of all acts of mis-governance and corruption.

National and State Level Perspectives

National and state level perspectives of the common person are required to identify;

1. Where is corruption.
2. Extent of corruption.
3. Forms of corruption.
4. Who and how many indulge in corruption.
5. Who are affected by corruption.

6. Why corruption.

7. How to eliminate corruption.

8. What people and civil societies institutions can do.

Approach Developed by Human Development Reports

World Human Development Reports also first developed and prepared international perspective and then subsequently several national and regional level studies were prepared which led to a new policy and programmes framework to deal with human development. National and regional perspectives substantiated the international perspective on human development. The same approach is required on corruption. The international perspective on corruption needs to be substantiated by national and regional level perspectives, for formulating approach, policy, and programme for combating corruption and for educating and empowering people. There is a very high rank correlation as well as coefficient of correlation between Corruption Perception Index and Human Development Index.

People's Perspective

Indians think that corruption cannot be eliminated from India—at least not in their lifetime. This pessimistic and cynical perception of the people is largely an outcome of confusing corruption with all kinds of illegal actions and activities like dishonesty, cheating, duping, etc. Most illegal actions, many of which are private actions, are confused with corruption. The Prevention of Corruption Act 1988 and Indian Penal Code clearly distinguish between corruption indulged by public servants for private gains and illegal actions by individuals. There are separate Acts in India for dealing with different kinds of illegal actions of private individuals. For example, if a public servant amasses wealth disproportionate to his known sources of income then he can be tried under Prevention of Corruption Act 1988. However, if a businessperson amasses wealth disproportionate to his known source of income he will be dealt under Income, Tax Act for concealing his income and not under Prevention of Corruption Act.

Types of Corruption

Corruption is defined as the use of public office for private gains. Scales of corruption can be Grand, Middling or Petty and payment of bribes can be due to collusion between the bribe taker and the bribe giver, due to coercion or even expectation.

Existence of corruption implies that there are corrupt people, there are also corrupt practices, and there is a corrupt system.

Therefore, all the three have to be fought simultaneously to eliminate the vice of corruption. The present system provides for taking on the corrupt persons through a legal mechanism, which has not been found to be very effective. Many corrupt practices fall outside the purview of existing laws and need to be tackled by people themselves. The responsibility for dealing with corrupt people, corrupt practices and corrupt systems devolves equally on individuals, civil society institutions, legislature, executive, and the judiciary.

Who indulges in Corruption

India is one of the most regulated economies of the world with powers concentrated in few hands. It is a poor country with scarce resources where demand is always more than supply. The receivers of the public services are largely poor, ignorant, and illiterate. There is also absence of transparency and accountability of the public servants. There is no system of rewards and punishments for the public servants. There is also no right to information. The licence-permit-quota-inspector regime is pervasive in India since independence and continues even after liberalization and globalization of 1991. In addition, there are 3,000 central statutes and 10 times as many state statutes plus subsidiary and administrative laws (most of them archaic), with several exemption clauses and discretionary powers sans accountability. All these conditions are fertile breeding grounds for corruption.

At present, 19.5 million people hold public office with Central and state governments, quasi-Central and quasi-state institutions, and rural and urban local bodies spread over 200,000 establishments and offices all over India.

CPI and HDI

A recent study on relationship between Corruption Perception Index (CPI) and Human Development Index (HDI) ranked the CPI and HDI of 102 countries and estimated the Spearman's Rank Correlation and Coefficient of Correlation for 2002. The Rank Correlation is estimated to be 0.788 and the coefficient of correlation 0.766. Linear relationship between HDI and CPI also exists.

The relationship is estimated to be $Y = 0.52 + 0.048 X$, where Y is HDI and X is CPI.

Armed with these thousands of laws, 19.5 million public servants exercise their powers, control and regulate the remaining thousand million citizens. Since 90 per cent of these 19.5 million public servants are, class III and class IV employees, power is concentrated in the hands of less than 2 million public servants who regulate and control the fate of a thousand million people. This minority has the potential to indulge in corruption in all its forms and scale giving India an image of one of the most corrupt countries of the world. The remaining 17.5 million public servants with limited powers can indulge in petty corruption only.

Corruption can be reduced considerably in India by merely

scrapping obsolete and archaic laws (majority of them are such) and rationalizing the remaining ones. This task should be taken up seriously and vigorously by civil society, institutions using committed judiciary and lawyers because the government functionaries alone can never do this.

At present, the perception is that government can eradicate corruption and responsibility for eradicating corruption is that of government alone. However, in view of the kind of corruption and the framework that we have in India, it is very clear that government alone cannot eradicate corruption. If the people and civil society institutions remain indifferent and show helplessness in combating corruption, it can never be eradicated or for that matter even reduced. Thus, the responsibility and the onus of combating corruption are as much of the people and the civil society institutions as that of the government.

Prevention of Corruption Act 1988

To deal with corruption amongst public servants India enacted Prevention of Corruption Act 1988, replacing Prevention of Corruption Act 1947. PCA 1988 incorporates provisions of chapter IX of the Indian Penal Code to deal with public servants and those who abet them by way of criminal misconduct and provide to enable attachment of their ill-gotten wealth obtained through corrupt means. This act also widens the scope of definition of Public servants. Public servant means any person in the service, pay of the government, or remunerated by the government by fees or commission for the performance of any public duty. Public duty means a duty in the discharge of which the state, the public, or the community at large has an interest. 'State' includes a corporation established by or under a central, provincial or state act or an authority or a body owned or controlled or aided by the government or a government company defined in Section 617 of the Company's Act 1956. In India, in addition to a large number of health and educational institutions, the government also aids many other kinds of organizations. Hence, the employees of such bodies are also covered by this act. Normally corruption is defined as using public office for private gains. In PCA 1988, public servant and public duty have very wide definitions covering every person who is in the actual possession of the situation of a public servant and discharging public duty which the state, public or the community at large has a interest. Persons holding various public offices are public servants, whether appointed by the government or not.

Citizens' Charter

The concept of Citizens' Charter has been introduced to improve the quality of public services. It ensures accountability, transparency and quality of services provided by various government organizations. It enables citizens to avail of services with minimum hassle, in reasonable time, and at a minimum cost. Effective implementation of Citizens' Charters will go a long way in controlling corruption. The Government of India has launched an ambitious programme for formulation and implementation of Citizens' Charters in all government departments.

To oversee the implementation and diffusion of these Charters, there must be Monitoring Committees consisting of both public service providers and service receivers.

The number of government establishments and offices have doubled from approximately 100,000 to 200,000 in the last two decades and the number of government servants has bloated from 15.5 million in 1981 to 19.5 million today.

British Citizens' Charter

In Britain, there are more than ten thousand Charters setting service standards at a level that has a direct impact on the quality of individual's life. For example, what an elderly person can expect from his/ her local social service departments. Few years ago, many doubters said that the performance of the public servants could never be measured. These Citizen's Charters set new standards and new targets. They give more information about the performance tables for schools, hospitals, local authorities, and police and fire services, to help them make choices and question the way things are run. By setting up measurable targets, the government is delivering concrete improvements in the quality and efficiency of services. The Charter Mark Award Scheme is now the focal point for recognizing the achievement of organizations that have made a special contribution to serve the public; it also demonstrates a strong public commitment to raise standards.

Say No to Bribes

In Sivaji, the software engineer-turned corruption crusader essayed by Rajinikanth in the blockbuster movie of the same name, 42-year-old Vijay Anand closed down his software solutions firm in Washington DC in 2004 and returned to Chennai to inspire Indians to fight corruption. What prompted the drastic step? "I was running a business in Coimbatore in the early 1990s. Every little thing I needed to get done was done only by paying a bribe. When 1 went to the US in 1997, getting my driving licence was a cinch. I made up my mind to do something to stem the rot in the system," he says.

In 1998, Anand launched the AIMS India project in Washington to donate desks and benches to schools and to build toilets in backward villages. Red tapism bogged down the popular project. "Carrying out these projects from the US was difficult. Government officials took credit for our work. I decided to return in 2005," Anand says. In 2007, he joined social activist M.B. Nirmal to revive Fifth Pillar, a non-profit advocacy group that fights corruption. In 2008, he finally worked out an arrangement to focus fully on social work. "My brother and cousins manage my business in the US which I revived in 2006," he says.

Fifth Pillar exhorts people to fight corruption in a non-confrontationist manner. Anand travels around the country, educating students on the Right To Information Act (RTI) and on the debilitating impact of political corruption on India's democracy. Anand's weapon of choice is a zero rupee note, a facsimile of the 50 rupee note, designed to be handed to officials who demand a bribe. Instead of the promissory note is the pledge "I promise to neither accept nor give bribe." Anand has distributed about 1.5 million such notes in Tamil Nadu. Fifth Pillar now has 1,200 members and 6,000 online subscribers worldwide. Its centres in Chennai and other districts of Tamil Nadu staffed by volunteers help people to leverage the RTI Act by drafting petitions and delivering them to the relevant government department. "We want to empower people to fight for their rights. There was this woman in Chennai who had been waiting a year for her land title and was told she would only receive it if she paid a 'fee' of ₹7,500. She then went to the office with one of our volunteers and got the document in 30 minutes without paying anything," says Anand. Anand has orchestrated large human chains on the beaches of Chennai. The next step, he says, is to expand his crusade worldwide.

One of the important elements, in any anti-corruption framework, involving multiple jurisdictions, is the effectiveness of cooperation amongst agencies involved in common goal of punishing the guilty. "The difficulties for jurisdiction, to act in a concerted and coordinated manner, may be many. There is thus, a need to look at the existing mechanisms of institutions and instrumentalities of international cooperation in cross border investigations and the necessity to evolve mechanisms for addressing the flaws. There is a need for an appropriate anti-corruption framework to ensure more effective international cooperation.

Corruption is an evil. There is a need for checking corruption in private sectors and public procurement which act as breeding ground for graft to thrive. The role of private sector has increasingly come into focus as one of the key players in the anti-corruption framework. Steps are required to be initiated to cover private sector bribery within a legislative framework. India's domestic laws governing the functioning of corporate bodies is robust and it has substantive provisions to ensure transparency, accountability and audit.

It's a misconception that punishing corrupt lower and middle level public officials will go a long way towards eradicating the problem. The solution lies in bringing corrupt politicians and senior bureaucrats to book. Also, formulating anti-corruption laws alone is not enough. Proper implementation is equally, if not more, important.

Anna Hazare has been successful because he has focused single-mindedly on one issue corruption. The Lokpal is only a beginning. It will catch crooks after the act. There is a need to prevent the disease. To make a real difference, reforming the bureaucracy, the police, the judiciary, and the electoral system is required. These reforms should be next on Anna Hazare's agenda. He should not get distracted by other problems, such as education, health, drinking water etc. Obviously, there is corruption in the delivery of these services— one in four teachers is absent in a state primary school; two in five doctors are absent in a primary health centre. But the answer is to make civil servants accountable— government teachers and doctors are civil servants, after all. The overhaul of the bureaucracy, for example, will entail reduction in administrative discretion swiftness and certainty of punishment in disciplinary proceedings; reduction in rent seeking opportunities; penalisation for delays; elimination of the seniority system. These ideas are not new—every administrative reforms commission has recommended them, but the bureaucracy has sabotaged them.

In this age of information technology, when one can blink and situations change every second like the position of the sun, it is our political establishment that has not been able to keep pace.

The era of idealistic nation building of the 50s and the 60s has been replaced by individual self-serving agenda of an aspiring and ambitious youth comprising more than half of India's population. The system itself has transformed to reflect and encourage these individuals to chart their own growth path. The change in demographics is not merely limited to age but is also reflected in the increase in education, awareness and urbanization of India. From the vast majority of the population living in rural areas, the aspiration of the rural youth continues to compel large migrations to cities. Focus has shifted from ensuring two square meals to attempting to lead the high life. The anonymity of the Internet and outreach of mobile telecommunications have ensured that information finds diverse platforms to reach out.

This means that political constituencies are fast evolving to accommodate this fast growing, well connected and easily dissatisfied Indian youth. A large number of parliamentary constituencies have now become urbanized after delimitation. The middle class, considered at one time to be on the fringes of democracy, has now found critical mass due to the massive swell in its numbers and a strong medium of communication via Twitter and Facebook. The evidence of its power was first demonstrated in the success of the 'Pink Chaddi' campaign. No one has heard of the Ram Sena since then.

However, the majority of the political establishments have failed to take into account the changing needs of its voters. And remnants of Nehru's socialistic rural agenda continue to dominate political strategy. Politics has been changing in slow phases. The first was characterized by single party dominance, which was followed by a multiparty system and then a phase where there is a predominance of regional political parties in the country. All through, it has been assumed that popular concerns are being addressed with the changing political scenario in the country. This was challenged by the fact that thousands of people were on the roads, in support of Anna Hazare, just to make sure that their voices are heard. Though we have a representative democratic system in place, Indians are striving for a more participative democracy. The role of civil society, visual and social media and other voluntary organizations is a manifestation of this fact. The participation of middle class and youth in support of the spirit of the Lokpal movement shows the changing political scenario in the country. India's democracy will now have to incorporate this new political class and allow them to participate. Political parties that do not accommodate these rising voices will fade into oblivion.

This effectively means that the face of the modern politician is going to change. As long as India believes in democracy, the focus needs to be on reforming rather than undermining its democratic institutions. Politics continues to impact the lives of almost every Indian in some way. It is here that why this movement instilled a threat perception within the Government. This has been a positive transformation that brought corruption to centre stage. The adversarial tone of Team Anna did contribute to the unproductive environment. Abusive language and name calling has only served to vitiate the atmosphere further. Yet listening to the voices would have been more politically prudent. After all, Parliament remains the sole harbinger of legislation.

There has been much talk of the sanctity of institutions of the republic to be respected and safeguarded. Some Hon'ble members of Parliament have accused some of the Anna Hazare team members and supporters of breach of privilege and denigration of the dignity of the House. Not un-often has many a minister decried judicial or CAG 'overreach'. Nobody disputes that laws have to be enacted by Parliament, not on Parliament Street. Shouldn't Hon'ble members introspect and ask why people across the land reposed faith in an Anna, not in Parliament, why the citizens laud judicial activism at time-bound induction of CNG in public transport vehicles in the capital city or its sealing of illegal properties, or obvious inaction against black money stacked in safe havens abroad? Parliamentarians themselves have denigrated the institution. More often they sneer and shout than discuss and legislate, and yearn for *lal batti* (Red Beacon) atop their vehicles. Inevitably, "We, the people", whom the Constitution places at the centre-stage, have little respect left for them.

Institutions are built up by great minds and nurtured by brave souls over a period of time. But they can be destroyed by petty self-serving Atillas in a single act of mindless vandalism. Shouldn't the country reflect how systematically some of the hallowed institutions have been assaulted by myopic opportunism. A brazen partisan advocacy of a committed bureaucracy has jeopardised the very system of governance in the country, nurturing a culture of flourishing graft as much as tyranny of *babus*, swelling ranks of slothful parasites. The role of CBI generate almost perennial cynicism and disbelief. Are people aware of the extra-constitutional games that are played every other day in the stately Raj Bhawans? The role of country's most exalted office.

President of the Republic has not always remained unsullied. Now not even the authority and aura of Prime Minister has been spared. Simultaneously, the countrymen take pride at what the CEC now symbolizes after an irrepressible Seshan lent it the sinews of moral strength. The Anna Hazare-led countrywide peaceful protests symbolised by multitudes converging at Ramlila Maidan signified a gathering distrust of our governance system and eroding faith in legislators. It is not only the ubiquity and magnitude of scandals and scams which have benumbed people's consciences, an unabated plunder of nation's resources, its forests and minerals, land grabs, rampant inequities, ostentation and greed have widened the gulf between the, ruler and the ruled, the rich and the poor, breeding cynicism and disaffection for the very institution of democracy—as practised in the country. Politicians across the spectrum have failed to fathom the intensity of people's angst. Although conceding that some pockets of the country have been transformed in terms of material gains, its GDP recording a high growth, people now living longer and better fed, the glass remains more than half empty. Large swathes of the land, hundreds of the districts for years beyond the writ of the state have been driven by avarice and exploitation of *Adivasis* and tribals to the Maoist and to the naxal fold.

An abiding popular impression is of politicians' intent being suspect, seen as they are playing their frolicsome fraud, ever since the Lokpal and Lokayuktas Bill was passed by Lok Sabha in 1969. Notwithstanding its clear avowal in September 2004 that would lose no time in enacting the bill, amnesia got the better of it; and, worse, its own *sarkari* Lokpal draft put out under duress made a mockery of an important issue bristling with an incendiary situation. Septuagenarian Hazare's incarceration by the beleaguered government provoked nation's revulsion as much as its rare resolve to force it out of its inertia, apathy and inaction. Several of its acts of omission and commission added fuel to fire, for example, inexplicable obduracy while selecting and defending the previous CVC, blocking the formation of JPC for le *affaire* 2G, uncalled for comments on CAG. Government has been failing to communicate as much as to listen and grasp. The only communication with people has generally been through narcissistic splashes across the print media or by fielding mercenary-like party spokesmen, many of whom first need to learn the virtues of restraint. And some seniors, when they condescended, smother themselves with a self-belief in omniscience and superciliousness. Over 30 per cent of the country's population is less than 16 years old; more than half of its population is 25 or younger. It is the young people who are the country's real strength, and hope. It is the young among the 400 million middle class with aspirations of a vibrant India free of corruption who seem to constitute the foot soldiers of the Anna brigade. Julia Preston and Samuel Dillon, in *Opening Mexico: The Making of a Democracy*, talk of the disgust and cynicism of Mexicans, which led to a standard formation of rescue brigades which later spawned grassroots political organizations, implying that unless democracy could deliver a better life, the public could opt for the facile promises of undemocratic populists along the lines of Hugo Chavez.

A former IPS officer has finally reversed the improper overcharges on her travel bills, albeit after a bit of dawdling defence of her actions. That should hopefully cool off some of the steam over the matter. Though why perfectly honourable and sensible people indulge in such lamentable actions, and do not immediately see the impropriety of it even when pointed out, is a wonderment of the Indian ethos. It appears to be more a rule than an exception among senior government functionaries —whether in the IAS, IFS, IPS or even in the higher judiciary to operate Trusts for some charitable cause or the other, even when still in service. True, some of these Trusts actually render excellent service to the society, while others may be far removed from such contribution. But even so, the practice itself raises several questions, especially at a time when the society as a whole is throwing up some fundamental questions about corruption. The most obvious face of corruption is when a government functionary demands and or receives explicit graft in exchange for favours rendered. But what happens when a government functionary asks the recipient of the favour to pay a consideration, not directly to him or her, but as a contribution to his or her Trust instead?

The question becomes even more difficult when the Trust actually renders valuable service to the society. After all, the officer is not asking anything, directly or indirectly, for self, but only for the Charitable Trust, for a good cause! He or she may be merely clearing a file of yours, but just before communicating the decision, you may receive a polite telephonic request for a contribution to the Trust from one of the functionaries of the Trust. How does one link or dissociate the 'services rendered' by the officer to the call for contribution to the 'Charitable Trust'? It is not as if these questions are theoretical or rhetorical. Many a senior official in powerful position is all too well known to use, or to have used—or rather misused —their positions to 'extort' contributions for their Trusts. In the same spirit as the officer's argument that she did not benefit personally —one may have little reason to disbelieve her—all these officials might believe, convince themselves to believe or just say they believe, that they have not benefited personally from such contributions to their Trusts, even when the contributions are de facto 'extorted'. Never mind that in most cases, in due course, these Trusts become their retirement havens and, more often than not, even a political platform should they choose to use it. At least these Trusts offer them that option.

The next question is what is 'personal benefit'? When you are seen as the founder benefactor of a significant Trust working for a good charitable cause, isn't the benefit of that charitable image available to you? Isn't the founder of the Trust a beneficiary of the retirement and political options that the Trust affords him or her? Of course these individuals usually represent the finest brains in the society and do these things very safely and quietly, so that 99.99 per cent of the times, they not only simply get away with these deeds, but get to enjoy the enormous social or even financial rewards (albeit indirect) of these Trusts. Some of them even ensure that their Trusts genuinely do good work. But 'is it extortion or indirect graft all right, by government servants, if it is for a genuine charitable cause; This raises the big question, whether government servants, who are supposed to devote their entire energies to serving the public, be allowed to operate Trusts. In this country, there are enough and more NGOs working on any number of social causes. Is it really necessary to allow government servants to found and operate more Trusts? When a government servant operates a Trust, even if it is in the name of the spouse, is it realistic to pretend that there is really no conflict of interest between his or her official duties and the existence of the Trust? Is there a case to ban allowing formation of Trusts to serving officers of the government or judiciary?

Imagine if, an honourable and upright officer by any reckoning, could bring to convince herself that there was nothing wrong in what she did, what allowance do we make for the morally lesser officers? Given the lack of transparency in the operations of Trusts and Societies, there is no amount of due diligence that can prevent the potential for misuse of such Trusts by civil servants. The government service conditions should simply ban formation of Trusts by government servants completely. A related question is whether even the near relatives, say, spouses and children, of serving government servants be allowed to form Trusts? Of course, the "obvious question that comes to mind is, if it is morally defensible for the government to prevent the relatives from pursuing their desired area of interest. But the fact is, there are already some restraints on what the immediate relatives can or cannot do. Adding another key item to the list should not be a big problem. No principle ever comes without a price and if members of the government or judiciary wish to remain above suspicion of misuse of their offices, selecting their spouses accordingly and advising their offspring suitably is a just expectation by the society.

Malum in se (plural *mala in se*) is a Latin phrase meaning wrong or evil in itself. The phrase is used to refer to conduct assessed as sinful or inherently wrong by nature, independent of regulations governing the conduct. It is distinguished from *malum* prohibitum, which is wrong only because it is prohibited.

For example, most human beings feel that murder, rape, and theft is wrong, regardless of whether a law governs such conduct or where the conduct occurs, and is thus recognizably *malum in se*. In contrast, consider driving laws. In the US., people drive on the right-hand side of the road, in the UK and other states of the Commonwealth, people drive on the left-hand side. Violation of these rules is an example of a *malum* prohibitum law because the act is not inherently bad, but is forbidden by law, as set forth by the lawmakers of the jurisdiction. *Malum* prohibitum crimes are criminal not because they are inherently bad, but because the act is prohibited by the law of the state.

This concept was used to develop the various common law offences.

Another way to describe the underlying conceptual difference between "*malum in se*" and "*malum prohibitum*" is "*iussum quia iustum*" and "*iustum quia iussum*," namely something that is commanded (*ius sum*) because it is just (*iustum*) and something that is just (*iustum*) because it is commanded (*iussum*).

Definition of Corruption

Corruption is often defined as the lack of integrity or honesty. It is also defined as "moral perversion; impairment of virtue and moral principles." However, morality is difficult to measure as it is quite subjective.

The Transparency International (TI) defines corruption as follows:

> Corruption is operationally defined as the misuse of entrusted power for private gain TI further differentiates between "according to rule" corruption and "against the rule" corruption. Facilitation payments, where a bribe is paid to receive preferential treatment for something that the bribe receiver is required to do by law, constitute the former. The latter, on the other hand, is a bribe paid to obtain services the bribe receiver is prohibited from being provided. Thus corruption as defined by TI is restricted to the services provided by government, though the same definition can be extended to any other organization as well. A country can fall or rise in the corruption index depending upon the laws of the land. For example, if the governments make the laws that give government officials little power or discretion, there is no question of misuse of power and hence no corruption. Thus the free economies are likely to be less corrupt than the controlled economies.

The issue of corruption is mainly related to the payment of bribe or illegal money to 'the government officials for doing a legal or illegal work'. Thus the root cause of corruption is money that flows illegally from a citizen to a government official. Therefore, if the salaries of the government employees can be increased substantially or their compensation package can be related to the power they enjoy, then the scope of corruption can be minimized. It is, therefore, noticed that the countries like Singapore or the USA that pays their employees well are rated as less corrupt. However, the payment capacities of the government depend on the prosperity of the nation. If the nation is poor, governments cannot afford to pay well to its employees. Thus, there must be a correlation between the per capita income of the country and the corruption index. Corruption is considered to be the biggest hindrance in the economic growth of the country. It is believed that if corruption is reduced, the economic growth of the country is increased. Corruption has also been one of the most important issues in all elections in India. Almost everyday, we hear the news regarding the arrest or prosecution of some government official or political leader in a corruption case. Yet corruption continues to be all pervasive in the public life of India. Citizens of India are getting impatient as they wish to see the end of corruption sooner than later. Often the intellectual class proposes severe punishment to deter the corruption in government. It is often hinted that India is not serious in fighting corruption as other countries like China, the USA, the UK, Russia or Israel are. Some people even blame democracy for corruption as the changes in democracies are slow.

Corruption Perception

Corruption is a matter of perception. The surveys of the Corruption Perception Index (CPI) by Transparency International every year is considered to be the most authentic indicator of corruption. The 2008 CPI scores 180 countries on a scale from zero (highly corrupt) to ten (highly clean). According to the report, Denmark, New Zealand and Sweden share the highest score at 9.3, followed immediately by Singapore at 9.2. Bringing up the rear is Somalia at 1.0, slightly trailing Iraq and Myanmar at 1.3 and Haiti at 1.4.

It is evident that no country in the world is free from corruption. The score of 9.3 by the least corrupt indicates that even in such countries, the government officials are not considered above board by the citizens of their countries.

The Economics of Corruption

The studies clearly establish that there is a direct correlation between the state of the economy and corruption. It can be established by comparing the per capita income of a country and the corruption index of the same country. The per capita income of the countries based by GDP (nominal) per capita by the World Bank Report for the least corrupt countries are as follows.

Per Capita Income of 10 least corrupt countries

Country rank (170)	Country	Per Capita (US$)
(1)	(2)	(3)
5	Denmark	62,327
23	New Zealand	30,614
8	Sweden	52,057
20	Singapore	37,600
9	Finland	51,060
3	Switzerland	64,011
6	Iceland	52,549
7	Netherlands	52,322
11	Australia	47,498
17	Canada	42,031

The per capita income of the countries based on the World Bank Report of 2008 (4) for the most corrupt countries are as follows:

Per Capita Income of 10 most corrupt countries

Country rank	Country	2008 CPI Score
(1)	(2)	(3)
169	Congo Democratic Republic	180
24	Equatorial	28,111
143	Chad	755
161	Guinea	434
119	Sudan	1,413
176	Afghanistan	NA
145	Haiti	711
178	Iraq	NA
178	Myanmar	NA
180	Somalia	NA

Thus it is evident from the comparison of above tables that all countries that are rated as the least corrupt those which are also the most prosperous countries and their per capita income is more than 100 times of the countries which are rated as the most corrupt. The above findings can be interpreted as following:

1. *If the country is corrupt, it is likely to be poor:* Therefore, reducing corruption is prerequisite for increasing prosperity.

2. *If the country is poor, it is more likely to be corrupt:* Therefore, the economic prosperity is the prerequisite for reducing corruption.

Thus the poor countries are trapped in a vicious circle. Unless they reduce corruption, they can't become prosperous and they can't become prosperous unless they reduce corruption.

Measuring the Success of Anti-Corruption

The study as discussed above shows that it is possible for a rich country to be corrupt (like Equatorial Guinea). However, it is almost impossible for a poor country to be free from corruption as there is no exception to this rule in the real world.

Yet, the study also establishes that poverty and corruption are not always correlated. Individual countries and leaderships can make a difference in reducing corruption and increasing the development and prosperity of a nation by taking suitable measures. As the economic prosperity comes only gradually, corruption can also be removed only gradually. It is not possible to remove corruption overnight by taking hard measures like imposing severe penalty against corrupt officials as the punishments to them shall again be done by the same government officials and judiciary who are not yet free from corruption. Thus the true effort of the government in fighting corruption is reflected in the difference between the position of a country in the prosperity and corruption.

Above tables calculate the difference between the Corruption Score and the Prosperity Score which measures the determination of the leadership in fighting corruption despite of the lower per capita income of their citizen. The difference is called the Anti-Corruption Score (ACS). The Honesty Score and the Prosperity Score of a country have been calculated on percentile basis, i.e., the percentage of countries whose scores are less than them. This has been done to remove the difference between the numbers of countries selected for the study in two cases.

India's Fight against Corruption

The position of India was 85 of the 180 countries surveyed by Transparency International in year 2008. It is still a matter of concern and corruption has to be reduced for bringing growth and prosperity in the country. Yet the same statistics shows that corruption in India is reducing consistently and today there is no major country in the world which is less corrupt than India at the same economic level. The Anti-Corruption Score of India is the highest amongst the major countries of the world. It can be, therefore, concluded that corruption in India is declining over the year. The progress of India in fighting corruption is reflected.

It is evident that India is making consistent progress in its war against corruption. It has not only reduced the CPI consistently over the year from 2.7 to 3.4 but also improved its ranking in the least corrupt countries. While in the year 2001, India was more honest than only 22 percentage countries of the world, it has become more honest than 47 percentage countries in 2008. Its high Anti-corruption Score indicates that India is fighting its battle against corruption far more sincerely than any other major country of the world.

The Anti-Corruption Score of Major Countries of the World

Country	Country Score	Rank (180)	Honesty Score (%tiles)	Per Capita	Rank (170)	Prosperity Score (%tiles)	Anti-corruption Score
India	3,4	85	52.78	1068	131	22.94	29.8
China	3,6	72	60	2912	98	42.35	17.6
Sri Lanka	3,2	92	48.89	2031	110	35.29	13.6
New Zealand	9,3	1	99.44	30614	23	86.47	13
Singapore	9,2	4	97.78	37600	20	88.24	9.54
Bangladesh	2,1	147	18.33	494	150	11.76	6.57
Canada	8,7	9	95	42.031	17	90	5
Pakistan	2,5	134	2556	1013	135	20.59	4.97
Sweden	9,3	1	99.44	52057	8	95.29	4.15
Denmark	9,3	1	99.44	62327	5	9706	2.39
Egypt	2,8	115	36.11	1997	112	34.12	1.99
Germany	7,9	14	92.22	44471	15	91.18	1.05
Japan	7,3	18	90	38443	18	89.41	0.59
United Kingdom	7,7	16	91.11	43089	16	90.59	0.52
USA	7,3	18	90	46716	12	92.94	-2.94
Israel	6,0	33	81.67	27299	25	85.29	-3.63
France	6,9	23	87.22	45982	14	91.76	-4.54
South Korea	5,6	40	77.78	19115	30	82.35	-4.58
Brazil	3,5	80	55.56	8400	54	68.25	-12.7
Italy	4,8	55	69.44	38.309	19	88.82	-19.4
Argentina	2,9	109	39.44	8235	55	67.65	-28.2
Iran	2,3	141	21.67	5.352	73	57.06	-35.4
Russia	2,1	147	18.33	11339	42	75.29	-57

Winning the War against Corruption

It is much easier to get frustrated from the corruption and blame the government for it. However, the studies indicate that the fight against corruption is slow as it is intimately connected with the economic prosperity of the nation. The Anti-Corruption Score of India is higher than any other major economy of the world and it has improved its score consistently over the years. The days are not far when India shall become a corruption-free country and a role model for the entire world.

The beginning of the last century witnessed the emergence of an Indian, referred to as 'half naked Fakir' by Winston Churchill. His philosophy was, "Means are more important than the end: it is only with the right means that the desired end will follow."

To the charge that, 'means are after all means', he would say, 'Means are, after all, everything'.

His name is `Mohandas Karamchand Gandhi,' known to the world as Mahatma Gandhi, father of our nation.

Mahatma Gandhi's saying is not only in the realm of philosophy, it is in legal jurisprudence too.

About three quarter of century ago Justice Gordon Hewart said, only justice must be done; it must also be seen to be done'.

A quarter of century ago, this is how Lord Denning put it, "But it is fundamental in our law that the means that are adopted to this end should be lawful means. A good end does not justify bad means. The means should not be such as to offend against the fundamental freedom, the privacy and elemental rights of property."

Principle of natural justice is universal. Here is a case from another part of the World.

In TVA v. Hill (57-L.Ed 2nd 117) the question involved before the US Supreme Court was, should the construction of a dam over Little Tennessee River be stopped? The reason was that it might end the natural habitat of an endangered snail darter, a three-inch tannish coloured fish, found in the river.

Traditionally, Attorney General of the US appears only once in his term. These cases are argued in the court by the Solicitor General. At that time, Griffin B. Bell was Attorney General of the US. He chose to appear in this case. He showed the fish to the court. According to him, dam almost complete and its construction should not be stopped merely for this three-inch fish.

The US Supreme Court did grant the injunction stopping the construction of the dam. The court quoted the following passage of Bolds (A man for all seasons Act Page 147) with approval.

"The law Roper the law I know what's legal not what's right and will stick to what's legal—I am not God. The currents and endless of rights and wrong which you find such plain sailing. I cannot navigate, I am not a voyager. I am a forester in the thickness of law—what would you do? Cut a great road through the law to get after the Devil and when the last law was down and Devil turned around on you, where would you hide, Roper the laws all being flat. This country's planned thick with the laws from coast to coast—Man's law not God's and if you cut them down, do you really think you can stand upright in the winds that would blow? Then yes, I would give the Devil benefit of law for my own safety's sake."

Ultimately the US Congress had to amend the law to get over the judgment. Snail darters, that had previously lived only on the Little Tennessee River, were transplanted to the Hiwassee River. It was only then they could complete the constructions.

Black Money

If the UK, the US and Germany can make such arrangements with Swiss banks, why can't India? Clearly, lack of political will and a conniving attitude towards corruption among our politicians are the major stumbling block.

The issue of black money has long been hushed up. Swiss and other overseas banks have become synonymous with safe havens for black money, which in the Indian context touches $1,456 billion by some estimates. Let alone the principal, even if annual interest accrued on this sum, or the related notional tax be made accessible, it will help turn around the country's economy and address corruption-engendered poverty.

Most of India's undisclosed wealth is stashed away abroad, in places like Switzerland and the Cayman Islands which call themselves 'tax havens', a euphemism for banking systems that turn a blind eye to the sources of clandestine riches. According to the Swiss Banking Association report of 2006, Indians have more undeclared booty hidden away in secret accounts than all the rest of the world combined. If the estimated $1,456 billion of Indian money secreted in offshore banks were to be brought back to the country, India's foreign debt would be wiped out some 13 times over, and there'd still be some spare change left.

The UK government has reportedly struck a deal with the Swiss authorities whereby, from 2013, Switzerland will tax the Swiss bank accounts of the UK citizens and transfer this money to the British exchequer. Though the names of the account holders will not be disclosed, the British taxman hopes to gain between £3 billion and £6 billion a year. Germany is said to have signed a similar agreement with Switzerland, and the US has managed to arm-twist the so-called 'gnomes of Zurich' into providing information about American citizens who have undisclosed Swiss accounts.

So, why doesn't the Indian government try and do something

along the same lines? According to Rudolf Elmer—a senior Swiss bank executive who was earlier arrested in Switzerland for being a whistleblower and releasing to Wikileaks a CD with the names of over 2,000 international tax evaders who had secret Swiss accounts, New Delhi "doesn't do enough" to pressure Switzerland into disclosing the details of Indian accounts in that country.

This reluctance on the part of the government to unearth undeclared wealth might seem curious to common citizens who only too often face harassment from Indian tax authorities even after they've paid their full dues to the exchequer. Why hound honest taxpayers for pennies here while ignoring literally billions of pounds lying abroad with impunity? This is not just a case of double standards; it's a case of no standards at all.

The reason for *sarkari* inaction on the issue of offshore accounts is the same as that for its feet-dragging approach to bring in effective Lokpal legislation so many years after the idea was first mooted. In both cases, there seems to be what is often called 'lack of political will' to do what obviously needs to be done. For 'lack of political will' read 'fear of consequences'. Political parties across the board are understandably both to open up cupboards out of which would tumble all manner of incriminating financial skeletons. This conspiracy of inaction is not just restricted to the political class. According to whistleblower Elmer, many rich Indians, including business magnates, film stars and sports celebrities, have wealth hidden away in tax havens. It's in no one's interest to rock the boat. Except, perhaps, the interest of the common citizen who, whether it's a question of black money kept abroad or any other form of graft and financial *hera-pheri*, is perhaps not so common as we might like to think. With so much of India literally in the black, should the rare honest citizen be more accurately described as the uncommon citizen?

Wah India, your myriad avatars, your million mutinies never cease to amaze. We try hard to hijack you. Some cry; "India is

Indira". Others sing, "You are my Sonia". Still others chant, "Saffron Shining". Then comes civil society's counter: "Anna is India". Yet you defy all labels. You're that *band baaja* and political *baraat* marrying all tunes—Anna's Ramlila marching song, Rahul's rejoinders from Lok Sabha, *aam admi's halla bol.* For you remain that battlefield where everything from roving *mantris* to reigning myths are challenged. And how deftly you go from *Gandhigiri* to *Annagiri* when power-wielders stumble from *hera-pheri* to *hara-kiriā*

Rewind to Gandhi. Who thought colonial India would turn into Free India thanks to the 'half-naked fakir' Churchill once derided? Yet that civil disobeyer went to Buckingham Palace to meet the king in the freezing English winter dressed in a loincloth and sandals, remarking "the king had on enough for both of us". It turned out to be the sartorial equivalent of fasting. Ever since he punctured martial machismo, that man from Sabarmati hasn't lacked fans. Ask Obama. He thinks Bapu's the ideal dinner date.

And what of Incredible India's incredible women? Who thought Nehru's quiet daughter would not only become the only 'man' in her kitchen cabinet but also be electorally chastened on an 'Emergency' basis? Certainly not the Congress's all-male Syndicate which believed a "gungi gudiya" PM would make politics a doll's house. The 'dumb doll' went on to put the fear of Indira into everyone from privy purse-holders to Pakistan's macho Yahya Khan. Equally, who'd have wagered Indira's quiet daughter-in-law would trump those who dubbed her Congress's phoren Hand? Or betted Maya and Mamata would turn political He-Men Mulayam and Marxists into Ex-Men?

If gender bromides go bust, so do class- and age-related cliches. Many Anna supporters are middle class. So eat crow, those who said the middle class is such an apolitical navelgazer that it won't go vote let alone champion popular causes. And, no, our youngsters don't just chase dollar dreams abroad when not swinging between Marx and Mammon at home. Haven't they wedded Gandhian idealism with crusading consumerism, lapping up all that Anna merchandise? Who says New India is no country for old men? Septuagenarian Anna's now a youth icon, cheered by protesters and picnickers, Bollywoodwallahs and Dabbawallahs. Think: despite Singh Isn't King and other *netas* avoiding the hippest headgear in town, the cost of 'Main Anna Hazare Hoon' caps have zoomed like *aloo-pyaaz* prices in these inflation-hit times. What does that make India in these inquilaab-hit times? Priceless. Political peccadilloes, fasting and feasting, lokpal and jokepal—India's effervescent, tropical spirit makes a carnival of it all. Look at our record. Salt marches or independence days, spiritual yatras or national elections, cricket matches or hunger strikes, we midnight's children laugh even as we cry (for) the beloved country.

If Group C staff is put under Lokpal, it will get bogged down in cases of petty corruption. Yet, corruption by Group C officials is a reality. The perpetrators are so blatant that a constable will hit a rickshaw puller even as he pays a bribe to the policeman. Go to a government office and you will find that Group C staff are a law unto themselves. The unwritten rule of Group C: if they work, you are lucky, if they don't, too bad. In an officer-versus-staff confrontation, the political executive support the staff, whatever be the merits of their case. But even without Lokpal, corruption can be effectively controlled if higher officers are given clear direction to enforce Civil Service Rules.

The 2G Scam

The 2G scam re-emerged to haunt the Government when a memorandum on the pricing of 2G spectrum written by an official of the finance ministry to an official in the PMO on March 25, 2011, came out in the public domain. The note, which was vetoed by Finance Minister, charged Union Home Minister with not doing enough (i.e., not insisting on an auction) in his capacity as the then finance minister to prevent telecom minister orchestrating the 2G scam. The note split the UPA at the very top, with home minister taking exception to its inferences. It took an intervention from Congress President to arrange a public truce between the two warring ministers. In the interim, finance minister sent a four-page note to the Prime Minister explaining how the finance ministry note blaming home minister was not the opinion of the finance ministry alone but also of the cabinet secretary, principal secretary PMO, telecom secretary and law secretary. It seemed home ministry was being set up as the fall guy for the Government's 2G mess.

Home Minister's complete silence that has followed seems out of character. He isn't one usually shy of defending his position. Instead, he has left the task to others in the Government, primarily Law Minister. The Law Minister has argued that the Government never intended to conduct 2G auctions as a matter of policy because it wanted to pass on maximum benefit to the final consumer. If there was any flaw it was in the process of implementing the first-come-first-served policy which was only Raja's responsibility.

New documents accessed by *India Today* tear apart the Government's defence. There is considerable evidence to show that the finance ministry, presided over by the Home Minister, argued strongly in favour of auctions starting in November 2007. On January 10,2008, the Telecom Minister ignored all advice on auctions and issued 121 letters of intent to licences on a first-come-first-served basis. The Home Minister was silent. Then, on January 15, 2008, the Home Minister wrote a note to the Prime Minister in which he spoke from both sides of his mouth. On the one hand, he endorsed Telecom Minister policy by referring to it as a closed chapter. On the other, he exalted the virtues of auction of telecom spectrum. He authorized senior officials to draft memorandums to that effect in the weeks that followed. The finance minister, as the guardian of Government revenues, was within his rights to reverse Telecom Minister's decision of January, 2008—only letters of intent had been signed at the time—right until April 2008, which is when spectrum was allocated to the licencees. But he did not. The questions around the double talk of January 15, 2008, remained unanswered.

The 2G spectrum controversy has become a global concern, given its enervating impact on governance and growth and the Indian economy's role in global growth. Clear answers are required for three questions: What is the precise nature of the scam? Who lost and who gained? Who is responsible for all this? The common understanding is that the Telecom Minister decided to give away valuable spectrum to new licensees for arbitrary rates. Other ministers including the Prime Minister failed to check him, and the exchequer allegedly lost up to an estimated ₹76,000 crores.

The facts are otherwise. The Prime Minister wrote to Telecom Minister on November 2, 2007, asking him to examine a number of issues in telecom including introduction of transparent methodology of auctions "wherever legally and technically feasible", and revision of the entry fee. The Telecom Minister wrote back that "the issue of auction of spectrum was considered by the TRAI and the Telecom Commission and was not recommended as the existing licence holders, who are already having Spectrum up to 10 MHz per circle, have got it without any spectrum charge. It will be unfair, discriminatory, arbitrary and capricious to auction the spectrum to new applicants as it will not give them level playing field. An increase in the number of operators will certainly bring real competition that will lead to better services and increased tele-density at lower tariff." After issuing new licences, operators did drop charges and the industry added some 500 million customers. Till now, to increase the total number of connections to over 800 million. The minister followed the advice of the telecom regulator, rather than the wishes of the finance ministry. The regulator, in turn, followed the mandate of the New Telecom Policy, 1999, which identifies as its goal the spread of telecom so as to increase the pace of social and economic development, rather than direct revenue accumulation. The policy has been a runaway success ever since it was regularized, in 2003, Reliance's back door entry into mobile telephony, removing an arbitrary restriction—on full deployment of licensed technology.

Whenever the government brings in new players, incumbents stand to lose and cry foul. This happened in 2003, but consumers gained big time and, for the first time the common man could afford mobile telephony. But at the end of 2006-07, the country had only 206 million phone subscribers and the number had gone up to some 300 million by end 2007. Since then, tariffs have plummeted and growth of the customer base has been explosive. The Comptroller and Auditor General (CAG)— assumed auctioning spectrum was the right policy and further assumed that 2G spectrum would have got the same amount as 3G spectrum and arrived at a loss of ₹76,000 crores. This conclusion is doubly faulty. For one, the CAG's job is not to question or formulate policy. The policy of the government is to price spectrum and licence to maximize telecom spread and not direct revenue. And this is the right policy for a developing country like India. The CAG's first fault lies in adopting a normative yardstick that is inappropriate and whose adequacy it does not have the authority to judge. The second fault is ignoring, altogether, the indirect accretion of revenue from the policy that the government followed. It makes intuitive sense that growth in telecom penetration accelerates economic growth. Empirical tests by academics suggest that the effect is more pronounced at low levels of income and industrial development, such as in India. It would be reasonable to assume that the pickup in telecom spread after 2003 raised the rate of economic growth. It would also be reasonable to assume that, but for the rapid spread in telecom networks, computerization of tax administration would have been far less efficient. If we arbitrarily assume that the GDP growth and tax-GDP ratio both would have been one percentage point lower than what they have been without the kind of telecom growth India has had, the additional revenue attributable to telecom spread would be close to ₹1,00,000 crores in just one year. Over a period, the additional revenue would exceed spectrum auction , proceeds by far.

Instead of these arbitrary assumptions, a proper econometric study would find out the actual incremental contribution of fast telecom spread to GDP growth and tax administration efficiency, and we could compare the trade off between upfront revenue from sale of high-cost spectrum and superior revenue collections over time from faster growth induced by low-cost telecom.

Prima facie, the exchequer has only gained from a policy of low-cost spectrum and low-cost telecom. Consumers gained. The only losers were incumbent operators. Some argue that competition would keep tariffs down, even if telcos had to pay hefty upfront payments for spectrum. If telcos do keep tariffs down, they would not be able to invest in fast rollout of networks. Making telecom more capital intensive than it needs to be and transferring large investable funds from the private sector to the government are socially and economically undesirable activities, not ideal policy goals to be pursued. In implementing the policy, there could have been attempts to rig the queue for a first-come, first-served grant of licences, and the scam lies in this, and that is what calls for thorough investigation. In addition, there was no policy in place to tax away undeserved capital gains by spectrum allottees—it was added only later. However, it turns out there were no capital it gains to be taxed away.

The BIG Reversal

Seventeen VIPs, from a Cabinet Minister to top private sector executives, were sent to jail because CAG reported in November

2010, that the Government had presumably lost ₹1,76,000 crores in the disbursement of 2G spectrum in 2008. This figure was a massive exaggeration, said R.P. Singh, author of the draft 2G report and a former director-general audit, post and telecommunications, in the CAG. The loss, he has told *India Today*, is not more than ₹2,645 crores. In other words, this was exaggerated nearly 80 times in the report sent by CAG chief Vinod Rai to Parliament.

The Supreme Court set in motion proceedings which have rocked Government and shaped the discourse on the basis of the ₹1,76,000 crores figure. Says Singh, "You know how the Government functions. I don't want to go into the whys and wherefores of what happened between my draft report and the final CAG report, but in Government, one has to kowtow to superior authorities."

Singh in his May 31, 2010, draft performance audit report on the 'issue of licences and allotment of 2G spectrum by the Department of Telecommunications (DOT)' pegs the loss at ₹2,645 crores and not ₹1,76,000 crores, the figure in the CAG report of October 2010 that rocked the country. Both are still notional losses. The CBI, which filed an FIR against unknown persons in October 2009, was galvanized into action after the Supreme Court took note of the report. Singh's note states, "The decision to adopt 2001 prices was taken in 2003 for early implementation of Unified Access Service (UAS) licence. The bidding pattern of 2001 would clearly indicate that the prices were discovered from a nascent market and did not reflect the true value of licences. DOT did not even consider factoring in inflation in the economy in six years. The cost inflation index which was 426 in 2001-02 had risen to 551 in 2007-08." Using the index, the entry fee of ₹ 1,658.57 crores for a pan Indian UAS licence in 2007-08 should have cost ₹486 crores more than the rate fixed in 2001. He said that DoT, taking into account the changes in the economy in general and the telecom market in particular, should have made an attempt to revise the entry fee for the 122 licences issued in January 2008. Singh further said, "I am very clear about the facts. I have said that in the absence of written recommendations from Telecom Regulatory Authority of India (TRAI), statements and observations of CAG post facto on 3G auction don't hold. Equally S Tel withdrew its case before the Delhi High Court, so how can that be factored in to quantify the loss?" He believed that the 'Performance audit report on the issue of licences and allocation of 2G spectrum by DOT was manipulated'. Singh reckoned the CAG headquarters did not bother to consider the loss calculation by the DG Audit, P&T. Instead, it took a completely different track and used its own criteria to inflate the loss figure. Using the 3G auction prices, S Tel's offer in the Delhi High Court and the purported sale of equity by Unitech and Swan Telecom (which ultimately turned out to be issue of fresh shares), in October 2010, the CAG arrived at the notional loss figure of ₹1,76,000 crores. Strangely this was done despite strong objections posted by Singh in his draft report. The loss to the Government due to the decision not to auction 2G spectrum had not been quantified in his draft audit report. However, based on the offer from telecom operator S Tel for a pan-India licence in court, the impact of non-revision of the price for 2G spectrum was shown to work out to ₹65,725 crores. Singh did not include this figure for the simple reason that S Tel withdrew its offer later. Nor did he peg the 2G rates to the rates discovered through the auction for 3G spectrum in May 2010, where the hit to the exchequer would have been ₹1,02,497 crores.

In the Joint Parliamentary Committee (JPC) meeting on 2G spectrum, Congress questioned the CAG'S figure of ₹1,76,000 crores as presumptive loss due to former Telecom Minister first-come-first-served issue of licences on January 10, 2008. He wanted the committee to examine the communication between the audit officers in the run-up to the computation of the loss. The JPC took note and now wants CAG Vinod Rai, Deputy CAG Rekha Gupta and Singh to depose before it for a better understanding of how the final figure was arrived at.

Congress who pointed out the dissonance within the CAG says in the JPC'S minutes: "Certain people who were a principal part of the audit had a significant difference of opinion with what finally emerged and was tabled in Parliament as the CAG report. They thought it was fairly tenable to examine the entire basis of what went into the formulation and preparation of that report. CAG sources, when contacted by *India Today*, put up a stout defence. "CAG will produce all the relevant documents whenever called for. There was no cover-up, no loopholes, records will speak for themselves. A mountain was made of a molehill. When Singh's draft report was sent to DOT in August 2010, Telecom Secretary R. Chandrashekhar responded saying that he did not agree with its contents. DoT trashed the ₹2,645 crores figure. It argued that entry fee was not revised because till 2006 there were not many companies interested in entering the telecom sector even at the entry fee level decided in 2001. Moreover, DoT stated that TRAI had not recommended revision of entry fees. As for the apprehension of its finance wing on the pricing of UAS licences, DoT said it was irrelevant and out of context because the Telecom Secretary had explained to the finance ministry that the Cabinet decision of October 2003 had authorized the Telecom Minister to decide on the pricing of UAS licences. The difference between ₹2,645 crores and ₹1,76,000 crores is an unbridgeable chasm. Conspiracy theorists believe that the CAG may have done this under pressure from elements in the Opposition but there is no proof to substantiate this amazing escalation in numbers by CAG.

A member of the JPC said, "Since October 2010, there has been this big hype about the ₹1,76.000 crores figure. The whole debate and discourse has centred around this mythical figure. The question is whether this loss is real or imaginary. The principal audit officer, the man who diligently conducted the audit and retired as recently as September 1, 2011, has said that the loss is far less than the stated figure. Even on the charge of dilution of equity by spectrum holders, it has been proved to be unfounded.

They issued fresh shares and did not sell equity. We are now skating on thin ice because these revelations affect the very edifice and constitution of the JPC." To think this issue disrupted the winter session of Parliament and has captured the collective consciousness of the nation. Coupled with TRAI'S response to CBI that it is not in a position to put a figure to 2G losses, this new revelation considerably weakens CBI'S case in Justice OP Saini's court. The JPC will meet on October 12 and 13 to decide whether it is worth continuing with the inquiry into the allocation of 2G spectrum.

A special court framed charges against former Telecom Minister and 16 other accused, including top executives of three telecom companies, in the multi-billion-dollar 2G spectrum scandal. Special Judge OP Saini ruled that there was sufficient evidence against all the accused to stand trial. Raja and former telecom secretary Siddarth Behura will be tried for "criminal breach of trust by a public servant", which if proved, could lead to life imprisonment. The Central Bureau of Investigation special court said the 14 other accused, including Rajya Sabha MP K Kanimozhi, Unitech Group MD Sanjay Chandra, DB Realty MD Vinod Goenka, three executives for the Reliance ADAG and promoters of Swan Telecom, among others will stand trial for criminal conspiracy, which also carries a maximum punishment of life imprisonment. Chandra, Goenka, Swan telecom promoter Shahid Balwa, Reliance ADAG MD Gautam Doshi and senior vice-presidents Hari Nair and Surendra Pipara have also been charged with cheating and causing loss to the public exchequer, according to the court order. Judge OP Saini also upheld all other charges levied by CBI in its charge sheets, including abetment to illegal gratification against K Kanimozhi, daughter of DMK chief M Karunanidhi.

The 2G scam has damaged the reputation of the coalition government. The special judge ordered trial in the case to commence from November 11 after all the accused refused to plead guilty. Raja and the officials are accused of conspiring with corporates to grant mobile licences and airwaves to companies that the CBI claims were ineligible. The Comptroller and Auditor General estimates Raja's decision cost the government a revenue loss of up to ₹ 1.76 lakh crores. All the accused deny any wrongdoing. Raja and Behura have been charged under section 409, which is a criminal breach of trust by a public servant. An equivalent charge (120-B) of criminal conspiracy has been slapped on all other accused because 409 is applicable only to government officials. "We will test these allegations with evidence when the trial begins next month. We are also waiting to see how the court reacts to the bail applications of Kanimozhi and others, now that charges are framed, " Raja's legal counsel Sushil Kumar told the press.

Besides corporate executives, the court also charged companies—Reliance Telecom Ltd, a unit of billionaire Anil Ambani's flagship Reliance Communications, Swan Telecom and Unitech Wireless. "The order framing charges is by no means of finding of guilt. Reliance Telecom and the three executives will immediately move the Delhi High Court for quashing of the charges framed. The bail petitions of the 3 Reliance executives are listed for hearing before the Supreme Court on October 31, 2011," the Reliance ADAG spokesperson said.

Judge Saini imposed an additional charge (under Section 193) on Shahid Balwa, Vinod Goenka, Kusegaon Fruits and Vegetable promoters Rajeev Agarwal and Asif Balwa, Cineyug Films director Karim Morani and Kalaignar TV director and co-promoter Sharad Kumar for forging documents while the investigations were on to be used in court proceedings. The six have been charged with forging documents to show an alleged bribe of ₹200 crores, as a loan from DB Realty to Kalaignar TV, a television channel in which co-accused DMK MP Kanimozhi is a 20 per cent shareholder.

In the first charge sheet, CBI alleged that a bribe of ₹200 crores was channelized from Balwa's DB Realty to DMK-run Kalaignar TV through a "circuitous route" via Cineyug Films and Kusegaon Fruits and Vegetables for mobile permits to Swan. "The charge of 'forgery' (Sec. 468) against Shahid Balwa and criminal breach of trust by a public servant against Raja's former secretary RK Chandolia, have been dropped. This marks a very important victory for us," Vijay Agarwal, the legal counsel for five of the accused said. All the accused have been lodged in jail for over six months and have been denied bail despite filing multiple petitions with different courts. Kanimozhi's bail application comes up before the CBI court on Monday (October 24), in what is seen a test case. Kanimozhi has been seeking bail on the grounds that she is a 'woman' and as Section 437 of the Criminal Procedure Code allows court to grant bail if the person is under 16 years of age or is a woman or is sick or infirm.

The special CBI court has finally framed charges in the 2G case and it strikes a significant departure from the tenor of accusations hitherto. The court omits to accuse Telecom Minister A Raja or others of causing any specified loss to the exchequer. The focus has shifted to manipulation of the queue of applicants for licence to favour Swan Telecom and Unitech Wireless. The decision to drop allegations of causing loss to the exchequer is entirely appropriate and punctures the notion that the policy not to auction spectrum for second-generation mobile telephony (2G) was itself the principal scam. The implication is that since the policy is no longer in the dock, Cabinet ministers who collectively are responsible for policy can no longer be dragged into the 2G mess. Yet, the court does observe that minister Raja deliberately refrained from either revising the entry fee fixed in 2001 and did not consider auctions. Why the entry fee was not revised defies explanation. But, on the question of why there were no auction of spectrum for allocation to new licensees, the framed charge glosses over one vital fact telecom regulator TRAI did not recommend, auctions and the department of telecom required such a recommendation to institute auctions. Mr. Raja wrote back to the Prime Minister, after the latter suggested exploring the use of auctions to allocate spectrum, saying that TRAI had opined that auctioning spectrum for new licensees would be anti-competitive and malafide, when the incumbents had been allocated spectrum as an entitlement of licence without a separate upfront charge. Given TRAI's sensible view on 2G spectrum auctions, it is difficult to find faults with Mr. Raja's decision as Telecom Minister not to hold auctions. The framed charge has other weaknesses. While Mr Raja is accused of receiving a bribe of ₹200 crores, there is no such charge against fellow government functionaries Behura and Chandolia. While the promoters of Swan are accused of giving the bribe, the promoters of Unitech face no such charge. The framing of charges opens the way for the accused to move court for bail.

Government Aid and Corruption

Aid for emergency relief and humanitarian purposes is particularly vulnerable to corruption. Food aid, too, is open to systematic abuse by officials and the private sector. Given present trends in the incidence of civil disorder and natural catastrophes, it is likely that such forms of aid will increase in importance in years to come.

Agencies help combat corruption in countries with support for 'good governance' (referring to elements such as pluralism, judicial reform and anti-corruption agencies); the market economy (demonstrated by practices such as privatization, liberalization and deregulation) and civil society (including civil society organizations, non-governmental organizations and the medial. Corruption is viewed as a process of individual "rent-seeking" that can be reduced, even eliminated, by changing incentive structures, including better salaries for officials, enhanced public access to information and more competition for markets and customers.

Political corruption, in which public resources are diverted for purposes of patronage and cronyism rather than for personal accumulation, is not a phenomenon aid agencies can address directly without getting embroiled in local politics. Yet if the political dimension of corruption is not addressed, it is difficult to see how the implementation of largely technical solutions to corruption can have a lasting impact.

Some agencies lack transparency and accountability in their own operations. Their anti-corruption policies should be judged accordingly. Furthermore, the degree of tolerance among some agencies for the misuse of donor funds by recipient governments is unacceptable, it is easy to conclude that the donor propensity to overlook corruption is directly proportionate to their need to lend or grant money. In that sense, there is a virtual conspiracy of silence between aid givers and takers that defines the aid relationship. Ending such a conspiracy would be a precondition for aid agencies to develop a comparative advantage in confronting corruption.

Defining Corruption in Aid

There are three possible forms of corruption—unilateral misuse of funds on the part of the donor; misuse of funds on the part of the recipient; and collusion between the two sides. Of those three, the second is the most common. In general, bilateral agencies harbour the least internal corruption. As a rule of thumb, the extent of corruption in donor country politics and the quality of public accountability in national life determine the degree of corruption in bilateral aid. Some donor countries have a unique profile in this context: official financial and political support has helped promote national commercial interest, rather than addressing the needs of recipient countries.

Lack of transparency and accountability, in particular in the multilateral agencies, the European Union and the United Nations system, present particular obstacles to efforts at corruption control.

Over the years, a number of United Nations entities have suffered from cronyism and corruption. Corruption and cronyism in the European Commission, climaxing in the resignation of the entire Commission, demonstrate how agencies may find it difficult to practise what they preach in their development ideology, namely, good governance, transparency and integrity.

After a devastating report on its lending performance in over 1,500 projects worth 28 billion United States dollars, the Abidjan-based African Development Bank was substantially restructured and its board of directors replaced. (Knox 1994).

Corruption among Aid Recipients

The most common form of corruption with respect to aid is the unilateral misuse of funds by recipients, ranging from widespread petty corruption to grand corruption and looting. As with donors, corruption among aid recipients reflects the degree of transparency and accountability in public affairs. Aid lends itself to the politics of patronage. Patronage, a common feature of politics, does not necessarily imply corruption. In practice, however, the dividing line is not easily identified. For example, a senior government official may use influence to have his or her home district chosen as a pilot for a project to co-finance a local education development fund. Such an exercise may be used to strengthen relations with local elites, including politicians, bureaucrats and businessmen, as well as to impress the local population. There may or may not be a concerted effort subsequently to misuse project funds or opportunities. The important point is that aid, in the form of project loans in particular, creates many opportunities for patronage, including project location, hiring project staff, training opportunities, procurement and purchases, and consultancy. In the process, covenants and conditions for loans may be systematically ignored or flaunted.

Furthermore, corruption and patronage should be distinguished from bureaucratic waste, which characterizes much project and other aid. Bureaucratic waste is the use of aid resources for legal but unnecessary or non-productive purposes. For example, projects often involve vehicles and civil work, computers and other office equipment and a battery of training activities, study tours, and workshops or seminars of dubious utility. Technical assistance and consultancy inputs—both of which make up large components of aid—often fall into the latter category. Though analytically distinct, corruption, patronage and bureaucratic waste are usually found together, feeding off and reinforcing one another in a systematic fashion. Patronage, corruption and waste slow down and distort project implementation and help explain the poor performance of most loan financed projects in the country.

The extent of official misuse of aid is not easily assessed since those managing the process are generally protected from public scrutiny. The phenomenal amount of unexplained and irregular government expenditure reported by CAG both recurrent and capital budgets, gives an impression of the extent of the problem. Even where aid money is not directly misappropriated, the conceptual "fungibility" of aid means that any misuse of government revenue implicates aid in proportion to aid's overall contribution to government revenues. Since aid accounts for about 90 per cent of public investment and 30 per cent of recurrent expenditure in country the implications of the misuse of government spending on aid are substantial.

Most vulnerable to local corruption are loans from the international finance institutions and regional development banks for projects implemented by Governments and sectoral ministries. That is the most crucial area for assessing the impact of corruption in aid, since the international finance institutions account for a growing proportion of total aid flows and external debt. Projects funded by the World Bank are frequently put in place through project implementation units based in central ministries. Such units are staffed by officials who may have to demonstrate allegiance to their hierarchical and political superiors. At the implementation phase, the imperatives of corruption, patronage and bureaucratic waste can easily take over from the formal project objectives, design and management in determining project outcomes.

Beneficiaries from corruption in aid-funded projects include the private contractors and procurement agents, both local and expatriate, who are awarded contracts through suspect tendering arrangements. Contacts from within the system provide intelligence on opportunities. The best placed businesses are politically well connected and may help fund the ruling party's electoral coffers from income from aid-related contracts. In that way, aid money helps keep ruling the elite in power. Donor-funded projects, for example, lôans to youth groups or women for income generation activities, are routinely manipulated by incumbent or aspiring politicians.

Corruption is found throughout the project cycle. Corruption may be involved in selecting the consultants who appraise, implement, evaluate or review a project and may allow projects to be used for illicit activities during implementation. Procurement contracts may be awarded to relatives and cronies, and project funds earmarked for particular purposes may be directed elsewhere.

The most pernicious form of corruption in aid concerns loans for essentially bogus projects involving collusion between agency and government officials. Agriculture, livestock and irrigation are favourite targets for such projects, though multi-sectoral projects are also found. That form of corruption takes place in projects that are typically located in remote regions, where the ostensible target group of beneficiaries is unlikely to complain that no benefits are forthcoming. Such projects are by definition impervious to public scrutiny.

Overfunding can encourage corruption by providing more aid than governments can effectively absorb. Sectoral overfunding may reflect a donor tendency to jump into "flavour-of-the-month" activities without considering their combined or aggregate impact. Recent examples include democratization and governance, including anti-corruption initiatives, small scale credit and support for non-governmental organizations. Competing for relatively small markets forces donors to ignore warning signs of lack of capacity, quality or integrity among recipients.

Joseph Warioba, Chairman of the 1996 Presidential Commission of Enquiry against Corruption of the United Republic of Tanzania, makes a strong case for tracing the source of corruption in aid to the aid agencies themselves (Warioba 1998). Warioba argues that aid to some countries "from bilateral donors and IFls consist of very large amounts of money and the sum that disappears through corruption is also very large". Warioba singles out aid for infrastructure projects and tied aid, giving the example of a road project funded by a bilateral donor in which the contractor had the support of the local development mission, despite its poor performance. The pervasiveness of aid means that any corruption related to implementing particular government policies usually involves aid money. Warioba relates examples of corruption in the privatization process and in contracting a dubious foreign firm to collect debts from a defunct government bank. The debts collected were less than the fees received.

Aid Industry's Response to Corruption Challenge

Having identified corruption, albeit belatedly, as a basic constraint on economic growth and social development, the aid industry has proceeded to sponsor a wide range of activities promoting improved state and private sector governance. Government is implementing donor-funded governance programmes covering anti-corruption, democratization, rule of law and support for civil society, including non-governmental organizations. Economic reforms are intended to level the economic playing field, eliminate unnecessary regulation and encourage investment and growth.

In addition, despite the recent rhetoric of partnership, all major donors still attach formal conditions to their aid, including respect for human rights, anti-corruption measures, gender equality, protection of the environment, democratization and liberalization. Such conditions are intended to send the message to governments receiving aid that they need to change their ways in order to qualify for further development assistance. Conditions have rarely been effective in forcing compliance to structural adjustment policies. Leaders of some country have been known to swallow their pride, take the aid and proceed more or less as usual, lacking either the will or the capacity (or both) to implement agreed policies. Chabal and Daloz (1999) suggest that "donors... seem on the whole to have accepted a degree of non-compliance with the stated aims of aid and a level of failure of targeted aid projects which beggar belief... African ruling elites were able to use foreign aid primarily as an additional source of revenue."

The "disbursement culture" of the "World Bank makes it difficult to place anti-corruption concerns into the mainstream in projects funded by the World Bank. External audits routinely fail to pick up or follow up evidence of corruption. One report on Uganda found that "World Bank employees have complained that projects are indifferently audited, or, even where audits reveal diversions, that there are no substantial consequences for diversion because the internal institutional incentives of the Bank spur lending." (Thomas and Barkan 1998, p. 27). Project supervisory functions of the World Bank are often inadequate to reveal or follow up effectively on instances of corruption, for example, in procurement. World Bank audits of procurement tend to focus excessively on processes: much more needs to be done on the quality of the physical work undertaken, by independent consultants where the World Bank lacks the technical staff required. This could have a large immediate impact on reducing the losses of corrupt and fraudulent practices.

To be fair, the World Bank and other donors are often actively involved in challenging acts of bad governance, including corruption, among aid recipients. In extreme circumstances, aid donors may cancel projects or entire programmes for the same reasons. Though aid recipients obviously resent interference in local politics, donors are sometimes the principal source of critical opposition to instances of grand corruption. As a result of aid dependency, donors feel they have a responsibility to oppose instances of grand corruption unless, of course, they are involved themselves. At the same time, donors are often reluctant to "blow the whistle" on corruption, even where it undermines their own programmes. Some donors may deny well-founded reports of major misuse of resources in activities that they fund, even when they are not directly implicated in any wrong-doing.

Since the International Monetary Fund does not lend money for projects, its concern with the impact of corruption on its lending programmes remains at a more general level. After much criticism of its willingness to fund corrupt regimes in the past, there are signs that the International Monetary Fund, like the World Bank, is beginning to take corruption more seriously. Kenya, where an Enhanced Structural Adjustment Facility loan was suspended in 1997, is a case in point. However, many including bilateral donors, find the International Monetary Fund's subsequent keenness to recommence lending to Kenya too hasty. (Githongo 200)

Whether combating corruption should be used by aid agencies as a condition is a complex issue, further complicated by current initiatives, known as the Heavily Indebted Poor Countries Debt Initiatives, that link debt relief to transparent and externally monitored poverty reduction programmes by the beneficiaries of debt relief. For the moment, the actual amounts of relief forthcoming under such a debt initiative are so small that they hardly constitute a major material incentive to relief seeking governments. The issue of writing off "odious debts" resulting from previous badly designed and implemented projects has been peripheral to the debt initiative debate, which has focused on the past failures of the borrowers, not the lenders. Furthermore, aid agencies have started to improve their own practices, including better staff supervision and stricter rules and penalties. In the late 1990s, the World Bank began to publish the names of procurement companies and contractors involved in malpractice, banning them from further bidding on projects financed by the World Bank. Enhanced internal controls have also unearthed maverick staff. It is generally accepted that [such measures] are beginning to have a significant deterrent effect in curbing corruption in operations" financed by the World Bank.

In many cases, anti-corruption exercises have led to mistrust, low morale among staff, the possibility of the development of other forms of corruption, unnecessary bureaucracy and new avoidance mechanisms. Anechiarico (1999) describes how anti-corruption initiatives have failed in public administration in the United States of America. Zero tolerance is the approach of the Government of the United States to drug trafficking. Yet half the corruption cases brought against police officers between 1993 and 1997 were drug related. Escalating public spending over 20 years coincides with a significant improvement in the quality and fall in the price of drugs. (Drug Policy Alliance 2000)

The zero tolerance option adopted by the World Bank has had all those predictable effects. Competitive bidding has been used for contracts worth just a few thousand dollars. Donors introduce procedures in order to remove the least suspicion of malpractice, succeeding in slowing down project implementation and frustrating the honest actors along with the rest. Existing onerous bureaucratic procedures become even more onerous. The costs involved in appearing squeaky clean are not counted, since aid is not organized around principles of efficiency or competition. Both aid workers and recipients resent the assumption that they are guilty until proven innocent.

The "islands of integrity" approach championed by the Global Coalition for Africa and Transparency International, which aims to clean up on procurement and tendering in major projects, addresses a very real and urgent issue. That worthwhile initiative "Islands of Integrity" or no bribery pledges are not viewed favourably by many World Bank procurement experts. Must be linked to a more general view of aid-related corruption along the lines described. That would allow the inclusion of projects and non-project loans where international procurement is not a central feature.

Options for Tracking Corruption

Before anything can be done to address corruption in aid, the problem needs to be fully defined. For that to happen, corruption must be conceptualized in systemic rather than individualistic terms. It is also important to try to delineate the relationship between corruption as a factor undermining aid and other factors working in the same direction. In practice, the proposition is problematic since so many factors are involved.

For both aid agencies and recipients, addressing corruption in aid requires evidence of the nature and scope of the problem, a broad commitment to solve it and a strategy to address it. Aid agencies need to realize that their own long-term legitimacy and perhaps survival require a radical revision in their mode of operation. That means, exposing their own integrity systems to the same rigours of transparency and accountability as are expected from their development partners. To help mainstream anti-corruption initiatives, moral leadership should be sought from within the donor community, the major foundations and non-governmental organizations that focus on development issues, the research and consultancy industries, the private sector, associations of aid workers and political parties.

Compiling an annual donor corruption index to complement the corruption perception index and bribery perception index as developed by Transparency International would be a promising measure (Fjeldstad 1999). The corruption perception index has had a dramatic impact on public discussions of corruption. The criticism that it is unfair in concentrating on the bribe-takers has now been addressed by ranking bribe-givers. In the same way, an aid corruption index would rank both recipient countries and agencies on their propensity to corruption. The question that remains, however, is who would compile such an index and defend its findings.

The pressures on academic and research organizations to earn their keep from contractual work allows donors to define research and consultancy priorities in ways that primarily serve their own interests. Academics from countries in Africa suffer from the same constraints. Establishing a standing committee in the Development Assistance Committee of the Organization for Economic Cooperation and Development to monitor corruption in aid, for example, would be a useful measure. The committee would refer grievous cases of corruption in aid agencies to international legal process and adjudication, with appropriate sanctions.

There is often opposition from Governments to attempt to raise the issue of corruption in aid, including aid-funded projects. The number of non-governmental organizations and grass-root community-based organizations with the capacity to take up the issue of aid transparency is limited. The national chapters of Transparency International could take up the issue of corruption in aid should they be convinced that the issue merits their attention. The difficulty is that Transparency International chapters rely on donors for their core funding and other activities; thus, there might be reluctance to bite the hand that feeds them.

The preventive measures that may be of value are:

- All proposed aid projects above a certain value, and all programmes, should be the subject of public discussion, including wide review by Parliament, the business community and civil society organizations of all kinds;
- Public expenditure reviews should include greater disclosure of aid inputs and the rationale for public investment choices;
- Regular publication of details of donor-funded projects and public access to data on aid and debt.

Research on corruption in aid can be included in integrity system and service delivery surveys. Such surveys document public opinion and the experience of corruption, including the impact of the latter on the availability, cost and quality of public services. Such surveys are already part of the battery of public service reform tools aimed at improving the performance of central and local governments. National integrity system research could include the issue of corruption in aid and constitute a possible source of the above-mentioned donor corruption index.

From the public's perspective, civil society and the private sector need to be involved in carrying out the surveys, whereas governments and donors see them as part of civil service reform, and therefore under government control. Surveys that investigate service quality and the role of aid, but are controlled by central or local government, are unlikely to be carried out objectively, since the real picture would predictably show up the poor performance of both governments and donors. It is also unlikely that donors would get away with funding independent and potentially shocking research for very long. Finding credible local researchers prepared to risk the consequences of being involved in such activities is problematic, for the reasons discussed above. The involvement of outside researchers and consultants could lead to the research being branded as a foreign plot designed to discredit the government.

For some time, the World Bank has been sponsoring workshops on investigative journalism, national integrity and other anti-corruption activities. A round of workshops on investigative journalism could be run on the theme of corruption. Corruption should figure in integrity workshops. There would be major risks to investigative journalists, editors and newspaper editors. "Whistle-blowers" also risk their lives if they start telling the truth about certain types of aid.

The following measures may be effective:

- Establishment of parliamentary committees empowered to review aid performance with powers to question senior officials on aid-funded projects and programmes (sessions should be held in public)
- Unannounced value for money audits of any loan-funded project by an official auditor or consultants
- Systematic assessments of the impact on the environment, the economy and poverty levels of aid programmes and projects in all sectors.

The last two measures are information-empowerment measures, giving all stakeholders the means to take an intelligent position on the impact of aid.

The mechanisms for identifying and dealing with corruption in aid-recipient relations are not difficult to identify. What appears to be currently lacking is the will to assimilate the lessons of the past in order to introduce reforms on the part of donors. That poses particular challenges for the international financial institutions. Given the unique position of the World Bank in defining the terms of the development debate, including corruption, it is worth asking whether a more fundamental critique of corruption can be invoked in the interest of good sense and in the search for practical solutions.

The aid industry, led by the World Bank, tends to define corruption found in some countries as a local issue that can be addressed by supporting diverse initiatives of a largely technical nature. It is also assumed that corruption is a largely individual process of rent-seeking that can be addressed by changing incentive structures, including wages, accountability and competition.

Thus, if corruption were to be viewed as a systemic political phenomenon, derived from complex patronage structures, aid agencies would have to ask who their local anti-corruption allies might be in any given context. It is not enough for a head of state to adopt a formally anti-corruption stance: that may be done just to placate donors. If aid agencies and their local partners have diametrically different definitions of the situation, it is difficult to see how the implementation of largely technical solutions to corruption can have a lasting impact.

It is a common, though unjustified, criticism of aid to countries that it has had no impact despite large transfers over a protracted period. The impact of aid has grown in direct proportion to the rise of aid dependency. Corruption as rent-seeking and political patronage have been major contributors to personal accumulation among ruling elites and political strategies to protect or advance their collective interests.

Political Reforms

WC Fields, American Comedian and writer once said, "Hell, I never vote for anybody, I always vote against". We urgently need electoral reforms that will clean up Indian politics.

Having captured the public mood against corruption and

stirred up Parliament over the Lokpal issue, social activist Anna Hazare and his team have now set their sights on electoral reforms. Anna's next campaign will focus on the right to recall elected representatives, the right to reject candidates contesting elections and demand MPs be subjected to annual performance audits. Election reforms with the aim of improving the quality of our legislators are long overdue. But here too an all-or-nothing attitude that typified the Jan Lokpal movement needs to be discouraged in favour of wider consultations with civil society.

Recalling elected representatives for perceived non-performance in the middle of their terms can be arbitrary and problematic, as it would motivate losing candidates and parties to keep making trouble for winning ones and thereby hamper governance. But the proposal to grant the voter the right to reject all candidates on the ballot is an excellent one. At present, the electorate has no say over the choice of nominees for elections. The latter are foisted on the people by political parties, leaving voters with the depressing task of electing the least unsuitable candidate. In fact, this lack of suitable choice discourages voters from exercising their franchise.

While Section 49(O) of current election rules does provide for an option where a voter may not vote for any of the candidates, the measure has no significant impact on the ground. By instructing voters to register their names separately if they wish to exercise the no-vote option, the provision goes against the fundamental principle of a secret ballot. It would be prudent to suitably amend the election rules and have the no-vote option enshrined in the voting machines themselves. In order to make the measure meaningful, if the number of no-votes polled exceeds that of all other candidates, the particular constituency should be obliged to conduct a fresh round of elections with a new set of nominees.

In strengthening the no-vote option, political parties will be forced to put up suitable candidates. If the measure is combined with the proposal to debar candidates charged with serious crimes—an amendment to the Representation of the People Act towards this end is currently under consideration—it would provide a powerful tool to check criminalization of politics and serve as an antidote to institutional corruption. Such reforms would go a long way towards making the political system vibrant, efficient and more in tune with what the people of India want. They deserve as much importance as a strengthened Lokpal.

Anna Hazare's anti-corruption movement has highlighted the need for lawmakers and policy framers to get more proactive than they've been so far on fighting graft. The Lokpal Bill, which is work in progress, is one key weapon in this combat. But other tools need deploying as well to boost systemic openness, which will force greater public accountability. Much of what anti-graft watchdogs do is detect malpractices as they occur and clean up the mess afterwards. Structural reform acts as a preventive; it reduces scope for the mess to be created in the first place. In this context, let's welcome the government's call for transparency in public procurement. WTO estimates our total government procurement as a percentage of GDP is around 20 per cent, roughly an annual ₹11 lakh crores. Courtesy red tape and opaque decision-making, award of government contracts offers huge avenues for graft. Be it rules-bending by the defence, power or telecom sector or as witnessed in the Commonwealth Games run-up, bidding and tender selection processes are routinely manipulated to favour palm-greasers. This impacts investor confidence, choking off funds that could help boost infrastructure and industry. It's good a roadmap is being envisaged to trim room for arbitrary decisions by, among other things, requiring digitized records of procurement-related official communications.

Discretionary allotment of land and housing in return for bribes is no secret. Government ownership of land in excess of need, regulatory complexity and outmoded land acquisition rules—all favour land mafias. A proportion of state-owned land sold on the market would help treat the problem of artificial scarcity pushing up prices. Land records too must be better kept and digitized to check fraud and land grabs. In the mining industry, a similar regulatory jungle facilitates graft-fuelled grant of leases and fronting by state mining firms for private commerce by politicians, bureaucrats and their cronies. Regulatory streamlining besides a crackdown on illegal mining is imperative.

As is tax reform. Introducing the goods and services tax will spur tax compliance while creating a common market that boosts revenue. If politicians were truly serious about curbing black money, they'd shout less about overseas tax havens and more about rolling out GST or reducing stamp duty. It's as important to link delivery of subsidy and welfare benefits to UID and financial inclusion projects, for routing via direct cash transfer or smart cards rather than leaky public distribution channels. Finally, Team Anna has talked about electoral reforms. The political class would do well to take the initiative here, pushing for strict auditing of party finances, mandatory disclosure of poll funding and greater checks on entry of criminal elements into politics.

The exertions of Anna Hazare might well fetch the nation a robust Lokpal Bill soon. In the bargain, however, we may have to contend with a lethal danger: saintliness in our public life. For, what Hazare has done is to act solely according to the dictates of his 'conscience', his 'inner voice', to attain his goal. He places those dictates well above Parliament—the repository of the will of the people and the Constitution—the touchstone of our Republic. Like other claimants to infallibility—the Pope, the Communist Commissar, the fascist ideologue, the jihadi theocrat Hazare too appears to abide by what he believes are self-evident propositions. He alone can distinguish between vice and virtue; he alone knows the truth; there is only one path to reach it and that is the path laid by him. In other words, he alone is entitled to deploy his very own means to eradicate corruption.

But this is not the only reason why he puts his critics and detractors on the defensive. What renders their task more difficult is the image Hazare projects: his meekness and humility, his austere demeanour, his home-spun homilies, his adherence to non-violence. Such trappings of saintliness have a wide and instant appeal in a country where religiosity has struck deep roots. Once you concede spiritual levity to anyone in order to cope with your own insecurities—as our middle class, abetted by hyper-moralistic sections of the media, does with abandon-yours is not to question why; yours is only to gawk and sing. This must be appreciated, in spite of huge gathering there was not a single incidence of violence and indiscipline. The large crowd was always well behaved.

And yet we have sterling examples of individuals who refused to succumb to the soothing seductions of saintliness. The most eloquent warning against them came from B.R. Ambedkar in a speech he gave in the Constituent Assembly in November 1949 after it had completed its labours. If India is to maintain democracy not merely in form but also in fact, he argued, the first thing that needs to be done is to "hold fast to constitutional methods of achieving our social and economic objectives. It means that we must abandon the bloody methods of revolution. It means that we must abandon the methods of civil disobedience, non-cooperation and satyagraha. Where constitutional methods are open, there can be no justification for them. These methods are nothing but the Grammar of Anarchy and the sooner they are abandoned, the better for us".

In the next paragraph, Ambedkar approvingly quoted John Stuart Mill's caution to all those who are interested in safeguarding democracy: not to "lay their liberties at the feet of even a great man, or to trust him with powers which enable him to subvert their institutions". Ambedkar then went on to assert that this caution is especially relevant in India where the "path of devotion or hero-worship plays a part in politics that is unequalled in magnitude to the part it plays in the politics of any other country in the world". In our country, he concluded, "*bhakti* or hero-worship is a sure road to degradation and to eventual dictatorship."

No one can deny the fact that Anna Hazare has raised public awareness about the need to combat the menace of corruption on a humongous scale. But when he seeks to emasculate Parliament's prerogative to legislate, when he refuses to grant that views on the Lokpal Bill other than his own, deserve equal respect, when he fails to educate his followers about the complexity of addressing the issue of corruption and when he embarks on a fast that places his life in jeopardy to get his way, he opens a Pandora's box. Imagine what will be in store for the nation should others emulate his example to demand instant legislation to allow khap justice (in the name of custom), the destruction of places of worship (in the name of religious faith), the banning of a film (in the name of 'hurt sentiments') or a shutting down of nuclear energy projects (in the name of ecological rectitude). Such zeal will take no time to give rise to a call for a muscular regime that will banish democratic politics into the wilderness.

Anna achievements are monumental. He managed to spur one of the most unapproachable governments in the world into positive action. Anna lit a desire for change in the youth's hearts. He also started the much-needed process of restoring good values in Indian people. Yes, many of us are still corrupt, whether forced by the system or otherwise, but a part of us yearns to be good. That part just became stronger. This mass booster shot of morality is the biggest contribution of the movement, apart from the Jan Lokpal.

Of course, these achievements did come at a cost. We saw a relatively long period of unsettling turmoil. We saw ugly, unpleasant human qualities like stubbornness, insolence and overaggressiveness on both sides, out for public display. In an ideal world, people would be reasonable, and irrespective of their position or power do the right thing. However, we live in a far from ideal world, and given the circumstances, we came out relatively unscathed. This time, our youth did not come on the streets to hurt people from another caste or religion. They came to simply demand a more fair and just society, in a peaceful manner. It is a proud moment for all of us, India's class of 2011 is different, and a salute to that.

However, it is shocking and disheartened by the intense criticism of Anna from certain sections of the English-speaking Indian intellectual circles. If the elite had backed Anna stronger, we could have had a faster and better consensus. Of course people have a right to an opinion. However, it is often found the opinions seemed more like a generic negative bias towards Anna, perhaps because of his background, rustic methods or sudden rise to fame, all irrelevant to the issue at hand.

The strongest anti-Anna argument was that Parliament cannot and should not be subverted. There is no doubt that Parliament and the Constitution are important and to be respected. However, these work on a basic assumption—confidence of the people. If confidence is lost, the institution does not work. And that is what we have to restore in Parliament now, before we ask people to respect it. To give an example on the importance of confidence, even a currency of the country works the same way. The paper notes we carry in our pocket have value, only if people believe they have value. In many global instances, people have lost faith in a country's currency. This normally happens when the government prints money without care, thereby devaluing it at a rapid pace. The most recent example is Zimbabwe. At one point in 2008, prices were doubling in Zimbabwe every 24 hours. The profligate government printed money in higher denominations. The price of a loaf of bread reached 10 billion Zimbabwe dollars. Eventually, people dumped the currency and switched to a barter system. Now imagine if elite Zimbabwe intellectuals came on TV and said that the monetary system of the country must be respected and the government and their currency are above all. What was needed was steps to ensure confidence. The government needed to commit that they would print money responsibly and put checks and balances in place. Zimbabwe didn't. People over there have now switched to foreign currencies.

Similar is the nature of the confidence crisis with politicians in India, particularly the government. Their constant lying has only made it worse. They keep saying corruption needs to be fixed, but do little. Even the PM says 'coalition compromises'. Lying is something politicians got away with for a long time. It came at the cost of losing people's trust. A good Lokpal Bill will actually bring back people's trust in the government. In fact, the government needs a Lokpal Bill almost more than the people. It also needs to be more open and approachable. Party spokepersons need to be people with personal conviction, who place what is right above the party, even if it means accepting mistakes. And while we love telling politicians how to do their job, we as citizens have to do our bit to restore confidence as well. We can't vote for candidates only because they are from a particular caste, religion or region. We have to place only one criterion—is he a good person? When we all send capable, honest people to Parliament, the trust and respect will return.

Anna Hazare said, it was a victory of every Indian. Parliament and people power came together. The Lokpal is an idea whose time has come. It's a point hammered home by Anna Hazare's anti-graft protest. If Parliament adopted a unanimous "sense of the House" resolution to break the Lokpal logjam, it's because Anna's done what politicians generally haven't saved when expedient: he's turned national spotlight on corruption. It's been a victory for the social activist, who ended his fast only when his key demands were met. Yet, we also witnessed lawmakers go beyond homilies to adopt a just cause backed by ordinary citizens: the creation of a strong antigraft watchdog. It was a memorable day: Parliament and people's power partnering each other in the dance of democracy.

With a fasting Anna standing firm, it had become untenable for the Government to prolong the face-off. But isn't there a larger lesson for those who set store by the fact that they're elected by the people? The democratic contract bonding citizens to their political representatives isn't just a matter of form; its substance is what political institutions deliver between—and irrespective of—periodic elections. Massive popular participation in Anna's campaign signals society's deep anguish at corruption-fuelled institutional rot. Let's wake up to that. Yes, it'll take time and collective effort to find remedies via legislative deterrence and systemic reform. That's no excuse for inaction. With its broad framework in place, disagreements on the Lokpal Bill's details shouldn't prompt renewed breakdown in negotiations. Drafting this legislation is a complex and onerous task, aimed at establishing an authority in sync with the system of checks and balances underpinning our democracy. No one as of now can claim to be the sole and final word on what the contours and powers of such an ombudsman should be. The government's proposed Lokpal is widely viewed as toothless, the Jan Lokpal version too harsh. Only flexibility will help find middle ground. Both government and civil society must be willing to consider all inputs so that the best possible Bill can be framed. As for the political class as a whole, it's time to demonstrate sincerity of purpose. The Lokpal Bill, hanging fire for over four decades, has come before Parliament nine times in different versions. That's a poor advertisement for politicians claiming to be as keen on fighting corruption as civil society. Anna has said that the battle to create a good, effective Lokpal is only half-won. Given that they assert parliamentary prerogative in lawmaking, legislators must help win the other half.

The best way to curb corruption is to use the calculus of

pleasure and pain. Shehla Masood was killed in Bhopal recently, yet another RTI activist who lost her life in the battle against corruption. The Lokayukta report had brought down the Chief Minister in Karnataka. A high court judge was being impeached in Parliament. The Comptroller and Auditor General and the Supreme Court were in hot pursuit of mega scams. The CBI has chargesheeted and locked up top executive honchos, MPs, even a cabinet minister. India is at war against corruption. Now we have Team Anna's much celebrated victory. His hunger strike and arrest galvanized a whole nation. Nothing like this had been seen since the freedom movement led by Gandhi, except perhaps the JP movement. As the rallies swelled and Team Anna grew more stubborn, the party swung from hard line to soft line to hard line again. Finally; it was Prime Minister much vilified in recent times even by his well-wishers for neither leading nor resigning, and presiding over a corrupt regime—who did the right thing. At his instance, alternative proposals for the Lokpal Bill were discussed in Parliament, and an all-party resolution passed that supports the three key issues raised by Team Anna. He then reached out to Anna, requesting him to withdraw his fast. Anna responded by congratulating Parliament and breaking his 12-day fast while the nation rejoiced and heaved a collective sigh of relief. The Prime Minister's approach preserved the authority of Parliament, yet ensured that Parliament was responsive to a popular non-violent movement. Between Anna and him, they have led the people and the Parliament of India to the finest moment of our democracy as the world has watched and applauded us. The Parliament resolution was a giant leap for Indian democracy, but only one big step in fighting corruption. The hard work then started. As the standing committee got down to the nitty-gritty of drafting the revised Lokpal Bill, it was a good time to look at the insights on corruption containment offered by a cross-over subject called Law and Economics.

The organizing theme underlying this approach was the plea

sure-pain calculus attributed to philosopher Jeremy Bentham. The idea that all human behaviour is driven by this calculus is controversial. But it seems reasonable to suggest that crimes like corruption are indeed driven by the criminal's perception of potential gain and the loss if caught: pleasure and pain. Much insight on how to contain corruption derives from this simple principle. However, corruption takes many forms and no matter how clever a policy, the criminal mind can be equally clever. Also, beyond a point, the costs of further reducing corruption could exceed the loss from corruption. Hence, corruption can be contained, possibly minimized, but not entirely eliminated.

First, there is the widespread phenomenon of citizens having to pay a bribe to get what they are entitled to by right, e.g., timely delivery of pensions, ration cards, passports, etc. or the timely restoration of power, phone lines, water supply, and so on. In such cases, the bribe payer is actually a victim of extortion. In a newspaper, economist Kaushik Basu had proposed that acts of bribe giving in such cases of 'harassment corruption' should not be considered a crime, as at present. Instead, the punishment for the bribe seeker should be significantly enhanced. Such an amendment of the relevant law could vastly reduce 'harassment corruption' because the potential extortionist would be deterred by his knowledge that bribe-givers are likely to blow the whistle after getting their job done. For other forms of major corruption, the pleasure-pain calculus has generated three basic approaches for containment: high civil service pay to moderate the lure of illegal gratification; laws prescribing very harsh punishment and/or strong law enforcement to enhance the probability and expected pain from being caught, compared to the potential gain; and strong competitive structures with transparent non-discretionary rules to minimize the opportunities for gain from bribe-driven decisions. International evidence reveals two cases of high civil service pay and low levels of corruption, Singapore and Hong Kong. However, both these places also have strong laws against corruption, strict enforcement and open, competitive market structures. Hence, the individual effects of each of the three approaches cannot be disentangled in either of these cases.

Evidence from other countries indicates that strong laws, strict enforcement and competitive structures individually and significantly contribute to curbing corruption. In most developing countries, including India, poor enforcement of laws is the norm. Turning that around would be very costly in resources and a great administrative challenge. By comparison, enacting strong laws or introducing reforms to strengthen competitiveness is relatively less costly and administratively less challenging. These should be our strategic priorities in fighting corruption. The former requires a revised Lokpal Bill that provides for very stiff punishment of corruption. The latter requires other urgent reforms to strengthen competitiveness through transparent, non-discretionary regulations that are not unduly restrictive. While these should be our priorities, enforcement too has to be strengthened to the extent our fiscal and administrative capacities permit.

The agitation for the Jan Lokpal Bill (JLB) was hailed as 'unprecedented' and as a 'second freedom struggle.' More grounded analysts have likened it to the Navanirman movement led by Jayaprakash Narayan in the 1970s. However, a more apt comparison lies closer at hand. Less than six years ago, Parliament enacted a national Right to Information Act. This was a major victory for the RTI campaign which aimed to empower people to fight corruption and maladministration. It mobilised a nationwide network of support, bringing together activists, NGOs and ordinary citizens, and effectively using media and middle-class interlocutors. India Against Corruption (IAC), the coalition leading the present campaign, shares the goals and the networking strategy of the earlier campaign, and its leaders Arvind Kejriwal, Prashant Bhushan and Anna Hazare were closely associated with it. Yet, the differences between the two campaigns are striking as well as instructive.

Both RTI and the JLB campaigns strive for greater government accountability, but their ideologies, modes of organization, support base and strategies diverge in important ways. Understanding these differences is crucial if the Lokpal Bill, once enacted, is to achieve its stated goal. The RTI campaign grew out of the experiences of the Mazdoor Kisan Shakti Sangathan (MKSS), the jan sangathan (people's organization) in rural Rajasthan which had, for two decades, fought corruption in village development work. The MKSS pioneered the use of *jan sunvai* or public hearings as a technique to empower villagers to 'speak truth to power', challenging an opaque, oppressive and corrupt system of governance. The *jan sunvai's* success depended on systematic preparation to mobilize people to testify, collect information and check its accuracy. The groundswell of public anger against abuse of public funds was harnessed to create a coordinated campaign led by trained local activists. From the villages, MKSS took its campaign to the district and state level, staging determined demonstrations that attracted the middle classes and intellectuals, before leading the national RTI campaign. The national network was more eclectic; it included not only *jan sangathans* like the MKSS; but also individual anti-corruption activists like Anna Hazare and Shailesh Gandhi. Notably, the RTI campaign aligned itself with the National Alliance of Peoples Movements, *sangathans* of the rural and urban poor fighting against dispossession. This organizational base gave the RTI campaign a solid political credibility.

The JLB campaign indicated a distinctly different trajectory. Even though Kejriwal's *Parivartan*, which battled corruption in ration shops in two Delhi slums, was a *jan sangathan*, its base was too limited to launch a nationwide campaign. The other campaign leaders—Prashant Bhushan, Kiran Bedi and Hazare—also cannot muster a trained cadre of activists. The JLB campaign has mobilized participants in two ways: through social networking and the media; and via regional chapters of Baba Ramdev and Sri Sri Ravi

Shankar's congregations. The coming together of a predominantly young, white-collar constituency that communicates through text messages and Face Book, lower-middle-class followers of Baba Ramdev and the professional classes that practise the Art of Living gives the JLB campaign the strength of numbers as well as the image of appearing all inclusive. However, this strength may dissipate once the Bill is passed. Mobilizing crowds for a successful agitation is one thing and having a committed and trained activist base to convert that success into a long-term institutional change is quite another.

If the RTI campaign embraced *sangathans* with an Independent Left ideology, the political beliefs of the participants in the JLB Campaign are harder to pin down. Eight of the 20 founders of India Against Corruption are religious figures, of whom only Swami Agnivesh can be described as a champion of *jan sangathans*. The rest voice patriotic sentiments and anti-government hostility without a clear analysis of how the systematic problems that plague public affairs will be tackled. Sri Sri Ravi Shankar's previous social initiatives have been of doubtful value (cleaning the sewage-laden Yamuna by picking up garbage from the riverfront) and marked by dubious claims (11,000 Naxalites 'converted' to the Art of Living). While other founders like Hazare and Bedi have a reputation for personal probity and courage, they endorse a form of individualist authoritarian action that's applauded by a public hungry for vigilante heroes. The JLB thus represents a shift in the political spectrum: from the left-of-centre democratic decentralization of the RTI campaign, to the right-of-centre legal-technical-fix of India Against Corruption. The test of any law lies in its implementation. Much disquiet has already been expressed about the overtly-centralized design of the JLB and the impracticability of the mammoth bureaucratic machinery it demands. However, making a law work also requires a mobilized public, a dedicated and organized network at every level that will keep up the pressure on public institutions. The ideologies, organizational structure and support base of the JLB campaign do not indicate that it is capable of such long-term and systematic social action. The RTI campaign's activist base has allowed it to sustain an arduous struggle against corruption, but the challenges have been formidable.

Miners Loot the Lost Paradise

The environmental impact of the mining is such that the Goa state is facing a water scarcity despite getting 120 inches of rain every year. The signs are everywhere. An hour into the narrow road from Margao railway station to the Netravali Wildlife Sanctuary at Colomba in South Goa, the Neem trees vanish. Hills of soil appear, along with pits created to dig for iron ore. With an annual legal turnover of around ₹18,000 crores, mining has led to rampant destruction of the environment. Goa has 20 per cent of the nation's iron and magnesium ore deposits. Since China started importing low-grade ore in 2005, exports from Goa have increased eight-fold. No surprise then that with little over 0.1 per cent of India's land mass, Goa accounts for 117 of 536 mining leases granted nationwide. These cover 259 sq km of land in the state, but there is an extensive mining that takes place outside the lease areas. Most of it in environmentally sensitive areas like prime forest land.

The loss is in terms of royalty at ₹10,000 crores in the last five years. Cheap excavation has made mining profitable in Goa. An operating lease for a mine comes for a one-time fee of ₹5,000. It costs ₹50 to excavate one tonne of iron ore. Refining and cleaning costs around ₹500 and transportation costs ₹200 per tonne. A royalty of ₹270 and 20 per cent customs duty takes the expenses to around ₹2,500 per tonne. In turn, the export of one tonne of iron ore fetches $180 (₹7,920). Rajendra Kakodkar, who has studied the mine economy from the National Institute of Oceanography (NIO), based in Goa, says the prices of iron ore have gone up 10-

fold and the profit has surged by 50 times in the last eight years. An operating profit margin of 75 per cent is unheard of in any legitimate business in India. Iron ore exports from Goa have gone up from 14 million tonnes in 2000 to 46 million tonnes in 2009-10. These are provisional figures based on royalty payments. Kakodkar suggests that these figures may be way off the mark. His calculation puts it at 64 million tonnes in 2009-10. Unlike Karnataka, where 70 per cent of ore extracted is processed by state-controlled public sector units, the entire haul in Goa passes through private parties dominated by a handful of families. The top four mine operators Sesa Goa, Salgaocars, Timblos and Chowgules—control 83 per cent of the overall mining business. The mine operator's financial figures are not in the public domain. Sesa Goa is the only company whose annual report is available. During 2009-10, it earned a pre-tax profit of ₹3,445 crores on an iron ore sale of 14 million tonnes. This translates into a profit per tonne of ₹2,500.

Illegalities in the mining business are not possible without the connivance of politicians, forest officials, police and the pollution control board. Politicians are directly involved in mining. Former Karnataka Lokayukta N. Santosh Hegde, who authored a damning indictment of then Chief Minister and others on illegal mining, said in Panaji that authorities in Goa were working with miners in Karnataka to funnel illegally mined iron ore through the state's ports. "There is a collusion here. We do not know who the officials involved in the illegalities are. It is for the Goa government to investigate," he said.

The illegalities start with excavating ore beyond the permissible quantity. The state government does not have a system to check whether the trucks carrying ore are overloaded. Environmentalist alleges that officials of the mining department and pollution control board never carry out inspections. There is a big disparity in the figures provided by miners, the state mining department and the Marmagao Port officials on the export of iron ore. It is claimed that from the 66 mining leases in Sattari and Sanguem talukas alone, 15 million tonnes of iron ore valued at ₹6,100 crores was illegally extracted over the last three years.

In 1987, Parliament passed the Goa, Daman and Mining Concessions Act and abolished concessions given to miners by the Portuguese. The miners challenged the Act, first in Bombay High Court and later in the Supreme Court. The matter is pending before a 13-member Bench. Only 500 mines were allowed to continue. The miners were asked to file an application before November 21, 1988 to regularize their mines and extend the lease for 10 years. Today, only 336 mines are legal. Alvares alleged that the Ministry of Environment and Forests (MOEF) never took environment assessments seriously. "When the Chinese boom started in 2005, the environment assessment was only on paper. During 2005-09, 169 clearances were given by MOEF in such a hurry that they did not even keep copies of clearances.

The environment impact has been so adverse that agricultural output has dipped in the last three years and horticultural income has reduced by 30 per cent. A 2010 report prepared for NIO by environmentalists Pranab Mukhopadhyay and Gopal K. Kadekodi on valuation of forest resources in Goa states that the state may face water scarcity in the near future. "The denudation of forest resources in Goa could have dramatic effects on the hydrological cycle of the state which relies largely on the perennial flow of fresh water from Mandovi, Zuari and other watersheds that lie in the Western Ghats," the report states. Mining is also leading to siltation of rivers. There are 30 mines in the catchment areas of Mandovi and 21 along the Zuari. A report by NIO says 70,000 tonnes of iron ore particles get deposited in the Mandovi every year, making the water hazardous for human use. Mining has destroyed farms too. Dumping of waste by mines has rendered his farm infertile and he has to work on other's farms to survive. A committee tasked with coming up with a plan for Goa 2021, has emphasized the need to map mines. The Committee comprises well-known architect Charles Correa and Chairman of the Indian Institute of Architects, Bryan Soares, besides eight others. "Mining has caused incalculable direct and indirect damage to both the environment and the people in these areas by affecting the quality of air, water and forests as well as health, agriculture, employment and living conditions," states the report of the committee. It has recommended shutting mines that are located within 200 metres of settlements, river banks and wildlife parks. The same holds for mines that are less than 2 km from reservoirs such as Selaulim and Anjunem.

The Union Government has appointed a commission under retired Supreme Court Justice MB Shah to study the state's mines. Faced with the threat of closure, mine owners warn that if mining is stopped the economy of the state will collapse. "More than 15,000 truck drivers will lose employment as well over two lakh villagers who do odd jobs in the mines," says a mine owner. No party wants mines to shut down. However, activists say if mining goes on for five more years, half of Goa will become a desert.

Mining Legislation

Revamped mining legislation can shore up transparency in the vexed sector that seems much prone to illegality, corruption and extensive fraud. Further, a well-crafted mining law can actually boost value-addition downstream in metals, for instance by incentivizing production of high-grade steels provided there's proper valuation of ore. The point is that proactive legislation would have a huge positive impact on mining, minerals and metals. And yet, the mining Bill may well defeat the policy purpose should it become law as per its present draft. For it appears to eschew international scarcity value and cross-border traded prices of ore, so as to determine royalty rates that are deemed adequate and just. Now for major minerals like iron ore, Section 43 does call upon the mining lease holder to pay annually to the District

Mineral Foundation an amount equivalent to the royalty paid (to the state government) during the financial year. Not that the second schedule of the draft Bill merely says that royalty on iron ore would be 10 per cent of sale price on an *ad valorem* basis. But with no explicit provision for taking into account going export prices to calculate royalty, the actual levies earmarked can well be a fraction of the potential sums envisaged. It is true that since the latter half of 2009, royalty on ferrous ore is supposed to be on an *ad valorem* basis, but the standard practice seems to be to use local prices, which can quote at a steep discount to the prevailing export price. Such pricing seems widespread: recently a steel ministry panel specifically recommended that NMDC, the miner in the public sector, values its ore for local deliveries at the export prices pegged for Japanese and Korean steel producers, which are revised quarterly. Such valuation for domestic ore is the way ahead to rightly determine scarcity; domestic steel quotes have been linked to internationally traded prices for two whole decades. And yet there seems no upfront provision in the draft Bill to peg domestic ore prices to the export rates for working out royalty payment for minerals.

The point remains that there are very many policy-induced distortions in the mining sector that need to be promptly removed. The fact is that until quite recently, the prices of mineral ore were depressed by flat and royalty was at rock bottom, which remained unrevised for years. In the days of pre-reform prior to the path breaking 1990s, the policy of artificially depressed ore was put in place in the mistaken belief that it would boost steel output. But with import duties on steel as absurdly high as 200 per cent, the policy outcome was a high-cost economy generally complete with stultified, pricey steel output and poor quality to boot. That was then. Fortunately, after opening and reforms of the early 1990s, duties on steel are down to a nominal 5 per cent, domestic output has gone up six fold and more and India seems set to be the second largest producer of the metal soon.

However, there's no parallel reform of mining and mineral pricing, and it is unfortunate that the draft Mining Bill prefers not to link domestic ore prices to export prices. For globally-traded commodities, such pricing surely ought to be standard policy. Our ore output can but be a fraction of global output, and it is sensible to determine domestic scarcity value by taking into account market-determined export prices. With sound pricing of domestic ore, up to 20 per cent of mineral value can be set aside as royalty, including for targeted social development and economic uplift. As for coal and lignite, where high-ash content and other rigidities limit valuation, apart from royalty, such levies as cess, surface rent and other charges can be clubbed together so that such imposts add up to 20 per cent of turnover, the same for other minerals. It would be far more transparent than the 26 per cent profit share mandated for coal mining for development purposes; profits after all can be so structured as to accrue to special purpose vehicles and the like.

It is notable that the draft Bill envisages a nominal central 'duty of excise' on ore output, as per Section 44. A central levy would mean keeping better tab on ore output, and the indirect tax can well be set-off against duties payable downstream in the production value chain and input credit availed. Additionally, to remove continuing distortions, captive mining ought to be subject to royalty, central excise, etc. complete with funds earmarked for development purposes. Actually, as captive mining can be inherently uneconomic and subscale from a national perspective, there's solid rationale for doing away with such mining norms once green field steel producers lacking access to infrastructure have fully depreciated plants.

Political Donation: Common Practices

It is reported (*The Economics Times*, dt. 16.10.2011) political parties requested Vedanta Resources-owned mining firm Sesa

Goa for donations as part of `common practice', the multinational group said on Friday as the spectrum of the massive illegal mining scandal loomed large in the state. In a newspaper advertisement in local newspapers, Sesa Goa admitted to political donations that the company claimed to have made with a sense of propriety and transparency and said that "it is extremely unfortunate that certain activists and sections of media are ascribing motives to such political donations". The advertisement came against the backdrop of TV channel CNN IBN running a story this week on millions of rupees shelled out by the company to national and local political parties in Goa, amid allegations of illegal mining against several corporates. Quoting from Sesa Goa's balance sheet, the channel said in 2009-10, the company paid ₹85 lakhs to the main opposition party, while the ruling party got only ₹30 lakhs. Maharashtrawadi Gomantak Party got ₹2 lakhs while Shiv Sena got ₹1 lakh. Similarly in 2007-08, the company had paid ₹28 lakhs each to the two national parties, which was also the year when the company got permission to enhance iron ore production from four million tonnes to seven million tonnes from its three mining sites. The company did not deny the report.

"Like many other corporate houses in India, Sesa indeed made donations to political parties, but strictly in accordance with due process prescribed under law, including the Companies Act and the Income Tax Act," it said, saying that the donations were made by account payee cheques. "It is common practice among political parties to approach business houses for donations at different points of time," it further said, adding the donations were made only after political parties made requests to the mining firm, the "biggest in operation in Goa." It is unfortunate allegations have been made against the company for excess production without checking and/or understanding basic facts," read the clarification, denying any link between the donations and the nod to enhance production. Sesa Goa has in part been charged with several allegations of illegal mining.

The ruling party simply goofed up, said a techie who participated in the Anna movement. Political analysts would probably say the ruling party did not display political sagacity. They belonged to the large, faceless, nameless, lower middle class—carpenters, masons, sales staff in garment shops, and malls fitters, welders, car mechanics—the people who work with their hands and really produce something. Here are some thoughts.

The Government and all of us must be thankful that Anna put a gun on the ruling party. We are fortunate that this gun does not kill. On the contrary like Gandhi, Anna said, "I am prepared to die for this cause, but l am not prepared to kill for any cause. If this is blackmail 1 will continue to blackmail as long as it takes to get the government to change laws that will enable elected representatives to be prosecuted and punished for corruption".

The ruling party was sinking in the quagmire of scandals, one following another. They could have turned the Anna movement to advantage by embracing all of Anna's suggestions and presenting his Bill in entirety for debate in the parliament and taken the wind out of the sails, of the opposition. For the PM, here was a golden opportunity to support Anna's Bill and turn the tide of public opinion in his and his party's favour. Anna's Bill may not be the best of the Bills. The ruling party's attempt to use that logic by inviting more ideas, from other civil society members by introducing bills of, people like Aruna Roy came a cropper. But why limit yourself to Aruna Roy? Why not Fali Nariman, Soli Sorabjee, Amartya Sen, Raghuram Rajan, Ramchandra Guha and so on? There is no dearth of talent or wisdom. That is what the government desired the 'argumentative Indian' will ensure the death of the Bill. Just as when the Constitution was written, Ambedkar drafted a Bill and a few good men—Nehru, Gandhi, Azad, Rajaji and others—blessed it. There was no referendum to consider if they were the best people in the country.

The ruling party forgot that it was through Gandhi, Nehru and others that the party gave the gift of non-violent civil disobedience (ahimsa and satyagraha) to the world as an effective tool of protest. The irony was lost on the Congress leadership that their erratic and high handed actions to stop Anna's army was only having the opposite effect. People had intuitively grasped that Anna was not undermining democracy. On the other hand it was the elected representatives who had subverted democracy through a lethal combination of money, muscle power, caste and vote-bank politics supported by the party machinery. They realized there has not been a single case in any party, where a party had expelled on its own, its members for corruption.

Many honest, well-meaning politicians felt stifled within the parties controlled by high command. So, the repeated taunt and challenge to Anna's team by leaders from many parties that Anna must fight elections if he wants to enact laws, cut no ice with the people, but only strengthened, and gave credence to Anna's demand that elected representatives have to be accountable and getting elected does not grant licence to loot. At a loftier level, Anna Hazare's call was also a call for transformation of not only the politician but also of society and a call to all of us to be honest in our dealings. The politician is one's inside in the mirror. He is the reflection of society. We have been narrow and selfish. We are all implicated. We have colluded with the system and we have looked the other way when it suited us. Edmund Burke said, "Among the people generally corrupt, liberty cannot long exist." In a society, where everything can be purchased and influenced, there will be no peace or stability, because true democracy is subverted and a large population will be left out of equitable growth and justice. All of us—the middle class, the corporates and elected representatives—have a stake in preserving stability. You cannot survive in isolation if a flame engulfs the whole country. Listening to public opinion is not cowardice, it is statesmanship and political wisdom and will only enhance: the stature and respect of the leaders in government. Anna Hazare gave hope to the youth of this country who were cynical, sceptical and enclosed in a cocoon of complacency. He infused optimism into them, united them across caste, creed and class and taught that they must participate in shaping democracy and their future or they will have no future. He imbued the indifferent youth and middle class with optimism and showed us all a way out of our helplessness. This may be his greatest gift.

But as he has cautioned, this is only the beginning of a long struggle and the first baby steps in a series of reforms in the days to come.

Agitation and Non-Violence

Today we see tens of thousands of citizens, including many youth taking to the streets for a better tomorrow. In a country with a sizeable young population, having youngsters in the forefront of a political agitation is not surprising. We only hope that the movement remains non-violent, for violence always ends in failure and it is truth that wins. The spectacle of families bringing their children to Anna Hazare's fast at the Ramlila Maidan in Delhi for a dose of morality and ethics raises fundamental questions. What is it that we can do to establish *ahimsa* in our youth? Since protest is here to stay as a vital tool in the political arena, education in non-violence becomes a priority. Gandhiji's *satyagraha* was influenced and inspired in part by religion, especially Jainism and his own Vaishnava upbringing and he held regular *satsangs*. Today, for young people, religious instruction is mostly a family affair, or is imbibed through popular television programmes.

School textbooks offer a rather dry history of religion without inspirational content. Since there is no structured discussion in a classroom environment, there is very little space for reflection with peer groups, or for discussion on how ancient wisdom can be applied to contemporary issues, for instance greed and corruption. Without a meaningful discussion and proper mentoring how can young people go deep within and create meaning for themselves?

It is this looking within is called introspection. We need to honour its wisdom. This self-enquiry is what helps us traverse the boundary between religion and spirituality. It was a spiritual force that guided our nation through non-violence to freedom. The fact that so many youth are taking to the streets in a spirit of *ahimsa* is commendable. The real test, however, is when non-violent protestors face resistance, opposition, or violence. With spiritual practices like meditation, we can go deep within and experience the space of silence and love. Anger and hatred come in the way of dialogue and conflict resolution. Patience is required for sustained negotiations. Spirituality can solve social problems. There is a need for a spiritual tsunami as the means of transforming people and creating a divine society. This should especially inspire youth, for they are eager to do something for society. The seed of the universe is deep inside and life is more than your activity. Life is not just about achieving, it is about contributing.

Without spiritual training, *ahimsa* is fragile. Let us hold our breath and pray that people fed up with corruption continue to hold onto spiritual values. Corruption happens where there is no belongingness and spirituality is experiencing belongingness with everyone. Nurturing the spirit of *ahimsa* and truth is what youth need. We need to recognize the divinity in everyone, including ourselves. Once we are in touch with ourselves and can celebrate the silence within, nothing can provoke us.

Transparency

In view of the popular movement for a stronger Lokpal Bill, India should consider how technology can help enable accountability and transparency. It is clear to any observer that the Indian government will seek to incorporate further measures that will help restore some confidence in the system.

Today, India already has an impressive growth of roughly 8.5 per cent and is one of the largest economies worldwide. It has achieved a remarkable transformation that has been much admired around the world. The economy seems poised to grow even more in the future. Given all this, the issue of fighting corruption is a serious one—one that India needs to address to maintain its long-term growth and economic success. Transparency, of course, helps to weed out any financial irregularities. Today, transparency is a talked-about issue around the world, particularly in countries that suffer the so-called "resource curse"—the paradox in which countries blessed with natural resources are often typically economic underachievers and suffer from corruption and conflict. In Africa today, accountability is being successfully provided using technology, and it is a model that could be instructive for the Indian government. Let's take the case of the Extractive Industries Transparency Initiative (EITI), a high-profile initiative backed by prominent leaders such as former UK Prime Minister Tony Blair. The initiative "encourages government, extractive companies, international agencies and NGOs to work together to develop a framework to promote transparency of payments in the extractive industries...[and] seeks to create missing transparency and accountability in revenue flows from the extractive industry". EITI is helping bring unprecedented transparency and an audit trail to important mining and oil industries in Africa. Ghana is the first nation that has adopted it, and is serving as a case study for some 20 other African nations.

Transparency and accountability always benefit the right people. Another example from Ghana has to do with software and mobile technology helping provide transparency to 1,500 impoverished rural shea nut pickers, improving their livelihoods and cutting out middle men and reducing graft. The 1,500 nut pickers, all women, were organized into 83 groups, with each group's leader possessing a mobile phone through which the women can get local market price information via SMS. Once they sell their produce, software helps them get a view into the global supply chain for shea butter. A Stanford University study found that the new technology has significantly improved the women's income—anywhere from between 59 per cent and 82 per cent. In the developed world, government organizations regularly use technology for visibility. Government agencies that have implemented software-tracking tools have seen increased revenue from past-owed taxes and reduction in fraud. When the US Congress allocated $787 billion for the recovery of the US economy in 2009 (formally, the American Recovery and Reinvestment Act), it instituted technology to track how the money was being spent, not just by lawmakers but by anyone interested. The Act said it would provide "unprecedented levels of accountability and transparency in government spending." Today, it is indeed possible to track online where that money went and how many jobs were created as a consequence in a particular region.

Information technology systems can enhance public administration by providing real-time insight into financial transactions and related outcomes, helping to manage internal risks, improving control over funds, enforcing standards and rules, and streamlining automated processes. IT systems offer countries not only the tools to make fiscally responsible policy for future generations, but also improve the abilities of policymakers to provide good public services and make well informed decisions. Newspapers recently carried the story of a poor man and his family committing suicide because the money sanctioned to him under the Indira Awas Yojana, a government housing programme, was siphoned off by middlemen. India has already implemented the Right to Information Act in 2005, which enshrines the right of a citizen to seek information from officials within 30 days; there are strict penalties for those officials who do not comply with. Although technology is not the panacea for everything, it has the ability to streamline processes, detect fraud and ensure fairness, providing efficiency transparency and accountability things which Indian citizens all over India seem to be demanding today. Best of all, the use of software technology plays to a key Indian strength: India's leadership in computer software. Of course, all this transparency will not happen overnight. While human efforts such as those by anti-corruption protesters remain crucial, technology can make a real difference in making people's lives more independent from the benevolence or malevolence of any kind of oligarchy. An automated fully open and transparent process set up to show how public funds are being used and how government is functioning will convince Indian citizens that the government is serious about providing transparency and accountability; and make the great Indian success story even better.

Civil Society Organizations

Recently, bribe-givers, particularly businesses, have come into limelight. Cases connected with mining and telecom have brought to the fore the active role of corporate, and whispers in the market have now become headlines in the media. Earlier, a financial fraud of massive proportions sent tremors through the corporate world, triggering many a discussion and report about corporate governance and ethics.

Issues related to corruption and fraud by the private sector have now turned the spotlight on governance in companies and led to new regulations, including strict norms—especially for listed companies—regarding board composition disclosures and transparency. Also ministry of corporate affairs has published voluntary guidelines, which raise the bar beyond what the law mandates. A new Companies Act is in the final stages of clearance and enactment; it seeks to strengthen various aspects of corporate governance. There is a lively debate about whether PPP projects should be covered by the right to information. Some would like the private sector too covered under RTI. So, there is much focus and regulatory activism aimed at enhancing accountability, transparency and honesty amongst companies.

At the same time, a Lokpal Bill—almost certainly, one expects come into existence in the near future, and will act on corruption in government. A similar law is likely to ensure that the judiciary too is covered. These are welcome developments while they are unlikely to end corruption, these could certainly help to curb it.

Apart from business, judiciary and government, there is now an increasingly important role being played by a media and civil society. The former wields disproportionate power, because of its ability to set agendas, steer discussion and influence opinion. As in other sectors, there are those who are corrupt and others who are honest. The ills range from paid news and an insider trading, to extortion and blackmail. Self-regulatory mechanisms are in place and seem to be making some impact also, private media is subject to the same laws and voluntary guidelines as corporates in other sectors.

Civil society organizations (CSOs), in contrast to the segments mentioned earlier, have far less regulation. They are under the ambit of the Societies Act (or its equivalents, depending on their organizational form) and constrained by limits on foreign donations. But they are rarely under the public scanner. So, one hears little about any corruption, fraud or malpractice amongst CSOs. While one explanation could be their innate honesty, few would attribute it to this. As in other fields, here too there are honest organizations run by selfless persons, and others who are there only to make money or seek undeserved fame by any means.

A recent high-profile case has highlighted ethical if not legal issues related to the operation and management of CSOs. Other attempts—many by motivated detractors—to defame CSOs or individuals connected with them, have raised doubts about their quality of governance. The laws relating to societies and trusts are often archaic, with periodic tinkering making them worse. Light-touch regulation is appropriate for this area however, there is a need for safeguard, checks and balances, and transparency. Governmental control in any form is contrary to the very purpose of such organizations, and regulations like the new apparently draconian ones in Gujarat, are definitely undesirable.

One cause for the clouds of suspicion is that this new growth sector has attracted many people out to make a quick buck. The dedicated, do-good, stereotyped *jholawala*—surviving on a pittance and commitment to a cause—yet exists, but has now been joined by those for whom CSOs are only a convenient mechanism to tap funds, mainly from government, and by socialites who are in CSOs for visibility or as an excuse for kitty parties. Some CSOs are but proxy marketing and public relations arms of companies that fund them, often with undeclared connections; others are used as a tool against corporate rivals; some are also being used as fronts by companies, political parties, and religious organizations. There are many that have become very important pillars of democracy and do outstanding work. While some have excellent governance with well-defined procedures and systems, many CSOs have poor accounting practices and petty frauds are common. Unlike company boards, there is no requirement for independent directors, and few have the equivalent of an audit committee. CSOs, which get substantial funding from the government and the public, need to be governed better. Mechanisms to ensure good governance and transparency, while safeguarding against financial impropriety and frauds, are necessary. Ideally, CSOs should come up with a self regulatory code, with efforts like the Credibility Alliance. It's time for genuine CSOs to stimulate a debate on ethics, good governance and ways of enforcing standards of transparency and probity in this sector.

Rent-seekers turned to natural resources after the reforms in the 1990s brought to an end the licence raj to a large extent. The natural resources include land, forests, minerals, oil, spectrum, etc, as the picking ground for their greed and need. Because they have to fight elections that cost humongous amounts nowadays. But state funding for elections will never be a panacea, because that will not satisfy their greed. Just take a look at the voluntary disclosures by ministers, which clearly show how rich they have become ever since they came into politics. And that is just the declared income and not their wealth, which is much more than their declared wealth, salted away insalubrious climes abroad. Why have exports to the Bahamas suddenly shot up 100 times in two years, from $2.2 million in 2008-09 to $2.2 billion in 2010-11? The answer: round tripping of black money stored abroad.

Another method of illegal wealth creation is our systems. Wherever discretion to the powers continues to operate, illegal wealth creation reaches alarming proportions. Many high court judges take bribes in double digit lakhs to write a favourable order. No court *babu* will move a file without a standard *bakshish*. The list is endless, but the gratification levels are steadily going north, with the excuse that if politicians can make thousands of crores, what is a few lakhs. The loss to the nation on account of the 2G spectrum scam has been estimated at ₹ 1,76,000 lakh crores, an incredible figure. But the fact is that bribes in thousands of crores were paid through various means to get the licences without going through the competitive bidding process. Now the government is talking about transparency in spectrum allocation under a new telecom policy. Few other things have started happening to address the morass, but they too are moving slowly due to the inertia, while rent-seekers and wheeler-dealers dominate the show. The spectrum conspirators are behind bars, though yet to be convicted. Even if they are convicted, our laws do not allow the disgorgement of their ill-gotten wealth. Very recently, Bihar has seized a corrupt bureaucrat's house and turned that into a school for the weaker sections. But that is perhaps a rare thing.

In between all this, an RTI application unearthed an inter-ministerial advice by the finance ministry to proceed with caution in the 2G scam. That created quite a furore. Suddenly, there were calls made to amend the RTI Act. Once again, the RTI Act was blamed for the policy paralysis. But wise counsel prevailed that one cannot unwind or dilute the RTI law. After all, why should honest officers be afraid. Fortunately, the RTI law has helped improve both transparency and, in turn, probity, which is what it aimed at. Babus dealing with public procurement functions are reported to be causing a loss estimated at ₹ 7,500 lakh crores per annum, or about 20 per cent of our GDP. Our procurement systems are not only opaque but out of sync. Just because the scams are not a one-time affair, they do not catch the public's attention unless they are funny ones like the CWG buying toilet rolls for ₹4,000 each. This is somewhat like the huge number of road accident deaths in our country, 1.18 lakh in 2008, which cost the GDP about 3 per cent, but they don't hit the headlines. The death figures translate to a number of people dying if two Boeing 737s (with about 160 passengers on-board) crash everyday, and even one air crash hits the headline news. As another step forward, the government has set in motion reforms in procurement policy and also drafting a procurement law. To ensure sound allocation of natural resources, the government has prepared an excellent draft report. Alas, the same is not in the public domain. The report seeks transparency and fairness in allocation of business licences through competitive bidding, etc. The reason that this is not yet public is because of many dissensions within the government for obvious reasons. The Committee headed by Ashok Chawla, inter alia, comprised the secretaries of the government dealing with these natural resources so that there could be a consensus report. Unfortunately, that did not happen. Sixty-eight of the 81 recommendations have been accepted but a few relating to coal, petroleum and land are still to be agreed upon. Evidently, political economy factors are holding up the proposal to discipline these sectors. In the ultimate analysis, it will be the implementation of all these measures that would matter more than drafting policies, laws and regulations.

Chapter 4

CRIME CONTROL

Harvard psychology professor Steven Pinker, in his latest book. "The Better Angels of Our Nature; Why Violence Has Declined," answers questions on the relationship between wealth and violence and whether there will ever be another great war. Peace would only lead to decadence, effeminacy, materialism, selfishness and intellectual and artistic stagnation. War was necessary for men to develop courage, manliness, self-sacrifice, loyalty, solidarity and obedience to authority. Many important artists and thinkers in the 19th century e.g., Alexis de Tocqueville, Emile Zola, Georg Hegel, Thomas Mann, Igor Stravinsky and Friedrich Nietzsche positively gushed about how holy and thrilling war was.

World War I pretty much put an end to all that. There are no downsides to peace. Unless one thinks that it's a good idea to control population size by machine-gunning or blowing up a random sample of the world's inhabitants, the moral harm of war will always outweigh any good it does in controlling population. Also, except for truly horrendous wars, population size depends far more on birth rates and on deaths from disease and famine than it does on deaths from war. "The survival of the fittest" is also a dubious benefit of war. Not only does war kill pretty indiscriminately, but it also makes no sense to think of Darwinian natural selection as an inherent human good, unless we believe that pumping out the maximum number of babies, killing people who get in our way, and letting sick and weak people die are positive things. The decrease in the number of political actors is one of the historical developments that have reduced the number of wars. Europe went from 5,000 political units in the 15th century to 500 in the 17th and about 30 in the 1950s. And holding territory constant, countries have fewer civil wars within their boundaries than interstate wars that cross them, since governments, armies and police are much better able to keep their own citizens from each other's throats. So fewer jurisdictions mean fewer wars.

The connection between violence and prosperity is more tenuous. Today, civil wars are certainly more common among more often countries at the very bottom of the economic scale, but this relationship quickly levels off as gross domestic product per capita increases. In the past, lots of rich countries waged war, often with each other and some periods of economic growth for these nations (like the 1960s) had far more violence, both international and domestic, than periods of recession, like the 2000s. Surprisingly, few wars are fought over control of resources; they are far more often fought over glory, honour, influence, ideology, emotion, security and other intangible issues. It's certainly possible that another horrendous war could break out; the observation that war has decreased a lot isn't the same as the prediction that it will never happen again. But if the question is whether war is cyclical, or whether during periods of peace the urge for war inexorably builds up until it bursts, the answer is no. Statistical studies of war show no reliable cycles and countries can remain at peace indefinitely. It's not as if Canada, the Netherlands, New Zealand, Sweden and other peaceable countries are feeling a greater and greater need for war with each passing year. There are many statistical predictors of violence that we choose not to use in our decision-making for moral and political reasons, because the ideal of fairness trumps the ideal of cost-effectiveness. A rational decision-maker using Baye's theorem would say, for example, that one should convict a poor defendant with less evidence than one needs to convict a rich defendant.

India can be called a soft state, because rule of law has been given a go by in many parts of the country. The spectre that haunts most political parties is the fear of losing their vote banks. They are hesitant to take action against criminals or gangs that can raise the banner of religious or regional identity. Everybody, regardless of religion or region is equal before the Indian law. Indian law provides that there should not be any discrimination against one or the other for political or any other considerations. But practically it is not found today in the country and actually it is not being practised also. Blatant violations by the rich and influential have become commonplace. And if the government turns a blind eye, it lays the foundation for the breakdown of the entire system of governance and theory of broken window syndrome truly applies. White collar crime is generally committed by the white collar criminals having influence in society either through power or money. In white collar crime too much money is spent. Their collar is white and always remains white even after committing the crime without getting any blot on it. White collar criminals are generally not engaged in criminal cases like murder, etc., but nowadays the earlier position has changed and they are also engaged in murder, etc., through hiring someone. Literally white collar means belonging or pertaining to the salaried or professional worker whose jobs generally do not involve manual labour. White collar crime is increasing day by day with the influence of computer and other advanced electronic technology and adoption of consumerism in the society. Businessmen are constantly discovering ways of influencing politicians and bureaucrats and engendering a whole new culture of disregard for the law of the land. They immediately obtain bail from the court or even if they stay in jail, procures five star facilities of comfort. Criminal minds have adopted noble modus operandi to become rich quickly. Recent example of some famous Rajya Sabha Members is a manifestation of this trend. They spent money like anything causing immense loss to the economy. The middle class people of the society try to copy them on the belief that even if Mr. X has committed crime of murder, law could not do any harm to him.

The USA and the UK police have a special status in the world. It is true that our policing system is the copy of Britain Police System and it is still unchanged. It is a false impression that our Police character and structure is not theirs. There are three organs of our criminal justice system—police, judiciary and jail. All of these are more or less in that form as were in British time. The British used to utilize these forces to crush the oppositions so as to keep their hold on the state safe and these we have copied from them after independence.

Number of police in the USA and the UK is more than that in India. Their structure of police is three times which includes Home Secretary, Police Authority and Chief Constable. Chief of Police is called Chief Constable in those countries like DGP in our country. Police Authority is a committee of public representative to whom chief constable is responsible. Chief constable has full control over the whole police system. Due to this there is no political interference. There is only one point of entrance as police constable in police and on promotion purely based on merit they can be promoted up to the Chief Constable. Police structure in those countries is like a pyramid. Chief Constable is empowered to promote up to the Chief Superintendent and above this post Police Authority is empowered to select the officers and after selection they do not interfere in their work. A constable is fully empowered to arrest a person on his own reasonable belief. There is an independent police complaint committee to investigate the complaint against individual police. In the UK public has full faith in police and judiciary. In the UK police is called Bobby.

The faults in the system are being exploited by forces hostile to India. Too many concessions are enjoyed by all sorts of people and groups to carry on their illegal activities. In such a situation the police which are required to maintain law and order are helpless and in dilemma to take appropriate stringent action against the law breakers. This attitude of the police is causing a frightening decline in the ability and willingness to do their job. The country is experiencing an unprecedented decline in the efficacy of the politico-administrative structure. Politicization of the state institutions has seriously eroded their credibility and effectiveness. All-pervasive corruption is eating into the vitals of the Indian state. Even judiciary is not free from it. For example, we have seen a famous film actor is being prosecuted in Rajasthan Court on the charge of killing a *chinkara*, while hunting for pleasure. The decision of the court is still awaited even hearing of the case is not yet finished. Every time when he appears for hearing in the court there is lot of pomp and show by the media. Whereas in the USA, a Sikh fellow charged by the public after 9/11 in rash, the accused has been sentenced. The final decision came in just nine months after the incident. With effective intelligence and controlled action by the army and police jointly the prolonged militancy in J&K has come to end. But ruling party is campaigning for abolition of Armed Forces Special Right Act only for their political gain.

The Hon'ble Supreme Court Bench, consisting of Justice Ajit Parsayat and Justice M Sharma, has delivered a remarkable and laudable judgment in regard to criminal justice administration. "Protection of society and stamping out criminal proclivity must be the object of law which must be achieved by imposing appropriate sentence."

India internal security challenges have become progressively more complex since the late 1970s. But the government is still looking for soft options and simplistic solutions by underplaying the problems or by trying to pass on the buck for the present mess to the states. It is evident that short term electoral advantages have taken precedence over the requirements of national security.

The growing ineffectiveness of the tools of governance, especially the police and criminal justice system is one of the major causes for the growth of extremists and militant forces. The increasing politicization and breakdown of the command and control system in the police and intelligence agencies have allowed the leadership in many states to pass into the hands of officers known for their flexibility than for their merit and leadership qualities. The perception that the state is weak and unable to provide protection of life and property of its people encourages the forces of lawlessness. The dissatisfaction of the people should be addressed by taking possible steps considering social, economic and political factors. Unfortunately, instead of concentrating on strategies to address these grievances, only enquiry commissions are being repeatedly appointed without taking any concrete steps. It has resulted in further reinforcing a sense of victimization among the alienated communities. Suffering from a sense of injustice, they readily believe the false propaganda that state is discriminating against them. Therefore, the government has only made the task of police of dealing with the secessionist and terrorist more difficult. Any action against the suspected persons is seen as an assault on the entire community by the large section of people in that community. With the state structure losing its credibility, legitimacy and effectiveness, the job of the police has become more difficult.

The security forces are stretched over vast areas in large parts of India's vast rural expanse and pitted against their own people. Large deployment of security forces suffering from a siege mentality in far flung areas in fact provides more targets to the extremists. An important point is that senior bureaucrats, police, intelligence officers required to be made accountable for their bad advice and failures in the field. Few blackships in the police who indulge in corruption have given bad name to it, which urgently required to be weeded out. There are still quite a few people in the police who are honest out of conviction and not fear. However, for the most of them honesty begins and ends with them. It may be advisable to keep one's integrity intact but it is not enough if corruption is flourishing right under your nose. They are obliged to catch and root out corruption and to protect the honest. They seem too much in love with their white clothes to take such a risk. One cannot fight corruption in white clothes, as it is inevitably involves mudslinging, white clothes and fighting corruption do not go hand in hand. To challenge corruption, one has to don khaki's or fatigues and take on mud and brickbats that come thick and fast. You take off your khakis only when the job is accomplished.

1993 Mumbai Serial Blasts

Among the blizzard of reactions to the terrorist blast in Delhi and other places, Muslims face a fresh wave of hate-mongering, taunts and vilification. Numerous terror attacks have forced the community to reconcile to the fact that Muslims must carry the albatross of being sympathizers of terrorist, if not actual terrorist themselves.

Muslim employees see the attitude of their colleagues change after the July 13 bomb blast in Mumbai. The co-workers always say, "all this is happening because of you people." Muslims have to endure an entire train journey listening to an angry co-passenger saying that Hindu youngsters would have to keep pistols to deal with these Pakistani (Muslims).

Muslims undeniably carry the guilt that Muslim terrorists are wreaking suffering on innocents. Even if the involvement of Muslims terrorists is not proved the impression is that Islamic terrorists are behind all blasts. Muslim Federations always condemn the blast through a press conference. The need to repeatedly condemn every act of terrorism shows the pit of fear that Muslims have fallen into the fear of being maligned and framed. The international conference against terrorism was held at Taj. Even Islamic seminary Darul Uloom Deoband sounded a Fatwa against terrorism. Today it has become a ritual to hold a conference against terrorism immediately after every attack. This betrays the fear in the Muslims psyche. Even in case of genuine need people do not help only due to fear that they may be framed for sheltering Muslims even if just for a few minutes. The antennae of anti Muslims folk also get activated after terror episodes and vitriol is spewed from different platforms. It is an open humiliation of Muslims and an attempt to create discord among communities yet police ignore it. Most of the Muslims now dread on their shadow and feel the need to reiterate their patriotism at every opportunity.

Crime is as old as the hills and so is organized crime. Many crime experts draw a similarity between today's multinational crime syndicates and the medieval gangs of robbers. The first large-scale organized groups of criminals in India were the thugs. Organized groups of criminals is a modern phenomenon. The members of this cult generally operated by joining caravans, getting accepted as member and then attacking the travellers at a suitable place. To keep their identity secret, it was not unusual for the thugs to kill the entire caravan. The typical method of killing was strangulation. Estimates of how many people the thugs killed between the 18th and the early 19th century vary widely, from about 50,000 to 20 lakh. The lack of any central leadership in India helped them thrive. The thugs were finally eradicated by the British. Like the thugs in India, there were various criminal organizations operating in pre-industrialized Japan and Italy.

In terms of pure economics, the motive of any criminal is

to increase profits and decrease risks. Crime is also, however, a social issue and hence social changes like centralization of the power at national and international level has an impact on crime. Although the concept of nation states became more prominent after industrialization, but closed national borders emerged only after the First World War. This resulted in giving more power to central governments in implementing law and order. In these circumstances, the chances of an individual criminal surviving became slimmer than for a criminal who was a member of some syndicate. That helped the growth of organized crime and the nexus between criminal groups, enforcement authorities, politicians and businessmen. Although this phenomenon may have emerged as a counter to the consolidation of power at the central level, it has also been observed that a central government losing its grip can lead to the formation of powerful criminal organizations as happened after the collapse of the Soviet Union in 1991.

Perhaps the most famous criminal organisations were the Italian American mafia, a word which has now become synonymous with organized crime in general. The group operated much like the Sicilian Mafia as the central control was held by specific families. In almost every group, the entry of non-Italians was restricted. Similar to the Italian mafia, the Irish Mob also originated in Irish American street gangs. The Chinese triads, criminal organizations of Chinese nationals, operate in Hong Kong, Vietnam, Macau, Taiwan, China and other countries with sizeable Chinese populations. Japan also has similar syndicates known as the Yakuza and it is estimated that these organizations have over 1 lakh members at present.

In India, crime started getting organized during the British Raj. In the early 1940s, some smuggling syndicates were formed in Mumbai. Initially dealing in petty stuff like transistors and watches, in the post-Independence period these gangs started smuggling gold and silver. Prohibition led to the rise of Karim

Lala who facilitated bootlegging and gambling dens. By the 1960s, Mumbai's underworld got its poster boy and Haji Mastan became a celebrity. Mastan and his accomplice Yusuf Patel specialized in smuggling gold and silver and it is reported that they invested their money in real estate. The 1970s saw the rise of Varadarajan Mudaliar, whose interests were bootlegging and *matka*, a form of gambling. In the late 1970s, Dawood Ibrahim Kaskar started gaining prominence in Mumbai's underworld and over the next decade he built India's largest crime syndicate. Starting with smuggling, Dawood soon specialized in extortion. In the mid-1980s, when his operations started coming under the police scanner, he shifted his base to Dubai. The shifting of base made some of his lieutenants more powerful and gang wars became common. The 1993 Mumbai bomb blasts communalized the underworld and his key aide Chota Rajan parted ways with Dawood. It is believed that the information revolution has been a great help for Dawood who is still believed to have substantial control over the Mumbai underworld even though he is physically not present in the country for some time now.

Socially beneficial tool turning into legal terrorism. Misuse of Section 498 A of the Indian Penal Code has resulted in innocent getting punished. It is too early to say whether Dominique Strauss Kahu was framed by a woman employee of a hotel. It cost him his job as IMF chief and cast a shadow on his ambition to become French President. After prosecutors developed doubts over veracity of the victim's charges, Kahu got unconditional bail. The relief cannot save his image, reputation and political prospects. It is difficult to say but, generally allegations of sexual assault or exploitation against the rich, powerful and famous are taken to be true. But the most equipped investigation, able prosecution and hawk-eyed judicial scrutiny sometimes fail to unravel the facts. Actor Shiney Ahuja, who probably would be finding similarities of his case with that of Strauss Kahu, will agree. The Supreme Court faced an identical dilemma just last year, relating to dowry harassment cases under Section 498A of Indian Penal Code. "It is common knowledge that unfortunately, matrimonial litigation is rapidly increasing in our country... this clearly demonstrates discontent and unrest in the family life of a large number of people of society," it said.

On the one hand, the law was the social legislation giving women protection against harassment at the hands of the husband and his relatives, who demand more and more dowry. The court was concerned with the rapid rise in such cases. But on the other hand, it was aware that "a large number of such complaints are not bona fide and are filed with oblique motive." It admitted, "To find out the truth is a herculean task in a majority of these complaints. The tendency of implicating husband and all his immediate relations is also not uncommon. At times, even after the conclusion of criminal trial, it is difficult to ascertain the real truth." The SC wanted a way out of the vicious cycle of litigation that mostly ruins innocent husbands and in-laws, who are falsely roped in, but seldom affects the real perpetrators who exploit loopholes in the system to escape.

The court was worried by the overkill of Section 498A. It did not want a socially beneficial legal framework to be turned into a mechanism of legal terrorism. It requested the Law Commission to examine the issue and suggest changes that could help create an ambience where the perpetrators could be adequately punished and at the same time, leave some room for negotiations to arrive at an amicable settlement. The Commission invited suggestions from all quarters, including NRIs. And the overwhelming response was in favour of thorough investigations into the complaint of the wife under Section 498A before police arrested the husband and in-laws.

The Commission is in the process of finalizing its decision which appears to be in favour of providing for a settlement clause between the victim and in-laws, which could be a welcome breather. However, it is against making the offence under Section 498A bailable. Before any change is made in the law that was enacted to protect women from dowry harassment, it needs to be debated, whether a woman's complaint under Section 498A be thoroughly probed before effecting arrest of the husband and her in-laws. Right now, once a Section 498A complaint is lodged, the police arrests the person named by the wife. The SC had said, "The allegations of harassment of husband's close relations who had been living in different cities and never visited or rarely visited the place where the complainant resided would have an entirely different complexion. The allegations of the complaint are required to be scrutinized with great care and circumspection." The commission, before sending its recommendation to the government, must examine this aspect—what should be the protection to husbands and in-laws who have been framed in a complaint under Section 498A. But it must also not forget and lose sight of the gruesome treatment meted out to women who fail to satisfy the greed of husbands and their in-laws.

Naxalites

The Maoist threat to the internal security of the country is unfortunately degenerating into a battle between robbers in the establishment and killers among the Naxalites. Both swear by ideology. Government spokespersons never tire of showing their great concern for the common men but the truth is that the heart of the ruling elite beats for corporate lobbies. On the other hand, the Maoist leaders pretend to champion the cause of the poor but their activities have only brought sufferings to the tribals. Both, tragically, indulge in extortion—one in the garb of development and the other to sustain its "protracted people's war" against a government it finds semi-colonial and semi-feudal.

The government, in pursuance of policy of "clear, hold and develop", launched a massive operation involving the police and paramilitary forces at the beginning of 2010 to quell the Maoist rebellion. Forces were deployed in significant numbers in Naxalite affected states of Chhattisgarh, Jharkhand, Bihar, Odisha, Maharashtra and West Bengal. The Home Minister stated that the Naxalite menace would be contained within the next couple of years. However, barely had the operations commenced that discordant voices began to be heard. Jharkhand was the first to express its opposition to the use of force.

The Chief Minister of Bihar expressed his apprehension that such action would lead to further alienation of the people. The Chief Minister of West Bengal has consistently shown a soft corner for the Maoists. The greatest dampener to the Home Ministry campaign, however, was the Congress general secretary's criticism of the Home Minister emphasizing the "hearts and minds approach." There is no doubt that development has to be given very high priority in any counter-insurgency plan. However, it can only supplement and not substitute the security approach. You cannot have a state within a state; an irregular army alongside the regular troops. There is no overall strategic plan and the state satraps are pursuing their own ad hoc policies. There is a lack of seriousness and absence of commitment at all levels in dealing with the Maoist threat. This is reflected at the ground level in the slow pace of modernization and expansion of the police forces, lackadaisical operations by field commanders and tardy work on the development front by a bureaucracy which thinks it is not its battle. The Maoists, taking advantage of the continuing confusion in government policy and the absence of coordination among the states, have established their presence over a huge territorial area —in 223 districts of 20 states of the Union and the wave continues to expand. Urban centres are their latest thrust areas. They have already penetrated Delhi and sneaked into the metropolitan cities of Mumbai, Kolkata and Bengaluru. The success of the Maoists is to be attributed not so much to the relevance of their political philosophy as to the inefficiency and corruption of the establishment. The Government has launched schemes which are perfect on paper to alleviate poverty, mitigate unemployment, uphold the rights of tribals, and rehabilitate and resettle those displaced as a consequence of development projects. But the tragedy is that none of the flagship schemes is having the intended impact, essentially because the bulk of the funds are either siphoned off or just embezzled. The government may as well re-write the Biblical sermon to say: "Blessed are the corrupt for they will inherit the earth". Monsters of corruption are exposed but they continue to hold high office. Politicians with links to Dawood Ibrahim manage to get away; those who destroyed the national carrier remain unscathed. The tragedy of the Indian state is that its people are sandwiched between robbers and killers. The Maoists might make spectacular noises now and then by ambushing the security forces or derailing a railway train, but beyond that it is unlikely that they will make any significant impact on the political horizon. Their thinking is completely out of sync with the dreams and aspirations of an emerging India. We will have to go back to the lesser evil, the political class, which will have to mend its ways, enforce accountability and improve governance, or else the volcano of popular anger will obliterate them.

Mumbai's crime ambience makes it easier for terrorists to operate. It was a recruitment centre for Pakistan's ISI even before the 1993 blasts. There is a high floating population of about 20 lakh persons who enter and leave every day, which provides very high anonymity for terrorists. One cannot have a city-wise response to terror and the government's total response to terror is inadequate.

The government is getting complacent at the state and Centre. Home Minister started well but now he wants to project a picture of all-is-well. The attitude seems to have percolated down. Terrorists need a structure of overground workers to support them. These overground workers are well known but for political reasons no obtrusive surveillance is being maintained on them.

On the evening of July, 13, 2011 three successive bomb blasts in south and central Mumbai shattered the calm that accompanied two and-a-half years of terror-free existence for the residents of India's commercial capital. Twentyone people had been killed and hundreds injured in the serial blasts at Opera House, Zaveri Bazaar and near the Kabutarkhana in Dadar. The return of terror followed an all too familiar pattern. The terrorists chose to target heavily congested areas in rush hour. The damage inflicted may not be as extensive as other such attacks but the psychological damage on India's financial capital is immense.

The last time terrorists struck Mumbai was on November 26, 2008. That was an act of some audacity as armed gunmen went on a killing spree at various locations in south Mumbai, including the iconic Taj Mahal Palace and Towers Hotel, before holding themselves up in three different venues for three days. By the time they were flushed out by NSG commandos, more than 160 people had lost their lives and more than 300 were injured. It was India's 9/11. A terrorist attack of that magnitude should have forced the Government to undertake a radical reform of its internal security apparatus. The US Government did just that after 9/11 creating a new Department of Homeland Security to coordinate the work of all intelligence agencies. The US has not suffered a terrorist strike in 10 years. It didn't take terrorists even three years to attack Mumbai again.

In the aftermath of 26/11, individuals, such as the then Union Home Minister Shivraj Patil and the then Maharashtra Chief Minister Vilasrao Deshmukh lost their jobs for their failure to anticipate the 26/11 attacks. New individuals have taken their place. It seems obvious that the system has remained much the same. Interestingly, the Ram Pradhan Committee that was set up by the Maharashtra government to examine the lapses made by the Mumbai police during 26/11, made a specific reference to the American experience after 9/11 and recommended ways to improve coordination in intelligence. Like most such reports it gathers dust. Mumbaikars, as always, stepped forward to help their unfortunate fellow citizens by even using cyberspace to offer food and shelter. Some news reports on the evening of the blasts suggested that many shops in the affected areas continued to remain open for business. That is admirable. The high threshold for suffering of the Indian citizen lulls the endemically inert police and politician into a false sense of complacency. Nothing is done and history repeats itself with dreadful monotony.

Extreme religious fundamentalism is one of the root causes of terrorism in urban areas. More so, after the communal divide in the 1990s, Left-wing extremism (LWE) is ideological and more in the rural areas. Both need different strategies but, unfortunately, we haven't been able to build a strong intelligence network in the country for both. Today, we have to look at the issue of intelligence, afresh. Police-to-people ratio is one of the lowest in our country. We have to go for fresh recruitment at all levels in the state and the Centre. Recruitment of IPS was slashed from 85 to 36 during 1998. We have to look at the demographic profile of the uniformed force. Our uniformed force hasn't been able to instill confidence among Muslims, and therefore we are not any intelligence input from this section. Media should not break news on unsubstantiated reports after a terror attack. This has really shaken the confidence of the Muslim community. We have to reach out to win their confidence, particularly lower middle class professionals, doctors, advocate, notary people, retired teachers and others. We have to look at the behavioural aspect in intelligence-gathering of policemen in their training module. We haven't been able to install "e-borders" as yet. David Headley entered India more than five times, and yet we couldn't keep track of him. Mohammad Athar involved in the 9/11 attack in the US was given a green card after the incident. This wouldn't have been possible if the software for e-borders had been installed.

Training of personnel in intelligence agencies has to be updated regularly with ever-changing technology. Procedure for procurement of equipment to keep pace with technology has to be different from routine procurement procedures. State and central agencies don't share information most of the time. One ex-DIB has gone on record that the government had been alerted nine months before hostilities broke out in Kargil. Different counter terrorism centres operate within their cocoon and the National Counter-Terrorism Centre announced in 2008 is yet to be created.

We have national commission report and 10 different committee reports on police reform on which we haven't acted in spite of the court order. We haven't been able to institutionalize the concept of community policing mentioned in the police commission report. This can be a very effective source of intelligence-gathering. We have a huge force of private security personnel who with a little bit of training can be a fairly reliable source of intelligence inputs. We should also institutionalize regular security audits of public places. There was a similar incident in the Delhi High Court sometime back. If there was a regular security audit, maybe this attack could have been avoided. Involvement of officers of Military Intelligence, in terrorist activity is a matter of serious concern. Shouldn't we purge such elements who have infiltrated our uniformed force? We need now is a comprehensive strategy to improve our intelligence network. Clear division of work and responsibility should be given for the internal security of the country.

The Male "Criminal" Mind

To control crime we have to first study the psychology of the criminal mind and its evolution. Army Gen. Omar Bradley, addressing West Point cadets, in 1952 have said, "Ours is a world of nuclear giants and ethical infants. We know more about war than we know about peace, more about killing than we know about living."

In the past several years, studies intended to ferret out the factors producing the male criminal mind seem to have focused upon low serotonin levels, low standing heart rates and high testosterone levels. These studies are being done as the social order seems to be crumbling beneath our feet. Our society, some social critics fear, is losing the battle of controlling and preventing violence in our culture. While politicians of the left and right cry that Hollywood, or the disintegration of the family, is to blame for the decline in morality, scientists, too, weigh in on the debate. Scientists, however, tend to believe that if they can just find the gene responsible for criminality, violence will become a thing of the past. There is in fact more than one gene responsible for "criminal aggression," and that these genes act in concert according to the environment in which the "criminal" finds himself. In short, we will find that a stressful environment creates a responsive behaviour adaptive to that environment. From the standpoint of evolutionary psychology, these behaviours, are innate, adaptive behaviours—their motive is not the commission of crimes, but survival. We have a brain and genes that were suited for the savanna of 25,000 years ago, and we still carry them with us today. We must readjust our thinking to reflect that admission.

As hunter-gatherers, our ancestors formed groups. We are social animals today because our hunter-gatherer ancestors found that, in forming groups, they could better provide for their own survival. In a group there are more eyes and ears to watch and listen, and more noses to smell for potential predators, an act of nature, or perhaps other tribes. In order to transmit the coming of a potential danger, our ancestors created cries in patterns by expelling air from their mouths. Later, these noise patterns were linked with hand motions as early sign language, which then developed into verbal language unique to the group. Additionally, by being in a group they found that they had a greater selection of females and males to choose from as potential mates. All of these factors gave our hunter-gatherer ancestors a common reason to be together: The social structure of the groupings provided better opportunities for food, mating, safety, and companionship.

There is no way to get around this: the majority cultural patterns of present-day males in society lead evolutionary psychologists to conclude that our ancestral hunter-gatherer social groups were dominated by the physical strength, stamina and stature of the males. Before plant domestication some 10,000 years ago, fruits, berries, and nuts were not always easily available. This problem-solving ability of learning to capture small animals, and then larger ones insured our survival as a species. Our ancestors survived on their hunting abilities, assisted by an adaptive "aggressive" tendency necessary to accomplish the task. Once the cultural habits of male dominance were established, they were reinforced by further continued successes; in most but not all cases, success in using force over females to dominate gene distribution. The adaptive response of the female to this aggressive tendency was to adapt to the trait, thus gaining resources for her children. Another possibility is that the male became aggressive to gain favour of the female and thus pass on his genes. Finding great advantage in this arrangement to their gender, males dominated by the use of strength and stamina in a harsh and unforgiving world. Since evolutionary success was built on the foundation of the aggressive male and responsive female, evolution continued to favour those social groups dominated by "naturally selecting" cultures in which this aggression and response dominated. However, because of child-rearing and the delicate task needed, males took the most and gave little back. Then, as today, males control most of the resources and they use those resources in a variety of manipulative methods. The species survived, and the survival behaviour became embedded into genetic instructions to ensure that survival.

This, of course, is not to posit the inevitability of the continued dominance of this male "aggression..." Just because this direction of evolution allowed us to arrive at this place in time successfully, does not mean it has to continue.

In any group, conditions vary, leading to various cumulative results. Some male hunters were more successful than others. Some clans had numerically more sons, who were engines of resource acquisition and, hence, an advantage in accumulating resources. (Also most likely giving rise to the concept of males as more desirable in childbirth in various cultures). Those combining the traits of strength, stamina, and cunning began to outperform and bring back more catches than others. Their stature grew, that of others withered. This male dominance in hunting led to battles for dominance in territory and the selection of females both essential elements in gene transference. In most cases, this led to the creation of a single dominant male who controlled access to the females; if other males wanted access, they found it necessary to form an alliance with the dominant male. Thankfully, this sexual dominance was eventually cracked by the cunning resourcefulness of the females. To do this, the females had to most likely "cheat" on their dominant male by stealing away from the group for a dalliance with a non-dominant male.

Today, there are three major internal indicators that scientists are focusing on which seem to contribute to male criminality. They are: 1) low serotonin levels; 2) low resting heart rate; and 3) high testosterone levels.

On study it has focus that:

- Serotonin levels are the lowest in adolescent males.
- Serotonin levels are 20 per cent to 30 per cent lower in men than women.
- Serotonin levels are lower in lab animals subjected to stressful environments.
- Serotonin levels are high in newborns.
- Serotonin levels rise again with maturity.
- Serotonin levels are low in depressed individuals

- Serotonin levels are low in lab animals with increased sex drives.

Now, though, let us move on to low resting heart rate and its link to criminal tendencies. In study after study, results have shown that petty criminals tend to have a significantly lower pulse rate than do their well-behaved counterparts. Psychologist Adrian Raine seems to think that lower heart rate probably reflects fearlessness.

Finally, high concentrates of testosterone have been found in those men who are more likely to have committed crimes of a violent nature. Testosterone levels are responsible for building muscle mass and strength. Scientific studies abound establishing the link of testosterone to criminality. Those of us in evolutionary psychology believe it is simply a "cunning manoeuvre" to avoid and control the more physically stronger testosterone-high male by weaker males. The objective would be to force society to look at overwhelming evidence of the link of criminality and high-testosterone and hence derogate the "fitter" male into oblivion and away from the females.

Theory, as seen through the eyes of evolutionary psychology, suggests that serotonin depletion in the "criminal" male is most likely "time-released," similar to puberty. This aggressiveness is activated by a brain that has adapted to its own unique environment. Lower serotonin levels in males causes "outward aggressive motion" to increase the "fight" or "aggressiveness" necessary to capture or kill food for the tribal clan, help establish territory area, and establish ranking through the acquisition of resources. In simpler terms, low serotonin levels, low standing heart rates, and high testosterone levels merely mean that "aggression" was and is used to obtain resources which ultimately attract the female. The primal motivation is not to commit "crime" but to attract a mate in order to pass one's genes on to the next generation.

The three indicators of "criminality" are activated by a cascade effect. Certain genes turn off and some turn on in order to produce the desired cryptic gene messaging to the brain. Today, as then, the most likely cascade scenario would depend on your socio-economic level and your immediate safety factor. Hence the "aggressive need" of your neighbourhood would determine and affect your serotonin levels. Your "aggressive need" most likely would be greater in where the stressful environment would be less secure than in the wealthy, peaceful,... Both, however, are still activated by mate attracting "requirements."

Speculation is that they are "deviant" behavioural responses to "fill-in" a blocked path —i.e.,depression is really inward aggression towards one's self vs. outward aggression.

To sum up, serotonin levels are lower in men because 30,000 years ago they usually did the hunting. Serotonin levels are lower in animals subjected to stressful environments because hunting is a violent exchange between prey and predator. Serotonin levels are high in newborns because they do not hunt. Serotonin levels are lowest in adolescents because 25,000 years ago, the best hunter had the best future. This corresponds with studies that show increased sexual activity and low serotonin levels in adolescents. Infants do not find and locate mates; males in the 16- to 26-year-old range do. Thirty thousand years ago, an old man was 35; hence the increase in serotonin levels and "less aggressive" tendencies when our present day males reach maturity. Do you need empirical evidence? Single young males between ages of 17 and 25 have the most accidents. And why do they have the most accidents? Because they are most aggressive drivers found on our nation's highways. As for the mature male, remember that most professional athletes retire by the age of 35 to 37 years of age.

Now, let's take low standing heart rates and high testosterone levels, both of which seem to be present in the modern day "criminal" man. As for a low heart rate: the successful hunter had to learn not to move, breathe heavily, or make any noise; any of these would alert prey and thus lessen the possibility of the successful kill. But, the hunter must still be ready to act "aggressively" in a moment's notice to catch the startled prey. The usefulness here of a high testosterone level is fairly obvious: muscle mass and stamina helped in the "catch." The bottom line is this: the better hunter our male "criminal" ancestor was, the more resources he acquired. The more resources our long ago male gathered, the better the chance of obtaining a higher-ranking female who would be lured by his comparatively large cache of resources. Men were aggressive then, and in most cases are aggressive today because it is this "aggression," that helps to acquire what females want most: resources. It is, however, a mistake to conclude that the young males in our inner-cities are more criminally prone and "aggressive" than their wealthy gender cousins in safe suburbs. Both are hunters—only the environment is different.

The augment of the male "criminal" mind and state that there are females who do commit crimes, but the overwhelmingly statistical evidence leaves little doubt about the males dominance in the crime statistics.

Richard Wrangham and Dale Peterson, Demonic Males and Houghton Mifflin, New York, have found in their studies that:

- Men are nine times as likely as a woman to commit murder,
- Men are 78 times as likely to rape,
- Men are 10 times more likely to commit armed robbery,
- Men are six and a half times as likely to commit aggravated assault,
- Altogether, American men are almost eight times as likely as women to commit violent crimes, FBI, 1991 as quoted.

Now that is violent crime. There still remains the statistical analysis of non-violent criminal activity, which although are not as destructive as violent crimes, are still behaviours that we in our moral societies have judged to be criminal in their actions and have passed laws to prevent those behaviours by passing judgement in courts of laws.

- Males are thirteen and a half times as likely to commit fraud.
- Males are thirteen times as likely to be arrested for carrying or possessing a weapon.
- Males are ten times as likely to steal a car.
- Males are nine times as likely to commit burglary.
- Males are 8 1/5 as likely to be arrested for drunkenness,
- Males are eight times more likely to be arrested for vagrancy.
- Males are eight times as likely to vandalize.
- Males are 7 1/5 more likely to fence stolen property.
- Males are seven times more likely to commit arson.
- Males are 6 1/2 as likely to be arrested for gambling offenses.
- Males are 6 1/2 as likely to be stopped for drunk driving.
- Males are 5 1/2 more likely to be arrested for sex offences (excluding prostitution and forcible rape).
- Males are 5 times more likely to be arrested for drug abuses.
- Males are four and a half times as likely for offences against children and other members of the family.
- Males are over twice as likely to commit larceny.

- Males are almost twice as likely to commit forgery
- Males are 1 1/2 more likely to commit embezzlement.

In only two categories do females lead males in "criminal" activity; running away from home, and "commercialized vice." Although not listed, it is believed that in the latter "crime," the female is helped and strongly influenced to commit the crime by a male "protector" and " solicitor agent." Now, it should be appropriate at this juncture to bring up the argument "that minorities commit more crimes then the dominating and controlling phenotype?

Despite the gloomy mood, the historical backdrop is stunning progress in human decency over recent centuries. War is declining, and humanity is becoming less violent, less racist and less sexist—and this moral progress has accelerated in recent decades. To put it bluntly, we humans seem to be getting nicer. Today, we may be living in the most peaceable era in our species existence. Pinker writes, and he describes this decline in violence as possibly "the most important thing that has ever happened in human history".

In a century that began with 9/11, Iraq and Darfur, the claim that we are living in an unusually peaceful time may strike you as somewhere between hallucinatory and obscene. Still, even in a 20th century notorious for world war and genocide, only around 3% of humans died from such man-made catastrophes. In contrast, a study of Native-American skeletons from hunter gather societies found that some 13% had died of trauma. And in the 17th century, the Thirty Years' War reduced Germany's population by as much as one-third. Wars make headlines, but there are fewer conflicts today and they typically don't kill as many people. It's a myth that civilians are more likely to die in modern wars. Look also at homicide rates, which are now far lower than in previous centuries. The murder rate in Britain seems to have fallen by more than 90% since the 14th century. Then there are the myriad forms of violence that were once the banal backdrop of daily life. One game in feudal Europe involved men competing to head-butt to death a cat that had been nailed alive to a post. One reason this was considered so entertaining: the possibility that it would claw out a competitor's eye. Think of fairy tales and nursery rhymes. One academic study found that modern children's television programmes have 4.8 violent scenes per hour, compared with nursery rhymes with 52.2. The decline in brutality is true of other cultures as well. In contrast, until modern times, genocide was simply a way of waging war.

The Bible repeatedly describes God as masterminding genocide ('thou shalt save alive nothing that breatheth'-Deuterono-my 20:16), and European-Americans saw nothing offensive about exterminating Native Americans. Theodore Roosevelt, later a winner of the Nobel Peace Prize, was unapologetic, "I don't go so far as to think that the only good Indians are the dead Indians, but I believe nine out of 10 are, and I shouldn't like to inquire too closely in the case of the 10th." The pace of moral progress has accelerated in the last few decades. Pinker notes that on issues such as civil rights, the role of women, equality for gays, beating of children and treatment of animals, "the attitudes of conservatives have followed the trajectory of liberals, with the result that today's conservatives are more liberal than yesterday's liberals." The reasons for these advances are complex but may have to do with the rise of education, the decline of chauvinism and a growing willingness to put ourselves in the shoes of others.

Granted, the world still faces brutality and cruelty. But let's pause for a moment to acknowledge remarkable progress and give thanks for the human capacity for compassion and moral growth.

Chapter 5

PURIFICATION OF MIND

The *Bhagvad Gita* is the holy text of the Hindus. We can explore from a scientific perspective, the mind as explained in the Gita. The self is the friend of the self for him who has conquered himself by the self. To the unconquered self, this self stands ir the position of the enemy like the external foe. (6:6)

God has given us the free will to adjust the mind to bring the whole if it is close to God, or to remain turned away from Him. The worldly man chooses the latter alternative and thus his own mind becomes his worst enemy, tormenting him with desires and cravings, love and hatred, likes and dislikes. In the case of the wise man, the whole mind is close to God; it is luminous with the knowledge of the indwelling- omnipresence.

The mind verily is restless, turbulent, strong and unyielding, O Krishna; I deem it as difficult to control as to control the wind. (6.34)

The fight is hard and long-drawn, but let us fight the good fight with faith in God, for once the mind itself is offered at the feet of the Almighty, to serve Him, it will become our best friend. This is the symbolism of Hanuman, the son of wind (the wind and mind are the same, only the first letter is upside down) in the *Ramayana*. This restless 'monkey', (the mind) is invincible, wise and heroic and is able to work wonders, once it is made to serve the Supreme.

According to the *Bhagavad Gita*, the mind could be your friend or foe, depending on how it is being controlled. Further, Krishna says that the mind is flickering, restless, yet strong and obstinate. Controlling the mind is harder than controlling the wind. Here the comparison is being made between mind and matter, the wind. While matter is a subject of Physics, the mind does not come under its purview. There are no physical methods of probing the mind. However, an attempt is made here to throw some light on the basis of science on the qualities attributed by Krishna to the mind.

First, let us focus on the flickering and restless nature of the mind. They denote the fluctuation of the mind that arises from indecision. Therefore, if a person is strong-willed, the mind can be controlled and put in order. The same thing happens in a material body. It can show interesting, ordered phenomena, induced by strong internal energy. Interesting material properties like magnetism and superconductivity are examples of order.

Waves and Particles

The two other qualities of strength and obstinacy denote the opposites. While strength of mind is a positive quality, obstinacy is an undesired quality. The achievements of a strong mind can overshadow the work done by the strongest of material energy sources. A bunch of skillfully programmed super computers cannot recreate what a Shakespeare or a Kalidas or, for that matter, an Einstein had created. This is the power of the mind.

In Physics, we come across matter waves. Light is a wave, but it has a particle nature. Both manifestations are complementary to each other. Similarly, an electron is a particle, but it is simultaneously a wave. These are facts of science, the particle-wave duality, understood only in the last century.

In the realm of spirituality, sometimes references are made to something that is akin to a mental wave. We are not sure whether or not it exists. If such a thing exists, what is its signature? Sometimes we experience an intense feeling about someone who is very dear to us. There is an indirect relationship. If the fluctuations of mind affect the heart, there is a change in the heart beat, that can be detected by an electrical analogue circuit.

Ravana was a wise man. Through his austerities he had acquired great capabilities. In spite of all this, due to his abominable behaviour, God himself had to take birth on the planet to kill him.

Example of Bhasmasur illustrates that even after having reached a high spiritual state without any compulsions, due to ill state of mind one digs a hole for himself. Similarly great powerful fighters likes Hiranayaksh and Hirankshpu had to die due to evil state of mind and behaviour.

Durga killed Shumbha-Nishumbha, Madhukaitava and Mahishashur. Parshuram Ji killed Shahasrabahu and Shri Krishna killed Vanashur.

Bhim killed Jarasandh, Shoopernkha used to tease Rishi performing austerities in Kharduson forest. Tadka used to disturb the yogies. Bali had overthrown his younger brother and kept his wife with him. Ram and Lakshman killed all of them and padded their tyranny.

Valmiki, the Great Poet

Valmiki (during Lord Rama's time) is celebrated as the poet harbinger in Sanskrit literature. He is the author of the epic *Ramayana*, based on the attribution in the text of the epic itself. He is revered as the Adi Kavi, which means First Poet, for he discovered the first Śloka i.e., first verse, which set the base and defined the form to Sanskrit poetry. The Yoga Vasistha is attributed to him. A religious movement called Valmikism is based on Valmiki's teachings as presented in the *Ramayana* and the Yoga Vasistha. At least by the 1st century AD, Valmiki's reputation as the father of Sanskrit classical poetry seems to have been legendary. Ashvagosha writes in the *Buddhacarita*:

"The voice of Valmiki uttered poetry which the great seer Chyavana could not compose."

This particular verse has been speculated to indicate a familial relationship between Valmiki and Chyavana, as implied by the previous and subsequent verses.

The Realization of Valmiki

The *Uttara Khanda* tells the story of Valmiki's early life, as an unnamed highway robber who used to rob people after killing them, however other versions name him Valya Koli. Once, the robber tried to rob the divine sage Narada for the benefit of his family. Narada asked him if his family would share the sin he was incurring due to the robbery. The robber replied positively, but Narada told him to confirm this with his family. The robber asked his family, but none agreed to bear the burden of sin. Dejected, the robber finally understood the truth of life and asked for Narada's forgiveness. Narada taught the robber to worship God. The robber meditated for many years, so much so that ant-hills grew around his body. Finally, a divine voice declared his penance successful, bestowing him with the name "Valmiki": "one born out of ant-hills" (Valmikam in Sanskrit means ant-hill). The Rishi only asked dacoit Valmiki who was blocking their way, "Will your relation be there with you in your sins as they are in good and prosperous time"? When wife and children reacted in negative, he realised his path. Getting the right direction from Rishis he became saint Valmiki. Using the guidance from Rishis and his own intellect, Valmiki got the right vision and became very famous poet and became immortal in history.

Once Valmiki was going to the river Ganga for his daily ablutions. A disciple by the name Bharadwaja was carrying his clothes. On the way, they came across the Tamas Stream. Looking at the stream, Valmiki said to his disciple, "Look, how clear is this water, like the mind of a good man! I will bathe here today." When he was looking for a suitable place to step into the stream, he heard the sweet chirping of birds. Looking up, he saw two birds flying together. Valmiki felt very pleased on seeing the happy bird couple. Suddenly, one of the birds fell down, hit by an arrow; it was the male bird. Seeing the wounded one, its mate screamed in agony. Valmiki's heart melted at this pitiful sight. He looked around to find out who had shot the bird. He saw a hunter with a bow and arrows, nearby. Valmiki became very angry. His lips opened and he uttered the following words:

> mā niṣāda pratiṣṭhāṁ tvamagamaḥ śāśvatīḥ samāḥ
>
> yat krauñcamithunādekam avadhīḥ kāmamohitam
>
> You will find no rest for the long years of Eternity
>
> For you killed a bird in love and unsuspecting

Emerging spontaneously from his rage and grief, this was the first śloka in Sanskrit literature. Later Valmiki composed the entire *Ramayana* with the blessings of Lord Brahma in the same meter that issued forth from him as the śloka. Thus this śloka is revered as the "first śloka" in Hindu literature. Valmiki is revered as the first poet, or Adi Kavi, and the *Ramayana*, the first kavya.

The Author of the *Ramayana*

The *Rāmāyana*, originally written by Valmiki, consists of

24,000 verses in seven cantos (some say six, i.e., excluding the *Uttara Ramayana*). The *Ramayana* tells the story of a prince, Rama of Ayodhya, whose wife Sita is abducted by the demon king of Lanka, Rāvana. The *Valmiki Ramayana* is dated variously from 500 BC to 100 BC, or about co-eval with early versions of the *Mahabharata*. As with many traditional epics, it has gone through a long process of interpolations and redactions, making it impossible to date accurately.

Notwithstanding the aforesaid, it is pertinent to note that Valmiki is also quoted to be the contemporary of Rama. Rama met Valmiki during his period of exile and had interacted with each other. Valmiki had Sita in his hermitage where Kusa and Lava were born to Sita. Valmiki taught The *Ramayana* to Kusa and Lava, who later sang the divine story in Ayodhya during the Aswamedha yaga congregation, to the pleasure of the audience, whereupon, King Rama summoned them to his royal palace. Kusa and Lava sang the story of Rama there, and Rama confirmed that whatever had been sung by these two children was entirely true.

With this backdrop, it needs review to establish the period of Valmiki, likely to date back to thousands of years, as Krishna incarnation followed Rama's incarnation

Ashoka Conquest of Kalinga

While the early part of Ashok regime was apparently quite blood thirsty, he became the follower of Buddha teaching after his conquest of Kalinga on the east coast of India in the present state of southern part of Odisha. Kalinga was a state that prided itself on its sovereignty and democracy. With its monarchial parliamentary democracy it was quite an exception in ancient India where there existed the concept of Rajdharma. Rajdharma means the duty of the rulers, which was intransitively enlivened with the concept of bravery as a Kshatriya Dharma. The Kalinga war happened eight years after his coronation. From his 13th inscription we come to know that battle was a massive one and caused the death of more than 1,00,000 soldiers and many civilians. Who rose up in defence, over 1,50,000 were departed. When he was walking through the battle ground of Kalinga after his conquest, rejoicing his victory, he was moved by the number of bodies strewn and wails of the kith and kin of the dead.

As the legend goes, one day after the war was over, Ashoka ventured out to roam the city and all he could see were burnt houses and scattered corpses. This sight made him sick and he cried the famous monologue:

> What have I done? If this is a victory, what's a defeat then? Is this a victory or a defeat? Is this justice or injustice? Is it gallantry or a rout? Is it a valour to kill innocent children and women? Do I do it to widen the empire and for prosperity or to destroy the other's kingdom and splendour? One has lost her husband, someone else father, someone child, someone an unborn infant.... What's this debris of the corpses? Are these marks of victory or defeat? Are these vultures, crows, eagles the messengers of death or evil?

The brutality of the conquest led him to adopt Buddhism, and he used his position to propagate the relatively new religion to new heights, as far as ancient Rome and Egypt. He made Buddhism his state religion around 260 BC, and propagated it and preached it within his domain and worldwide from about 250 BC. Emperor Ashoka undoubtedly has to be credited with the first serious attempt to develop a Buddhist policy.

Prominent in this cause were his son venerable Mahindra and daughter Sanghamitra (whose name means "friend of the Sangha"), who established Buddhism in Ceylon (now Sri Lanka). He built thousands of Stupas and Viharas for Buddhist followers. The Stupas of Sanchi are world famous and the stupa named Sanchi Stupa was built by Emperor Ashoka. During the remaining portion of Ashoka's reign, he pursued an official policy of non-violence (ahimsa). Even the unnecessary slaughter or mutilation of animals was immediately abolished. Everyone became protected by the king's law against sport hunting and branding. Limited hunting was permitted for consumption reasons. Ashoka also promoted the concept of vegetarianism. Ashoka also showed mercy to those imprisoned, allowing them leave for the outside a day of the year. He attempted to raise the professional ambition of the common man by building universities for study, and water transit and irrigation systems for trade and agriculture. He treated his subjects as equals regardless of their religion, politics and caste. The kingdoms surrounding his, so easily overthrown, were instead made to be well-respected allies.

He is acclaimed for constructing hospitals for animals and renovating major roads throughout India. After this transformation, Ashoka came to be known as Dhammashoka (Sanskrit), meaning Ashoka, the follower of Dharma. Ashoka defined the main principles of *dharma* (dhamma) as non-violence, tolerance of all sects and opinions, obedience to parents, respect for the Brahmans and other religious teachers and priests, liberality towards friends, humane treatment of servants, and generosity towards all. These principles suggest a general ethic of behaviour to which no religious or social group could object.

The source of much of our knowledge of Ashoka is the many inscriptions he had carved on pillars and rocks throughout the empire. All his inscriptions have the imperial touch and show compassionate loving. He addressed his people as his "children". These inscriptions promoted Buddhist morality and encouraged non-violence and adherence to Dharma (duty or proper behaviour), and they talk of his fame and conquered lands as well as the neighbouring kingdoms holding up his might. One also gets some primary information about the Kalinga War and Ashoka's allies plus some useful knowledge on the civil administration.

The Ashoka Pillar at Sarnath is the most popular of the relics left by Ashoka. Made of sandstone, this pillar records the visit of the Emperor to Sarnath, in the 3rd century BC. It has a four-lion capital (four lions standing back to back) which was adopted as the emblem of the modern Indian Republic. The lion symbolizes both Ashoka's imperial rule and the kingship of the Buddha. In translating these monuments, historians learn the bulk of what is assumed to have been true of the Mauryan Empire. It is difficult to determine whether or not some actual events ever happened, but the stone etchings clearly depict how Ashoka wanted to be, thought of and remembered.

Ashoka's own words as known from his Edicts are: "All men are my children. I am like a father to them. As every father desires the good and the happiness of his children, I wish that all men should be happy always." Edward D'Cruz interprets the Ashokan dharma as a "religion to be used as a symbol of a new imperial unity and a cementing force to weld the diverse and heterogeneous elements of the empire."

Also, in the Edicts, Ashoka mentions that some of the people living in Hellenic countries as convert to Buddhism, although no Hellenic historical record of this event remains.

Now it is conquest by Dhamma [(here conquest means peaceful conversion, not military conquest)] that Beloved-of-the-Gods considers to be the best conquest. And it (conquest by Dhamma) has been won here, on the borders, even six hundred yojanas away, where the Greek king Antiochos rules, beyond there where the four kings named Ptolemy, Antigonos, Magas and Alexander rule, likewise in the south among the Cholas, the Pandyas, and as far as Tamraparni. Here in the king's domain among the Greeks, the Kambojas, the Nabhakas, the Nabhapamkits, the Bhojas, the Pitinikas, the Andhras and the Palidas, everywhere people are following Beloved-of-the-Gods' instructions in Dhamma. Even where Beloved-of-the-Gods' envoys have not been, these people too, having heard of the practice of Dhamma and the ordinances and instructions in Dhamma given by Beloved-of-the-Gods, are following it and will continue to do so. Ashoka also claims that he encouraged the development of herbal medicine, for human and non-human animals, in their territories:

> Everywhere within Beloved-of-the-Gods, King Piyadasi's [Ashoka's] domain, and among the people beyond the borders, the Cholas, the Pandyas, the Satiyaputras, the Keralaputras, as far as Tamraparni and where the Greek King Antiochos rules, and among the kings who are neighbours of Antiochos, everywhere has Beloved-of-the-Gods, King Piyadasi, made provision for two types of medical treatment: medical treatment for humans and medical treatment for animals. Wherever medical herbs suitable for humans or animals are not available, it were imported and grown. Along roads wells dug and trees planted for the benefit of humans and animals. The Greeks in India even seem to have played an active role in the propagation of Buddhism, as some of the emissaries of Ashoka, such as Dharmaraksita, are described in Pali sources as leading Greek Buddhist monks, active in spreading Buddhism.

Raja Rammohun Roy

Raja Rammohun Roy (22 May 1772-27 September 1833) was an Indian religious, social, and educational reformer who challenged traditional Hindu culture and indicated the lines of progress for Indian society under British rule. He is sometimes called the father of modern India. He founded, along with Dwarkanath Tagore and other Bengalis, the Brahmo Sabha in 1828, which engendered an influential Indian socio-religious reform movement during the Bengal Renaissance. His influence was apparent in the fields of politics, public administration, and education, as well as religion. He is known for his efforts to abolish the practice of *sati*, the Hindu funeral practice in which the widow immolated herself on her husband's funeral pyre (*Sati Pratha*).

Roy believed education to be an implement for social reform. In 1817, in collaboration with David Hare, he set up Hindu College in Calcutta. In 1822, Roy founded the Anglo-Hindu school, followed four years later by the Vedanta College, where he insisted that his teachings of monotheistic doctrines be incorporated with "modern, western curriculum"; the Vedanta College offered courses as a synthesis of Western and Indian learning. In 1830, he helped Alexander Duff in establishing the General Assembly's Institution, by providing him the venue vacated by Brahma Sabha and getting the first batch of students. Roy supported induction of western learning into Indian education. He advocated the study of English, science, western medicine and technology. He spent his money on a college to promote these studies

Social Reforms of Rammohun Roy

Roy demanded property inheritance rights for women and, in 1828, set up the Brahmo Sabha, which was a movement of reformist Bengalis formed to fight against social evils. Roy's political background influenced his social and religious to reforms of Hinduism. He wrote: "The present system of Hindus is not well calculated to promote their political interests. It is necessary that some change should take place in their religion, at least for the sake of their political advantage and social comfort."

Rammohun Roy's experience working with the British government taught him that Hindu traditions were often not respected or thought as credible by Western standards; this affected his religious reforms. He wanted to legitimize Hindu traditions to his European acquaintances by proving that "superstitious practices which deform the Hindu religion have nothing to do with the pure spirit of its dictates. The "superstitious practices" Rammohun Roy objected included sati, caste rigidity, polygamy and child marriages. These practices were often the reasons British officials claimed superiority over the Indian nation. Rammohun

Roy's ideas of religion sought to create a fair and just society by implementing humanitarian practices similar to Christian ideals and thus legitimize Hinduism in the modern world. It is theorized that *sati*, enforced widowhood, and girl marriage were customs that were primarily intended to solve the problem of surplus women and surplus men in a caste and to maintain its endogamy.

During the Mughal rule, *sati* became more widely practised, especially in the north. Humayun issued a royal fiat against *sati*, which he later withdrew. Akbar required that permission be granted by his officials, and these officials were instructed to delay the woman's decision for as long as possible. The reasoning was that she was less likely to choose to die once the emotions of the moment had passed. In the reign of Shah Jahan, widows with children were not allowed to burn under any circumstances. In other cases, governors did not readily give permission, but could be bribed to do so. Later on in the Mughal period, pensions, gifts and rehabilitative help were offered to the potential *sati* to wean her away from committing the act. Children were strictly forbidden from following the practice. The later Moghul rulers continued to put obstacles in the way but the practice still persisted in areas outside their capitals.

Guru Nanak, the first Guru of the Sikhs, spoke out against the practice of *sati*.

The strongest attempts under the Mughals to control it were made by Aurangzeb. In 1663, he "issued an order that in all lands under Mughal control, never again should the officials allow a woman to be burnt." Despite such attempts however, the practice continued, especially during periods of war and upheaval.

By the end of the 18th century, the practice had been banned in territories held by some European powers. The Portuguese banned the practice in Goa by about 1515, though it is not believed to have been especially prevalent there. The Dutch and the French also banned it in Chinsurah and Pondicherry. The British who by then ruled much of the subcontinent, and the Danes, who held the small territories of Tranquebar and Serampore, permitted it until the 19th century. Attempts to limit or ban the practice had been made by individual British officers in the 18th century, but without the backing of the British East India Company. The first formal British ban was imposed in 1798, in the city of Calcutta only. The practice continued in surrounding regions. Towards the end of the 18th century, the Evangelical Church in Britain, and its members in India, started campaigns against *sati*. Leaders of these campaigns included William Carey and William Wilberforce, and both appeared to be motivated by their love for the Indian people and their desire to introduce Indians to Christianity. These movements put pressure on the company to ban the act, and the Bengal Presidency started collecting figures on the practice in 1813.

The leader of the burgeoning Swaminarayan Sect, Sahajanand Swami, was influential in the eventual eradication of sati. He argued that the practice had no Vedic standing and only God could take a life he had given. He also argued that widows could lead a life that would eventually lead to salvation. Governor Malcolm supported Sahajanand in this endeavour, whose domino effect led to other social reforms.

From about 1812, the Bengali reformer Raja Rammohun Roy started his own campaign against the practice. He was motivated by the experience of seeing his own sister-in-law being forced to commit *sati*. Among his actions, he visited Calcutta cremation grounds to persuade widows not to so die, formed watch groups to do the same, and wrote and disseminated articles to show that it was not required by scripture. On 4 December 1829, the practice was formally banned in the Bengal Presidency lands, by the then Governor, Lord William Bentinck. The ban was challenged in the courts, and the matter went to the Privy Council in London, but was upheld in 1832. Other company territories also banned it shortly after. Although the original ban in Bengal was fairly uncompromising, later in the century British laws included provisions that provided mitigation for murder when the person whose death is caused, being above the age of 18 years, suffers death or takes the risk of death with his own consent. *Sati* remained legal in some princely states for a time after it had been abolished in lands under British control. Jaipur banned the practice in 1846. Nepal continued to practice *sati* well into the 20th century. On the Indonesian island of Bali, *sati* (known as masatya) was practised by the aristocracy as late as 1905, until Dutch colonial rule pushed for its termination.

Power of The Mind

We often talk about mind power. Something which does work is power. Much of our action or inaction is induced by the mind. Therefore, the mind is definitely a power but it is something that does not come under the realm of the laws of Physics. The equivalence of matter and energy is well established. Is there an equivalence of matter and mind? Some mystics and their supporters claim that matter can be created out of nothing, because of mind power. If the nothingness is a physical vacuum, yes, there is a possibility, since it has zero-point energy.

The answers to the above possibilities could be explored meaningfully, if a quantum theory of mind could be developed. The topic has occupied a few theorists. Let us wait and see if there could be a unity between mind and matter. But as of now; it is not known.

A Material Conjunction

Mind has attributes that can reasonably be compared with some of the properties of material devices. Consider, for example, a p-n junction diode. One of its uses is rectification—a process by which an AC current is converted into a DC current. The AC current is a fluctuating current, whereas the DC current is a steady one. A strong mind, likewise, can convert the vicissitudes of life into a steady state of peace and harmony.

An intelligent mind has alertness. It can sense external stimuli and direct the body to act appropriately. In this way, it acts as a sensor. It has also the attribute of a solid state oscillator. An oscillator generates electromagnetic waves which can be detected by another device, a detector, if it is tuned to the frequency of the wave. Since these devices are electronic in nature and follow quantum laws, perhaps, there could be a possibility of the role of quantum theory in the understanding and analyzing of the mind.

Liberation from Personhood

The brain's various centres are each designated for a specific function. The senses take cognition of the environment. The anthropological basis of the nervous system was to facilitate an interaction with the environment, based on the individual's awareness of being separate from the environment. All senses subserve the function of underlining a sense of discreteness. Touch, taste, sound, smell and vision are instruments of discrimination. The entity that integrates these inputs and collectively coordinates them as a subject is the assumed 'identity.' The coordinated output of separateness that the senses keep generating is ego.

The brain helps fragment awareness into the subjective 'self' and objective 'non-self'—the observed world. This split awareness is switched on continuously and both the 'self' and the 'non-self' are vital for each other's symbiotic existence. Our own identity relies on our ability to perceive our self as uniquely different and distanced from the environment. Various decremental states of consciousness, such as feeling drowsy, deep sleep, semiconsciousness or even an unconscious state are familiar. Therefore, it is only logical to believe in states where there is an incremental increase in the level of consciousness.

If identity was based merely on a deep-rooted sense of discreteness that the senses generate, would a person, alone in a dark, quiet room—whose brain is not being fed with sensory inputs—consider himself as non-existent? An unconscious person doesn't interact with the environment but might be assumed to possess an 'am-ness' that is partial and aware of only the 'self' without comprehending or interacting with the environment. It's a state of partial awareness.

A seizure that arises in the portions of the limbic system—phylogenetically one of the oldest groups of neurons—could give rise to profound spiritual experiences. Repeated bursts of abnormal electrical activity can facilitate a new pathway within the complex network of neurons. This is called 'kindling' where consciousness may be getting defragmented leading to an un-split awareness.

All sense organs route their inputs through the limbic system and to various designated areas. The sensation of extreme bliss generated by an un-split awareness gets triggered by the limbic system and not in the frontal lobes, the seats of intelligence and logical analysis. Such experience are hence states of altered awareness rather than conclusions arising as a result of intellectual thought processing of the brain. The experience or realization that the am-ness of subject and object are of the same essence could be that final frontier of consciousness evolution the attainment of state of super consciousness. Faith and devotion as ways to salvation rely on the dismantling of the worshipper's identity and becoming one with the worshipped.

That is, perhaps inputs that serve to generate and maintain a separateness of the self are modulated or filtered within the limbic system a state of comprehensive, unrestricted oneness. It's a paradoxical situation of the observer becoming the observed without the mediation of sense organs, by expanding awareness to a supra-sensory level. Realization may well be a modulation and 'kindling' of the neural pathways leading to a perception of oneness with the entire cosmos. It would then really be more a liberation from the person rather than of the person.

To bring a sense of purpose and better quality into our lives we must look at the nature and working of our very mind itself. The mind is meant to absorb information, transform it into knowledge and lead it into action. Action and speech determine the quality of our life and these come from the mind itself.

Most people's minds are as hard as a rock. Just as a rock is impervious to water, information that falls on a hard mind bounces off without a trace. A hard mind offers immense resistance to previously absorbed information that prevents the flow of knowledge and action. Our mind must be as soft as a sponge for maximum absorption. Just as water can be easily absorbed by the sponge and squeezed out, a soft mind easily absorbs information and allows free flow of knowledge into action. The two processes are reversible; a soft or open mind can be easily hardened and a hard or closed mind can be easily softened. What makes our mind hard or closed? Ancient sages have said that this is an automatic, front-line defence mechanism for the protection of our belief systems based on our state of ego. If we encounter an idea or a situation that is not in line with our thinking, we immediately close our mind by putting up a block against it. Ego creates mindset. Mindset is a protective mechanism of self-defence because we are scared of what others think about our notions and beliefs. This mindset is self destructive. For example, a simple discussion develops into an argument and leads to a verbal or physical fight. Mere gathering of information by our mind is useless. We must transform this into knowledge. Our mind must be extremely pure to be able to perform this conversion efficiently. The results of an impure mind will rebound while the work of a pure mind will reach out for common welfare.

A pure, soft mind is a gateway to divine living. Thinking positive isn't enough, you need to think divine. Only then can we soften and purify our mind. We should review the working of our mind at least three times a day. Was my mind aggressive or calm? Did my words and actions hurt or bring joy to people? An object that slips out of our hand can be recovered, but an inappropriate word that slips out of our tongue cannot be erased. Self-review will free our mind of all obstruction. Ideas and inspiration flash freely in a pure mind to transform information to knowledge.

Three basic steps can be followed: First, allow others the freedom to be as they are, without imposing your mindset of thoughts and ideas. Second, have faith and belief that ideal person is within you. Third, spend some time quietly everyday thinking about your inner self. This way our mind which seeks information can be changed into a mind meant for the transformation of our very life itself from human to idealism.

That knowledge is different from that derived from testimony or through inference, because it relates to particulars of objects.

Yog Sutra

Whenever you are in doubt, or when the self becomes too much with you, apply the following: est. Recall the face of the poorest and the weakest man whom you may have been, and ask yourself, if the step you contemplate is going to be of any use to him..... Then you will find your doubts and yourself melt away.

Mahatma Gandhi

When you meet someone not as good as you are, look within

and examine your own self. Famous Economist Chankya has said, "As gold is tested in four ways by rubbing, cutting, heating and beating—so a man should be tested by the four things, viz, his renunciation, his conduct, his qualities and his actions."

Meditation is the highest spiritual technique that needs to be practised diligently and devotedly by qualified practitioners. The essential prerequisite is a calm mind. A mind burdened with desires and attachments is unable to take off into subtler realms of concentration and meditation. Entitled 'The Yoga of Meditation", chapter 6 of the *Bhagavad Gita* elucidates meditation as the final gateway to Self-realization.

Krishna begins with the definition of a *sannyasi*, a renounced person. Renunciation is not giving up enjoyments, abandoning one's duties and escaping to a safe sanctuary. It is this misunderstanding that has turned away genuine seekers and prevented them from accessing the benefits of renunciation. Krishna describes a *sannyasi* as one who does what one ought to do, fulfil one's duties and responsibilities fully, without depending on the fruit of action. A *sannyasi* is not one without a higher ideal, nor is he an inactive person. Krishna describes the three stages of spiritual evolution, from an active yogi to a meditative *sannyasi* and, finally, to the exalted state of a *jnani*, the enlightened one. A *sannyasi* has off-loaded the bulk of his desires and is in contemplation of the higher. He is fit for meditation and embarks on the path of deep reflection and focus on reality. A *jnani* has reached the exalted state of enlightenment. Krishna describes the three stages in terms of mental states rather than external appearances. Step by step, Krishna takes us through the preparatory disciplines as well as disqualifications for meditation. One must have a balanced contact with the world—neither too much nor too little. Every activity must be carefully supervised by the intellect so that no desire interrupts the subtle practice of meditation. Krishna then gives the test of enlightenment. A realized soul is one who feels one with everyone. He sees his Self as the self in all beings. In the end he worships God not in a temple, church or mosque, but in every living being. Thereafter, he lives in *Atman*, whatever his lifestyle is. It is pointless to declare love for God when you cannot connect with His images everywhere. Arjuna, like us, is afraid of leaving the safe confines of his present existence to discover the unknown realm of the Infinite. He asks Krishna what the fate is of those who commit themselves to a spiritual life but die before realization. Krishna gives a fitting reply to reveal one of the most insightful laws of life. He says, "One who is righteous will never come to grief—either now or in the future. Your efforts will not go in vain. You will carry forward the credits to your future life."

A spiritually evolved person who falls short of realisation will either be born in the home of the happy and wealthy or in a family of wise *yogis*. There, endowed with the wisdom acquired in previous lives, he will strive even more to attain enlightenment. Thus the diligent seeker effortlessly reaches Brahmin. The key words are *vairagya*, dispassion and *abhyasa*, practice. One must be convinced of the futility of worldly passions and pursue the necessary spiritual practices consistently.

Osho has said love is painful, but the pain is certainly a blessing. Love is painful because love brings growth. Love demands, transforms and is painful because love gives you a new birth. Love brings your heart into relationship and when the heart is in relationship there is always pain. If you avoid the pain, you will miss all pleasures of life. With love you become human; you stand erect on earth. With love you are vertical. With love there are problems. But with problems these is growth—the greater the problem, the greater the opportunity. More and more pain, too.

That's why many people never love—it is so painful. They never become vertical. Love never shatters you completely. It simply shatters you a little, a little bit. It shatters the crust of your ego, but the centre of the ego remains intact. Then there is a deeper pain, deeper than love, and that is of prayer—it shatters you utterly. It is death. When you have learnt how to love, and you have learnt that the pain that love brings is a blessing in disguise, it is beautiful, then you become able and you take another step—that step is prayer. All lovers feel a little miserable. They would like to disappear completely; but it is not possible in human relationships. Human relationship is limited. But one learns from it, that there is a possibility: if it can happen so much in a human relationship, how much more can happen in a relationship with the Divine?

Love makes you ready to take the final jump, the quantum leap. That's called prayer, or you can call it meditation. You have to disappear for existence to be. Love is a training ground, a school, to learn first lessons of beauty, of the blessing and benediction of disappearance; to learn that pain is blessed.

So when you are in love, or when love arises, cooperate with it, don't try resisting. People come to a compromise. The basic problem that being looked at is that lovers by and by come to a compromise. The compromise is: You don't hurt me, I will not hurt you. That's what marriage is. 'Then people become settled. They become so afraid of pain that they say, "Don't hurt me and I will not hurt you. "But then when pain disappears, love also disappears. They exist together."

When you are in love, love hurts. It hurts terribly. But never resist, never create any barrier for pain. Allow it. And by and by you will see that it was a wrong interpretation. It is not really a pain. It is just that something is going so deep in you that you interpret it like a pain. You don't know anything else. You are only aware of pain in your past life, in your past experience. Whenever something penetrates deep, you interpret it as pain. Don't use the word 'pain.' When love and love's arrow goes deep into your heart, close your eyes and don't use words—just see what it is, and you will never see it is pain. You will see it is a benediction. You will be tremendously moved by it. You will feel joyous. Don't use words. When something new happens to you, always allow a deep look into it without any language.

Mind Guard Tibetan Kadampa

Generally, people keep all the doors of their senses open. Seeing this as an opportunity, troublemakers—*klesha* in Sanskrit —make their way into the mind. According to Buddhist Sutras, the job of these troublemakers is "to churn the mind." This means that the nature of the mind is peaceful and calm, but when churning takes place, it gets aggravated and agitated, resulting in the performing of aggressive acts that cause hurt to self and others, speech that is not the truth, or which makes no sense, and acts that foster hatred. Hence, looking inward is the essence of spirituality. *Adhyatma vidya* or inner science is what helps us overcome all these negativities. Observation of moral codes facilitates the mind to remain focussed on the work at hand. Mindfulness and awareness are the guards employed at the door of the senses. When the mind is protected from external interventions, it facilitates concentration on the work at hand. It also results in further perfecting moral practices and rectitude, thus generating higher spiritual qualities like *samadhi* or equilibrium, and *prajnaparamita*, perfected wisdom. Earlier Tibetan Kadampa masters laid emphasis so much on the importance of guarding the mind that a whole body of literature—today known as Lojong— came into being. These teachings originally came from the subcontinental region. Acharya Shantideva of the 11th century states: "Except the conduct of guarding the mind, where is the need of many conducts?" A Kadampa master said, "I have no other practice except standing at the approach point of troublemakers, waiting for them with a spear of antidote." Formerly a notorious thief in Tibet, Ben Gungyal went on to become a great teacher. After renouncing thieving and cheating and after spending long hours in solitude doing meditation, he became a respected yogi. Once he was invited by a family to their house for a day-long recitation of scriptures. At a point when the family members stepped out of the house for some work, the yogi, who was a tea lover, found the tea he was served a bit too weak. Looking around, when he found no one nearby, he walked directly into the kitchen and located the tea container in which dried tea leaves were kept. He decided to take some tea leaves without telling the householder. This act was a result of the instinct left behind as residual of his previous deeds. As soon as he put his hand into the container, his awareness came to rescue him. He became aware of this act of his and found himself shouting: "Thief! Thief!"

When others came running towards him in response to his call, they were surprised to find him holding his own hand. He told them "I have caught the culprit."

This story is often cited as an example of self-restraint, awareness and guarding the door of senses. It is a good thing to apportion a fixed time for spiritual pursuits such as prayer, chanting and meditation. But if the doors of the senses are not guarded for the rest of the time, you could become vulnerable to *klesha*. It will hunt you down and churn your mind. Then the few hours of prayer or meditation are less likely to have the desired effect. That is why sages and seers recommend continuous practice and mindfulness.

Religion and Life

The subject of the *Bhagawad Gita* entails the comprehension of basic truths of human life. First of all, the science of God is explained and then the constitutional position of the living entities. There is God, which means the controller of the living entities. If a living entity says that he is not controlled but that he is free, he is insane. The living being is controlled in every respect, at least in his conditioned life. Material nature and time, the duration of existence of the whole universe or the manifestation of material nature, and *karma* (activity) are also discussed. The cosmic manifestation is full of different activities. The living beings are in quality like the supreme controller. Material nature is not independent, acting under the directions of the Supreme Lord. (mayadhyaksena prakrtih suyate sacracaram: The material nature is working under My direction) Nothing could be manifested without being controlled.

In this world men are not meant for quarrelling like animals. Men must be intelligent enough to realize the importance of human life and refuse to act like ordinary animals. A human being should realize the aim of his life, and this direction is given in the Vedic literatures, and essence is given in the *Bhagawad Gita*. Animals can kill other living animals, and there is no question of sin on their part, but if a man kills an animal for the satisfaction of his uncontrolled taste, he must be responsible for breaking the laws of the nature. There are three kinds of activities according to the different modes of nature: the activities of goodness, of passion and of ignorance. Similarly, there are three kinds of eatables also: eatables in goodness, passion and ignorance. If we properly utilize the instructions, our whole life will become purified, and ultimately we will be able to reach the destination which is beyond this material sky, i.e. the eternal or spiritual sky.

We work not with our body, actually, but with our mind and intelligence. So if the intelligence and the mind are always engaged in thoughts of God, naturally the senses are also engaged in His service. Superficially, the activities of the senses remain the same, but the consciousness is changed. Religion teaches us how to absorb the mind and intelligence in the thought of the Lord. Such absorption will enable one to transfer himself to the kingdom of the Lord. The absorption of mind in God's service and automatic engagement of senses in His service is an art.

Movements of the Mind

Hen Edward De Bono, while inventing lateral thinking said everyone has become complacent about the way they think. "We believe it (our thinking) is wonderful, but it is not, we need to work on it to make it better. All our success in the fields of science and technology are a result of how we think, which is why we feel that our system of thinking is adequate. However, all the disruptions and human conflicts that we have been witness to are also a result of the way we think." The human mind has been taught to think rationally instead of creatively, and according to De Bono, that is the source of the problem. "Over centuries, the human mind has been trained to think logically, in terms of what is right and wrong, and pass judgment on a situation, but not think of a solution to a problem." The brain is excellent at forming patterns and establishing paths. Lateral thinking is about moving across these set paths." The biggest problem in the world today is that we operate on a system of judgments not design. Design is the key to find the way forward.

Using the analogy of driving a car with three wheels, de Bono points out that our current manner of thinking is rather impoverished. "Just as you need the fourth wheel to be able to drive the car, similarly without design, our conventional thinking is inadequate." Design, a critical aspect of thinking, is often overlooked by most people. But alongside analysis, design is what makes a thought process complete. Society has a great system for finding the truth, but systems for thinking about how to create value is missing. One, whether professional or entrepreneur, should always create value in his doings. "Analysis forms a significant aspect of how we think, but it is not enough. Analyzing standard situations to find standard responses that fit works to an extent, but it doesn't create any value. While analysis and knowledge dominate in the schools, in the real world, it is design", according to de Bono.

The Guilty Feeling

You cannot be happy with guilt, remember, you, cannot dance with guilt. Guilt will paralyse you: wherever you go, cannot laugh, you cannot move in ecstasy, because you will always be afraid of the suppressed. You ask a criminal, "Did you do this?" He will reply; "No, it happened! What could I do?" Knowledge of the Self is the only thing that can take you from imperfection to perfection. I don't believe in guilt, I believe in living on impulse as long as you never intentionally hurt another person, and don't judge people in your life. I think you should live completely free. A crust eaten in peace is better than a banquet partaken in anxiety.

Guilt is an emotion that all of us have felt at various times of our lives. And this is one emotion which can be draining and depressing and can rob us, to a great extent, of our mental peace and energy. In order to be able to overcome guilt, one first needs to understand why we feel guilty. Once the understanding comes, it becomes easier to tackle this problem. We feel guilty whenever we think we should have done something but did not do it, or whenever we should not have done something, but went ahead and did just that. Hence, the starting point of all guilt is in our minds. We have an ideal, which is either inborn or which has been taught to us by our parents, teachers and society. If we stick to this ideal, if we perform our duties as we have been conditioned to, there is no guilt. But as and when a discrepancy creeps in between our concepts of what is ideal and what we did, this discrepancy or gap gets transformed into guilt, making us feel miserable and depressed. Guilt has very little to do with the trigger or the circumstances that come from the outside. The environment is constantly changing. We are not affected by all changes. But if we have strong beliefs about right and wrong, duty and rights and what is good and bad, it is likely that whenever events occur that challenge our beliefs, we would either react with anger and aggression or with guilt and frustration. To get rid of guilt, we need to first understand what is right and wrong, good and bad, moral and immoral but these are not absolutes. What is considered good at a particular time or place could be bad at another time or place. If we cling to our parents at the age of two, it is considered normal. But if we cling to them at the age of 40, obviously something is wrong. If a man kills another, it is a crime. But if a policeman on duty kills a criminal or a soldier kills the enemy, he is honoured with medals. Therefore, in order to remove guilt, we need to first understand what it is that we feel guilty about.

The worst thing one can do to oneself, while feeling guilty, is inaction. If we acknowledge the mistake which has led to our guilt, we can go about correcting it. If we accept that mistakes happen and that to err is human, then too we can go about reducing our guilt, through acceptance. But to neither acknowledge nor accept our mistake is foolish, as we have to carry the guilt without there being any solution. It is like putting our car in neutral gear and pumping the accelerator. It gets us nowhere but ensures that we lose a lot of energy and we end up polluting the environment literally or virtually. Left unaddressed, guilt pollutes the atmosphere.

Life unfolds in accordance with a divine plan. We are only actors in a play and someone else is the scriptwriter. If we can put our complete trust in a higher power, it becomes relatively easy to get rid of guilt, and a whole lot of our negative emotions, which torment us on a daily basis. We come to understand what is right and wrong in absolute terms and also what the grey areas and then deal with them accordingly.

Self-Cleansing

Mahatma Gandhi advocated self-cleansing. It is a process that leads to self transformation. Self-purification is a process of cleansing the body and mind. It's about flushing the toxins out of the body and purging the mind of all self-defeating thoughts.

The process is simple, but it has a great ritual significance. Self-cleansing is also an integral part of Patanjali's *yoga*: the first component of the eight-fold practice that Patanjali prescribes is *niyam* or rules and the topmost among them is *saucha* or cleanliness both internal and external. Without observing *yam* or precepts and *niyam*, a *yogi* cannot reach the advanced stages of *dhyan*, *dharana* and *samadhi*—meditation, concentration and deep absorption.

"Identification with everything that lives is impossible without self-purification," said M K Gandhi. "Without self -purification the observance of the law of *ahimsa* or non-violence must remain an empty dream; God can never be realized by one who is not pure of heart. Self-purification, therefore, must mean purification in all walks of life." Gandhi constantly strove for self-cleansing; he was obsessed with it to the point of being ridiculed by his contemporaries. Gandhi was a spiritual practitioner arid a politician; from saintly practices he drew political insights and mental clarity. Just like Gandhi, a seeker can observe different aspects of self purification for a healthier body and mind. Gandhi took cleanliness seriously. In South Africa, he would often inspect the houses of his supporters to check for sanitation. He would also force his wife Kasturba to clean the chamber pot in their house. In a South African jail, Gandhi once volunteered to clean water closets. Eventually, he was asked to do a sweeper's work by jail authorities. For Gandhi, self-purification started by cleaning up the toilets, which he felt were causes of disease.

Clean surroundings are a prerequisite for the process of self-cleansing. Practising good hygiene protects you from disease and saves the environment from degenerating. Criental thinkers often say that energy circulates freely in clutter-free surroundings. Fasting and vegetarianism are some of the ways that Gandhi used to cleanse the body. Vegetarianism helps in reducing unwanted chemicals and hormones from entering the body. Fasting, on the other hand, de-toxifies your system and gives rest to your digestive system. Gandhi promised his mother that he would refrain from eating meat. He fasted for purification. For him, fasting wasn't something to be done mechanically; it required strict control of the senses.

Gandhi was also a great believer in nature cure and would use hydrotherapy to cure ailments like fever. He would use enemas to cure headaches. Enemas were a persistent part of ashram life, and had apparently been so since South Africa. Gandhi used to tell the story of a European girl who was close to him in South Africa and who suffered from persistent headaches. He said to her: "You must be constipated, I'll give you an enema," writes Jad Adams in his book *Gandhi: Naked Ambition.*

Self-purification also requires a strong will power, which is a product of a healthy mind. It requires shedding of ego and observance of equanimity, the ability to remain unaffected by joy or sorrow. "The path of purification is hard and steep. To attain to perfect purity, one has to become absolutely passion-free in thought, speech and action; I know that I have not in me as yet that triple purity, in spite of constant, ceaseless striving for it", Gandhi confesses. For him non-violence was also a part of the self-purification process; he believed in winning over the enemy not with the help of a gun but with compassion. Before attempting to win over the enemy, an individual has to first purify himself of anguish and animosity through a process of self-examination.

"Gandhi considered self-examination the keystone of self-purification. Recognising the triviality of all passing material interests constitutes more than half the moral battle," says William Borman in the book *Gandhi and Non-violence.* Spiritual rebirth takes place when there is a complete transformation. It requires dissolution of old habits and breaking-flee of old-patterns of thought. This is a state of being that can be achieved through the cleansing process. Gandhi did it to draw strength to our struggle for freedom. You can do it too, to break the mould of existence and transform into a newer you.

Who is Mahatma

The difference between an ordinary man and a saint or a man of God is that the ordinary man goes about doing his work without awareness, but men of God, whatever they do, right from their daily personal chores to their spiritual disciplines, do so with awareness. A *siddhapurush* or a saint is one whose thoughts are pure and who lives constantly in the awareness that God is Omnipresent. The mark of one who loves God and saints is sacrifice. If my love is without sacrifice, it is selfish. Such a love is barter, for there is exchange of love and devotion in return for something. It is a conditional love.

Virtue of Sacrifice

True love is selfless. It is prepared to sacrifice. Ascetics and *fakirs* come to mitigate human suffering; to heal us and lead us on the path. They put up with criticism; they go through many worldly trials. Some of them have even become martyrs for our sake. But they have done all this with a smile and with gratitude to God. Hence sacrifice is a great virtue.

Miss Madeleine Slade was a devoted disciple of M K Gandhi. She came from a wealthy English family. Her father was an Admiral in the Royal Navy. She was brought up in the lap of luxury and opulence. Yet she left everything—her home, parents, and country in order to live in Gandhi's ashram. When she met Gandhi and sought his permission to join his ashram, Gandhi tried his best to dissuade her. He told her that she would not be able to live a life of austerity that his ashram demanded of all inmates. He said, "Many women from royal families have come to live in this ashram. But without exception, they have found it difficult to live under the rules, regulations and the strict discipline of our way of life." But Miss Slade was adamant. She had come to India to live for her ideals, and no discipline could be too tough for her. In fact, the call to go and serve the Mahatma had come to her even when she was a young woman. Having read his biography by Romain Rolland, she was inspired to dedicate her life to the service of this extraordinary human being. In preparation, she had practised austerity. She went through all the chores of spinning, became a vegetarian and a teetotaller, started learning the language, taught herself to squat and sleep on the floor. She subscribed to *Young India*. She spent a part of her training programme in Paris, where she read the *Bhagavad Gita*, and part of the *Rigveda*, both in French. And now, standing before Gandhiji, she said to him, "My Gurudev, I am willing to bear any hardship, if I am allowed to be with you." Gandhi, looking at her beautiful cascading hair, said to her, "Can you sacrifice your crowning glory for me? Can you sacrifice your hair?" She left without replying. Everyone thought she was so taken aback that she had to leave. However, the determined Miss Slade went straight to a barber's shop and shaved off her hair. Placing the golden brown hair at the feet of Gandhi she said, "Bapuji, this sacrifice is for you."

Miss Slade bore witness to the teachings of Gandhi in deeds of daily living. After India won its Independence, Gandhi's associates demanded high positions in the government and in the party. But, Miss Slade whom out of affection, Gandhi named 'Mirabehn', did not wish for anything. She wished to continue Gandhi's work in village development. She went to a remote corner in the sub-Himalayan region and lived a life of obscurity, offering her service and love to the poor people of the area.

Miss Slade had true love for Gandhi and his ideals. She served him faithfully till the end and bore witness to his ideals.

Forgiveness

Rosh-ha-shana, the New Year that commenced this year on September 28-29, marks the beginning of the annual cycle of the

Jewish Religious Year. The ten days from New Year's Day through Yom Kippur, the Day of Atonement are known as the Ten Days of Repentance. Rosh-ha-shana is the Day of Judgement, when decree is inscribed, and on the Day of Atonement, it is sealed.

During prayers on Rosh-ha-shana, Jews say, Teshuva, Tifila and Tzedakah, Moavereem Es Roah Hagezairah—that repentance, prayer and charity nullify the evil decree because they together constitute what is necessary for us to lead good lives. The Shofar or horn of the Ram is blown on the two special days to call us to repent. Teshuva or repentance reminds us that we need to have control over our lives. We can change. Tifila or prayer is a ladder which takes us closer to God.

Prayers constitute an individual as well as community approach to God through meditation, pleas, requests, confession, supplication and expression of praise and thanks giving, all ways of communication between us and the Creator. Tefila says that we can have relationships, a relationship with God and with fellow human beings. Tzedakah or charity redeems us. Charity must be practised and a proportion of one's income should be earmarked for this purpose, as a visible expression of universal love. Charity also says that we ought to help the poor. We can help alleviate suffering. All these three are necessary in order to achieve common benefit.

Rosh-ha-shana celebrates the fact that your word is true and exists for ever. It is a unique combination of solemnity and rejoicing. The penitential mood of the day is ushered in by a month of Selihoth, confessional devotion of self-examination and supplication for forgiveness. Rosh-ha-shana is also Yom Hazikkaron, the day of Remembrance, and 'Yom Hadin' or Day of Judgement. On this day, the Book of Life is opened in the heavenly court and as we begin a new year, our *yeaming* and prayer to be inscribed in God's Book of Life, gives added solemnity to the blessings of the prayers. The home ceremonial of the Kiddush or sanctification is associated with the New Year and it expresses the joyousness of the festival.

The readings of the Torah on Rosh-ha-shana recalls the promise of the continuity of Jewish tradition through the birth of Isaac and how he was saved from sacrifice through God's mercy as well as the celebration of the birth of Samuel. On the first day of Rosh-ha-shana, Jews go to the seashore or a stream of running water, recollecting the words of the Prophet, "Thou will cast their sins into the depths of the sea."

On the Day of Atonement, obligation rests on each to cleanse his own soul through his communing and his own inward struggle. On New Year's Day, Jews think of God as dispenser of justice, for without justice the world could not endure. But on the Day of Atonement, Jews think of God as the God of mercy, love, understanding and forgiveness. In every service of the day, Jews recall this revelation of His nature in the 13 attributes perceived by the spiritual vision of Prophet Moses: "The Lord, the Lord our God is compassionate and gracious, long suffering and abundant in mercy and truth." During the Yom Kippur Service, every Jew makes Viddui or confession by saying, "I have been guilty and my guilt has piled up in dishonesty and in profaning that which is sacred. I have dealt falsely, dishonesty. I have spoken evil and slander with false and misleading tongue. I have perverted and twisted the right by my words. I have been vicious, arrogant, and violent." Thereafter the Jews seek God's forgiveness to release and pardon them from guilt and perverseness—remove their sins and forgive iniquity and transgressions. After concluding the Kol Nidre prayer, Jews say, "May all the people of Israel be forgiven."

We need not get overwhelmed by guilt. We can rid ourselves of our guilt if we will, like Prophet Joseph, respond to our past positively, not by denying our guilt but by embracing it and using it as a way of improving ourselves and working towards a better future.

Forgiveness of ourselves and of others releases us from the past. The Course in Miracles says over and over that forgiveness is the answer to almost everything. When we are stuck, it usually means there is some more forgivings to be done. When we do not flow freely with life in the present moment, it usually means we are holding on to a past moment. It can be regret, sadness, hurt, fear, or guilt, blame, anger, resentment and sometimes even the desire for revenge. Each one of these states comes from a space of un-forgiveness, a refusal to let go and come into the present moment. Love is always the answer to healing of any sort. And the pathway to love is forgiveness. Forgiveness dissolves resentment. There are several ways to approach this.

There is an old Emmet Fox exercise for dissolving resentment that always works. He recommends that you sit quietly, close your eyes, and allow your mind and body to relax. Then, imagine yourself sitting in a darkened theatre, and in front of you is a small stage. On that stage, place the person you resent the most. It could be someone in the past or present, living or dead. When you see this person clearly, visualize good things happening to this person —things that would be meaningful to him. See him smiling and happy. Hold this image for a few minutes, then let it fade away. As this person leaves the stage, put yourself up there. See good things happening to you. See yourself smiling and happy. Be aware that the abundance of the Universe is available to all of us. The above exercise dissolves the dark clouds of resentment most of us carry. For some, it will be very difficult to do. Each time you do it, you may get a different person. Do it once a day for a month, and notice how much lighter you feel.

Chapter 6

DISSOLVING MENTAL IMPURITY

The present day increase in crime rate, corruption, etc., are all result of impure mind. Though strict law can control them to some extent, it cannot completely uproot them. It can only be abolished until and unless there is a desire from the inner core of the heart of each individual. Such desire can be generated as we have seen in our past in case of Rishi Valmiki, King Ashoka and others. Rishi Valmiki was a robber but after realization of his misdeeds he became a great poet and wrote a unforgettable epic the *Ramayan*. King Ashok was very cruel in his early age but after the Kalinga war his cruelty got melted and he adopted Boudh Dharm and spent rest of his life in doing welfare of the people. Presently we all have impurity of crime, corruption, cheating, jealousy, lies, enmity in our mind and as a result we find 2G scam, illegal mining scam, etc. C.B.I. is continuously putting the guilty in jail. Have we thought how and when this will end? We will have to think and remove all these impurities of mind, then only we can handover a great and modern economically powerful and developed nation to our children in the next generation.

It is said, " Bad se badnam hue to kya naam nahi hua". Either very good people or very bad people are remembered for their deeds. Robbers and cheaters are very talented and due to their extra ordinary talent they are able to successfully do crime and escape the law. Their talent is utilized in negative works, it is required to be utilized only in positive work. The talent of Indian 'Jugaad' is famous in the world. We have to develop this negative mind to positive mind systematically.

(*Manyete Papkam Kritwa Na Kashchdweti Mamati*

Vedanti chainan devashcha yashchaiwanta Purushah)

Every human being thinks after committing crime that nobody knows about his sin. But only the Almighty knows and also the God sitting inside his heart is well aware of his sin. He cannot escape from his self.

About Buddhist Meditation

There are many different forms of meditation in Buddhism. Some go back to the Buddha himself (and possibly further back in time than that) while others are more recent developments. But what is meditation? Meditation is the conscious cultivation of mindfulness, positive emotion and clear perception of the ways things are.

Meditation is not a form of prayer, in which we call upon an external agency, but a form of inner training, in which we cultivate new ways of being. In meditation we consciously cultivate positive mental habits. The term meditation encompasses many different techniques that facilitate the cultivation of, amongst other things, calmness, relaxation, one-pointed concentration, loving kindness, compassion, a sense of wellbeing and insight into the impermanent and interconnected nature of reality.

In meditating we use some object on which we direct our attention. We can use the sensations of the breath, our emotional connection with ourselves and others, the physical sensations of the body, sounds, visualized images, etc.

Buddhist meditation is broadly divided into *Shamatha* and *Vipashyana* practices. *Shamatha* (Pali:*Samatha*) practice calms the mind and helps develop one-pointed concentration and positive emotions. *Vipashyana* (Pali: *Vipassana*) practice builds on the calmness, focus, and positive emotion generated in *Shamatha* and helps to develop an awareness of the impermanence, interconnectedness, and the contingent nature of our experience. On Wild mind we follow the traditional approach of cultivating *Shamatha* before approaching *Vipashyana*. In traditional Buddhist teaching there is a great emphasis on learning to calm the mind so that we can then go on to insight practices.

Vipassana meditation is a form of *Yoga*. It helps to manage stress, attain self-control and increase concentration. *Vipassana* is an ancient technique of meditation. *Vipassana* means an insight in Pali language. It was rediscovered and taught by Gautama Buddha as a technique of defeating universal ills and soon became an art of living. It is described as "the ability to see things as they really are, through a process of self-observation." According to *Vipassana* experts, it is a process by which one can recognize and eliminate the course of suffering.

While one is on his way to discover *Vipassana*, understanding *Yoga* can let him make the most of the practice. "*Yoga kameshu kaushalam*" which means that when one does any activity with full concentration and devotion, it becomes immortal and is liked by everyone. It is *Yoga* in its truest form. It can be writing a poem, cleaning one's closet or even brushing his teeth. Any activity with complete concentration and focus is considered as *Yoga*. If any work is done through complete integration of soul, mind, and heart it becomes *Yoga*. With a short insight to *Yoga*, *Vipassana* meditation can help in dissolving mental impurity in the following ways:

- Self transformation and self observation.
- Takes through the common spot shared by mind and body.
- Removes impurities of mind
- Enables concentration on interrelations between mind and body
- Helps to understand the mental process
- Helps to go deep within self and discover oneself
- Helps to heal from one's sufferings

Instructions for practising Vipassana

Before practising *Vipassana* meditation, keeping a few instructions in mind can help. Follow them to a 'T' and it will enable to make the most of *Vipassana* practice. *Vipassana* can be practised during any time of the day. Consult a Vipassana instructor or join a *Vipassana* Ashram if anyone is a beginner. *Vipassana* is so simple and beneficial that even children can practise it.

- Create a calm atmosphere of meditation around. It helps to concentrate better. For example, one can sit in a room with a dim light in a quiet environment.
- Wear loose clothes to be comfortable while practising *Vipassana*.
- Avoid smoking, alcoholism and indulging in illicit behaviour while practising Vipassana.
- Concentrate on breathing from nostrils.
- Pay attention on different parts of your body from head to toe. For example, start from your forehead then come to eyebrows, then cheeks, then nose, lips and in this way

continue till you reach your toes. Observe sensation of each part.

- Avoid reacting to the sensations of body and just observe them.
- Avoid paying attention to any one part of the body for a longer time.
- Try practising this activity daily for 45 to 60 minutes
- Seek help of an instructor for guidance.
- Avoid practising this activity immediately after a meal. Take a half an hour break between a meal and *Vipassana* practice.

Each Moment Is a New Beginning

The *Point of Power is always in the present moment. You are never stuck.* This is where the changes take place, right here and right now in our own minds. It doesn't matter how long we've had a negative pattern or an illness or a poor relationship or lack of finances or self-hatred. We can begin to make a shift today. Your problem no longer needs to be the truth for you. It can now fade back to the nothingness from whence it came. You can do it, you are the only person who thinks in your mind. You are the power and authority in your world. Your thoughts and beliefs of the past have created this moment and all the moments up to this moment. What you are now choosing to believe and think and say will create the next moment and the next day and the next month and the next year. You are the power in your world. You get to have whatever you choose to think! This moment begins the new process. Each moment is a new beginning, and this moment is a new beginning for you right here and right now! Isn't that great to know! This moment is the Point of Power. This moment is where the change begins.

There is an incredible power and intelligence within you constantly responding to your thoughts and words. As you learn to control your mind by the conscious choice of thoughts, you align yourself with this power. Do not think your mind is in control. You are in control of your mind. You use your mind. You can stop thinking those old thoughts. When your old thinking tries to come back and say, "It's so hard to change," take mental control. Say to your mind, "I now choose to believe it is becoming easier for me to make changes." You may have to have this conversation with your mind several times for it to acknowledge that you are in control and that what you say goes.

The Courses

The technique is taught in the courses during which participants follow a prescribed Code of Discipline, learn the basics of the method, and practise sufficiently to experience its beneficial results. The course requires hard, serious work. There are three steps to the training. The first step is, for the period of the course, to abstain from killing, stealing, sexual activity, speaking falsely, and intoxicants. This simple code of moral conduct serves to calm the mind, which otherwise would be too agitated to perform the task of self-observation. The next step is to develop some mastery over the mind by learning to fix one's attention on the natural reality of the ever changing flow of breath as it enters and leaves the nostrils. By the fourth day the mind is calmer and more focused, better able to undertake the practice of *Vipassana* itself: observing sensations throughout the body, understanding their nature, and developing equanimity by learning not to react to them. Finally, on the last full day participants learn the meditation of loving kindness or goodwill towards all, in which the purity developed during the course is shared with all beings.

Of course, the results come gradually through continued practice. It is unrealistic to expect all problems to be solved in ten days. Within that time, however, the essentials of *Vipassana* can be learned so that it can be applied in daily life. The more the technique is practised, the greater the freedom from misery, and the closer the approach to the ultimate goal of full liberation. Even ten days can provide results which are vivid and obviously beneficial in everyday life.

Benefits of Vipassana

Following are the benefits that practising *Vipassana* meditaion provides. Remember, it takes only about half an hour everyday to get these benefits and live a better life.

- Practice of *Vipassana* regularly helps control greed
- Helps face tensions and problems
- Increases awareness and helps make peace with yourself
- Helps attain self-control
- Helps control or stop day dreaming
- Helps face fear
- Helpful for stress management and anger management

Each one of us might be facing some or the other problem while coping with our daily lives. So, to stop coping and start living, try practising *Vipassana* meditation. Millions of people around the world have discovered the way of living life, through *Vipassana*.

Vipassana Meditation

Vipassana, which means to see things as they really are, was rediscovered by Gautam Buddha more than 2500 years ago and was taught by him as a universal remedy for universal ills, i.e., an Art of Living. This non-sectarian technique aims for the total eradication of mental impurities and the resultant highest happiness of full liberation. Healing, not merely the curing of diseases, but the essential healing of human suffering, is its purpose. *Vipassana* is a way of self-transformation through self-observation. It focuses on the deep interconnection between mind and body, which can be experienced directly by disciplined attention to the physical sensations that form the life of the body, and that continuously interconnect and condition the life of the mind. It is this observation-based, self-exploratory journey to the common root of mind and body that dissolves mental impurity, resulting in a balanced mind full of love and compassion. The scientific laws that operate one's thoughts, feelings, judgements and sensations become clear. Through direct experience, the nature of how one grows or regresses, how one produces suffering or frees oneself from suffering is understood. Life becomes characterized by increased awareness, non-delusion, self-control and peace.

Meditation is a mental exercise in which we direct our mind to think inwardly by shutting our sense organs to external stimulations. It is a Vedic exercise which can be used as a powerful instrument to restrain sense organs, control autonomic nervous system and also to attain superconsciousness. Ordinarily there are two planes in which the mind functions, the conscious and unconscious. Yet there can be one more plane which is higher than both, one where the mind goes beyond the level of self consciousness called super consciousness. When a man goes to sleep he enters the plane of subconsciousness; on waking up he regains his consciousness and becomes a normal person. But when a person has attained superconsciousness, usually through the prolonged practice of meditation, on returning to the conscious state he becomes a different person having acquired greater knowledge and wisdom. After practising *kundalini* type of meditation for many years, Gopikrishnan described his great experience of attaining superconsciousness and the subsequent remarkable events that occurred in his life. Still recently Maharishi

Mahesh Yogi described a simple method popularly known as transcendental meditation for attaining self consciousness to be guided by the law of Nature.

Methods of Meditation

There are many methods of meditation. Sage Patanjali described eight steps in *yoga* to achieve the goal of superconsciousness. *Vipassana* meditation of Lord Buddha (500 BC) and other types of meditation have been reviewed recently.

In order to study the utility of these methods and also to know the degree of attainment in each individual case a biofeedback system has been introduced, using an electronic instrument that can amplify the various psychosomatic changes in the body such as blood pressure, heart rate, muscle tension, skin temperature and brainwave patterns. By observing one's own bodily functions with this device, one can gradually, through meditation, develop a mental power to control the involuntary functions.

Studies on normal individuals have indicated that a regular practice of *yogic* postures (physical) leads to psychological improvement in the intelligence and memory quotient and a decrease in the pulse rate, blood pressure, respiration and body weight. The biochemical examination of blood has shown decrease in blood sugar and serum cholesterol and a rise in the serum protein level. However, practice of breathing exercise *Pranayam*, etc., alone produces similar results except that fall in serum lipids was more marked than was noted in the practice of physical postures. After intensive meditation for 10 days, there was a marked rise of neurohumours and their enzymes such as acetylcholine, catecholamine, cholinesterases and monoamine oxidases with a fall of plasma cortisol. When all the three integrated *yogic* practices, namely physical postures, breathing exercises and meditation were combined it was found that there was a decrease in the neurohumours and their related enzymes and an increase in the plasma cortisol levels. Based on these findings it can be postulated that the regular practice of integrated *yoga* can promote tranquillity of mind and increase resistance to stress. Kundalini meditation has been used with great benefit not only for improving the level of consciousness, but also in the treatment of certain mental illnesses. Recently mindfulness meditation of *yoga* has been shown to reduce stress in psychological symptomatology and suggested that mindfulness meditation course can be an effective stress reduction programme in a healthcare setting.

In recent years *vipassana* meditation of Lord Buddha (500 BC) has been used for clinical utility in terms of providing a general psychological pattern of positive mental stress particularly as a perfect antistress remedy. Biochemical studies have indicated that after ten days of intensive *Vipassana* type of meditation produces similar changes in neurohumoral contents of the blood as in integrated *yoga*. Wallace and Benson who conducted extensive studies on transcendental meditation observed that the electroencephalograph showed an increase in the alpha wave activity indicating greater tranquillity of mind. They also observed a decrease in the heart beat and a 20 per cent decrease in oxygen consumption. There was also a marked increase in skin resistance. In several subsequent studies this method has been used clinically in cases of hypertension, drug addiction, alcoholism and smoking, serum cholesterol, bronchial asthma, insomnia, etc., with significant results. It has been demonstrated that practice of transcendental meditation in morning and evening significantly reduces anxiety, decreases incidence of disease and causes reversal of aging process. It has also been shown that regular practice of transcendental meditation improves intelligence (IQ), academic performance and alertness. These effects have recently been reviewed. The promotion of mental health can also be obtained by using other methods of meditation, e.g., Zen meditation as practised in Japan, Sufism in the Middle east, and autogenic training in western countries. Recently Lama Gangchen has described five limitless meditation—love, compassion, joy, equanimity and peace and cures many diseases of body and mind.

Although *yogic* exercises are effective in certain diseases e.g., hypertension, anxiety neurosis, mucous colitis, bronchial asthma, diabetes mellitus, thyrotoxicosis migraine and rheumatic disorders, it cannot be practised by elderly subjects, in debilitate conditions and even in young women during pregnancy and menstruation. But meditation particularly, transcendental meditation, in a comfortable sitting position and Benson's meditation for beginners even in lying down position short of sleep can be practised in all conditions and at all ages. It has been suggested that regular meditation is the key to health (mental, physical and social well being) in elderly subjects. Balanced diet and moderate exercise are complimentary to the effects of meditation.

Everyone seeks peace and harmony, because this is what we lack in our lives. From time to time we all experience agitation, irritation, disharmony. And when we suffer from these miseries, we don't keep them to ourselves; we often distribute them to others as well. Unhappiness permeates the atmosphere around someone who is miserable, and those who come in contact with such a person also become affected. Certainly this is not a skillful way to live.

We ought to live at peace with ourselves, and at peace with others. After all, human beings are social beings, having to live in society and deal with each other. But how are we to live peacefully? How are we to remain harmonious within, and maintain peace and harmony around us, so that others can also live peacefully and harmoniously?

In order to be relieved of our misery, we have to know the basic reason for it, the cause of suffering. If we investigate the problem, it becomes clear that whenever we start generating any negativity or impurity in the mind, we are bound to become unhappy. A negativity in the mind, a mental defilement or impurity, cannot coexist with peace and harmony. How do we start generating negativity? Again, by investigation, it becomes clear. We become unhappy when we find someone behaving in a way that we don't like, or when we find something happening which we don't like. Unwanted things happen and we create tension within. Wanted things do not happen, some obstacle comes in the way, and again we create tension within; we start tying knots within. And throughout life, unwanted things keep on happening, wanted things may or may not happen, and this process of reaction, of tying knots—Gordian knots—makes the entire mental and physical structure so tense, so full of negativity, that life becomes miserable.

Now, one way to solve this problem is to arrange that nothing unwanted happens in life, that everything keeps on happening exactly as we desire. Either we must develop the power, or somebody else who will come to our aid must have the power, to see that unwanted things do not happen and that everything we want happens. But this is impossible. There is no one in the world whose desires are always fulfilled, in whose life everything happens according to his or her wishes, without anything unwanted happening. Things constantly occur that are contrary to our desires and wishes. So the question arises: how can we stop reacting blindly when confronted with things that we don't like? How can we stop creating tension and remain peaceful and harmonious?

In India, as well as in other countries, wise saintly persons of the past studied this problem—the problem of human suffering—and found a solution: if something unwanted happens and you start to react by generating anger, fear or any negativity, then, as soon as possible, you should divert your attention to something else. For example, get up, take a glass of water, start drinking—your anger won't multiply; on the other hand, it'll begin to subside.

Or start counting: one, two, three, four. Or start repeating a word, or a phrase, or some *mantra*, perhaps the name of a god or saintly person towards whom you have devotion; the mind is diverted, and to some extent you'll be free of the negativity, free of the anger. This solution was helpful; it worked. It still works. Responding like this, the mind feels free from agitation. However, the solution works only at the conscious level. In fact, by diverting the attention you push the negativity deep into the unconscious, and there you continue to generate and multiply the same defilement. On the surface there is a layer of peace and harmony, but in the depths of the mind there is a sleeping volcano of suppressed negativity which sooner or later may erupt in a violent explosion.

Other explorers of inner truth went still further in their search and, by experiencing the reality of mind and matter within themselves, recognized that diverting the attention is only running away from the problem. Escape is no solution; you have to face the problem. Whenever negativity arises in the mind, just observe it, face it. As soon as you start to observe a mental impurity, it begins to lose its strength and slowly withers away.

A good solution; it avoids both extremes—suppression and expression. Burying the negativity in the unconscious will not eradicate it, and allowing it to manifest as unwholesome physical or vocal actions will only create more problems. But if you just observe, the defilement passes away and you are free of it.

This sounds wonderful, but is it really practical? It's not easy to face one's own impurities. When anger arises, it so quickly overwhelms us that we don't even notice. Then, overpowered by anger, we perform physical or vocal actions which harm ourselves and others. Later, when the anger has passed, we start crying and repenting, begging pardon from this or that person or from God: "Oh, I made a mistake, please excuse me!" But the next time we are in a similar situation, we again react in the same way. This continual repenting doesn't help at all.

The difficulty is that we are not aware when negativity starts. It begins deep in the unconscious mind, and by the time it reaches the conscious level it has gained so much strength that it overwhelms us, and we cannot observe it. Suppose wisdom does prevail when anger arises, I say, "Thank you very much. Now I must sit down and observe my anger." Yet, is it possible? As soon as I close my eyes and try to observe anger, the object of the anger immediately comes into my mind—the person or incident which initiated the anger. Then I'm not observing the anger itself; I'm merely observing the external stimulus of that emotion. This will only serve to multiply the anger, and is therefore no solution. It is very difficult to observe any abstract negativity, abstract emotion, divorced from the external object which originally caused it to arise. However, someone who reached the ultimate truth found a real solution. He discovered that whenever any impurity arises in the mind, physically two things start happening simultaneously. One is that the breath loses its normal rhythm. We start breathing harder whenever negativity comes into the mind. This is easy to observe. At a subtler level, a biochemical reaction starts in the body, resulting in some sensation. Every impurity will generate some sensation or the other within the body.

This presents a practical solution. An ordinary person cannot observe abstract defilements of the mind—abstract fear, anger or passion. But with proper training and practice it is very easy to observe respiration and body sensations, both of which are directly related to mental defilements.

Respiration and sensations will help in two ways. First, they will be like private secretaries. As soon as a negativity arises in the mind, the breath will lose its normality; it will start shouting, "Look, something has gone wrong!" And we cannot scold the breath; we have to accept the warning. Similarly, the sensations will tell us that something has gone wrong. Then, having been warned, we can start observing the respiration, start observing the sensations, and very quickly we find that the negativity passes away.

Any thoughts or emotions, any mental impurities that arise manifest themselves in the breath and the sensations of that moment. Thus, by observing the respiration or the sensations, we are in fact observing mental impurities. Instead of running away from the problem, we are facing reality as it is. As a result, we discover that these impurities lose their strength; they no longer overpower us as they did in the past. If we persist, they eventually disappear altogether and we begin to live a peaceful and happy life, a life increasingly free of negativities.

In this way the technique of self-observation shows us reality in its two aspects, inner and outer. Previously we only looked outward, missing the inner truth. We always looked outside for the cause of our unhappiness; we always blamed and tried to change the reality outside. Being ignorant of the inner reality, we never understood that the cause of suffering lies within, in our own blind reactions towards pleasant and unpleasant sensations. Now, with training, we can see the other side of the coin. We can be aware of our breathing and also of what is happening inside. Whatever it is, breath or sensation, we learn just to observe it without losing our mental balance. We stop reacting and multiplying our misery. Instead, we allow the defilements to manifest and pass away.

The more one practises this technique, the more quickly negativities will dissolve. Gradually the mind becomes free of defilements, becomes pure. A pure mind is always full of love—selfless love for all others, full of compassion for the failings and sufferings of others, full of joy at their success and happiness, full of equanimity in the face of any situation.

When one reaches this stage, the entire pattern of one's life changes. It is no longer possible to do anything vocally or physically which will disturb the peace and happiness of others. Instead, a balanced mind not only becomes peaceful, but the surrounding atmosphere also becomes permeated with peace and harmony, and this will start affecting others, helping others too. By learning to remain balanced in the face of everything experienced inside, one develops detachment towards all that one encounters in external situations as well. However, this detachment is not escapism or indifference to the problems of the world. Those who regularly practise *Vipassana* become more sensitive to the sufferings of others, and do their utmost to relieve suffering in whatever way they can—not with any agitation, but with a mind full of love, compassion and equanimity. They learn holy indifference—how to be fully committed, fully involved in helping others, while at the same time maintaining balance of mind. In this way they remain peaceful and happy, while working for the peace and happiness of others.

This is what the Buddha taught: an art of living. He never established or taught any religion, any "ism". He never instructed those who came to him to practise any rites or rituals, any empty formalities. Instead, he taught them just to observe nature as it is, by observing the reality inside. Out of ignorance we keep reacting in ways which harm ourselves and others. But when wisdom arises—the wisdom of observing reality as it is—this habit of reacting falls away. When we cease to react blindly, we are capable of real action—action proceeding from a balanced mind, a mind which sees and understands the truth. Such action can only be positive, creative, helpful to ourselves and to others.

What is necessary, then, is to "know thyself"—advice which every wise person has given. We must know ourselves, not just intellectually in the realm of ideas and theories, and not just emotionally or devotionally, simply accepting blindly what we have heard or read. Such knowledge is not enough. Rather, we must know reality experientially. We must experience directly the reality of this mental-physical phenomenon. This alone is what will help us be free of our suffering.

This direct experience of our own inner reality, this technique of self-observation, is what is called *Vipassana* meditation. In Pali language *Passana* means seeing in the ordinary way, with one's eyes open; but *Vipassana* is observing things as they actually are, not just as they appear to be. Apparent truth has to be penetrated, until we reach the ultimate truth of the entire psycho-physical structure. When we experience this truth, we learn to stop reacting blindly, to stop creating negativities—and naturally the old ones are gradually eradicated. We become liberated from misery and experience true happiness. There are three steps to the training given in a meditation course. First, one must abstain from any action, physical or vocal, which disturbs the peace and harmony of others. One cannot work to liberate oneself from impurities of the mind while at the same time continuing to perform deeds of body and speech which only multiply them. Therefore, a code of morality is the essential first step of the practice. One undertakes not to kill, not to steal, not to commit sexual misconduct, not to tell lies, and not to use intoxicants. By abstaining from such actions, one allows the mind to quiet down sufficiently in order to proceed further.

The next step is to develop some mastery over this wild mind by training it to remain fixed on a single object, the breath. One tries to keep one's attention on the respiration for as long as possible. This is not a breathing exercise; one does not regulate the breath. Instead, one observes natural respiration as it is, as it comes in, as it goes out. In this way one further calms the mind so that it is no longer overpowered by intense negativities. At the same time, one is concentrating the mind, making it sharp and penetrating, capable of the work of insight.

These first two steps, living a moral life, and controlling the mind, are very necessary and beneficial in themselves, but they will lead to suppression of negativities unless one takes the third step: purifying the mind of defilements by developing insight into one's own nature. This is *Vipassana*: experiencing one's own reality by the systematic and dispassionate observation within oneself of the ever-changing mind-matter phenomenon manifesting itself as sensations. This is the culmination of the teaching of the Buddha: self-purification by self-observation.

It can be practised by one and all. Everyone faces the problem of suffering. It is a universal malady which requires a universal remedy, not a sectarian one. When one suffers from anger, it's not Buddhist anger, Hindu anger or Christian anger. Anger is anger. When one becomes agitated as a result of this anger, this agitation is not Christian, or Jewish, or Muslim. The malady is universal. The remedy must also be universal.

Vipassana is such a remedy. No one will object to a code of living which respects the peace and harmony of others. No one will object to developing control over the mind. No one will object to developing insight into one's own nature, by which it is possible to free the mind of negativities. *Vipassana* is a universal path.

Observing reality as it is by observing the truth inside—this is knowing oneself directly and experientially. As one practises, one keeps freeing oneself from the misery of mental impurities. From the gross, external, apparent truth, one penetrates to the ultimate truth of mind and matter. Then one transcends that, and experiences a truth which is beyond mind and matter, beyond time and space, beyond the conditioned field of relativity: the truth of total liberation from all defilements, all impurities, all sufferings. Whatever name one gives this ultimate truth is irrelevant; it is the final goal of everyone.

Current Research

In a recent study using 10 channel polygraphs, recording respiratory and autonomic variables, ECG, recording standard limb I, photo-electric plethysmograph, recording skin blood flow, nasal thermisters, recording breath cycle and closed circuit Benedict-Roth apparatus, recording oxygen consumption; it has been shown that 'OM' meditation compared to non-targeted thinking caused increased mental alertness, even while being physiologically relaxed. Still recently same group of authors have demonstrated that mental repetition of 'OM' caused a significant decrease in skin resistance and heart rate.

Presently controlled studies are going on in the Medical Research Centre of Bombay Hospital, amongst the Nursing students on meditation in relation to improved intelligence, performance and alertness and in the elderly subjects in relation to improved health and reversal of aging process.

Three Methods of Vipassana Meditation

There are three ways of doing *Vipassana*. In all the three methods explained below, the main focus is on breathing. What is different are the points on which we should focus our attention while breathing. Initially one is required to try this method in a separate, silent room. However, as one practises them regularly, he will be able to use them at any place, anytime.

(1) Watching the belly

Have you seen the pictures of laughing Buddha? These pictures are the speciality of Japanese traditions. In contrast to the image of Buddha as a serene enlightened prince, this images depicted him as a jovial, corpulent person who has a significantly large belly. Though the picture seems funny, in reality it contains a very subtle message. The message that the belly has an important role to play in meditation.

The belly is considered as the location of the *hara* centre. Just behind and below your navel (belly button) lies the *hara*, which is a point of consciousness that is considered as the centre of your subtle body. By focussing our attention on the *hara* centre, we can easily attain a meditative state of mind. As you meditate upon *hara*, your thinking process starts slowing down on its own. You achieve a state of choiceless awareness.

The 'belly watching' form of *Vipassana* meditation involves focussing our attention on the breathing process felt around the belly. Whenever we breath, our belly moves up and down. This movement of belly is a continuous process. Just like breathing, this movement (of belly) also goes on continuously. And we can use this movement to attain a meditative state. Let's see how:

Sit quietly at a comfortable, peaceful place. Close your eyes and take few deep breath. Now focus your attention on the area around the belly. See how it goes up and down along with the breath. Just be watchful of the belly movement as it comes upward & downward during the breathing. Focus your whole attention on this belly movement.

Keep watching this belly movement. Within a span of few minutes, you will realize that your thoughts have gradually started disappearing from your mind. You will feel a state of increased awareness. Be a witness to the changes in your body during this meditation. After 15-20 minutes, stop this belly meditation stop watching the belly movement and come out of this meditation.

Practise the above meditation daily. As you practise daily, soon you'll start recognizing the presence of a *hara* centre—a sort of ball of consciousness around the belly. That will help you increase the awareness of your inner self which is the main thing in meditation.

(2) Watching the Coolness in the Nostril

This is the second method of *Vipassana*. If you observe your breathing closely, you will find that whenever the air enters inside our body through nostril, it produces a little soothing coolness in the nostrils. Experience it right now. As you breath, see that whenever you inhale the air, it produces a sensation of slight coolness in the nostril. Though it is a very little, almost unnoticeable coolness, it does exist.

The second method of *Vipassana* involves focussing the attention on this coolness during breathing. Our breathing is a continuous process. It just goes on. And along with the breathing, the soothing coolness in our nostrils also keeps emanating itself as if it is a by-product of inhalation. If we focus our attention on this coolness we can achieve a meditative state.

Find a comfortable, peaceful place. Sit there silently in a comfortable position. Close your eyes and take some deep breath. Now start observing your breathing. Concentrate on the easily felt and comforting sensation of slight coolness that you feel inside the nose whenever breath goes in. Repeatedly engaging the mind in feeling this coolness relaxes the mind. It works as if an air conditioner has been fitted in the mind.

At least for a period of 15-20 minutes, continue experiencing this coolness in the nose. Just like the above method of 'Belly watching' this wonderful method will take you into a deep meditating state.

Slowly-slowly as you practise this method, your meditation session will improve in quality and you will start achieving an enhanced state of awareness. This is a simple method but a very powerful one.

(3) Watching the Breathing like a river

This is the third method of *Vipassana*. The main thing to focus upon in this meditation technique is the breath itself. This method is the most basic form of *Vipassana*. You have to watch your breath as it comes inside your body and then goes outside.

Just like the above two methods, find a comfortable, peaceful place. Sit their silently in a comfortable position. Now close your eyes and take some deep breath. Now start observing your breathing. Focus your entire attention on the breathing and follow it as it travels inside your body and comes out. Follow the breath in its entire route of inhalation and exhalation. Watch the breath as if you are watching a river.

A river is flowing and you are sitting on its bank. You are watching the water as it flows in the river. However, you are just a watcher. You are not concerned with the speed of the flow. Neither you are concerned with the quality of water nor whether it has ripple in it or not. You are just watching the river without involving yourself in the flow.

Similarly, just watch your breath as it moves in your body. Don't be attached with it.

When it comes—watch it.

When it goes—watch it.

Be a watcher, be a witness.

This is not easy. There will be distractions as you watch. There will be floods of thoughts. You will be carried away by different kinds of thoughts. But don't get discouraged. If your attention is diverted 100 times, bring it back to breathing 100 times. Slowly all thoughts will start settling down. As you watch your breath, soon you will realize the witness in you. The one who is watching the watcher itself. Your true identity. You are not body, you are not mind, you are not breathing. You are self. The knower who knows everything. Yet remains pure and unattached. Watch your breathing. Keep watching and you will be in meditation.

Chapter 7

CONCLUSION

Neither corruption nor hard outs are required to succeed. Take one portion of courage, one point of integrity, one portion of dynamism and add a pinch of foolhardiness and you may become a successful person.

The truth is: if you bend they will kick. In a democracy the political executive is supreme. They are accountable to the people. They are accountable to Parliament and the Assembly. They have to get re-elected. But the role of the political executive is to take policy decisions. It is the job of the bureaucracy to implement the policy decision. Why have the bureaucracy allowed the political executive to trespass onto their turf? The simple answer is lack of backbone.

To be able to stand up, one needs to have personal integrity, both financial and intellectual. Few people are financially honest. A good percentage of people have impeccable financial integrity. And possibly very less percentage of people have intellectual integrity. It is not enough to be financially honest, it is equally important that you do not allow others to make money. If somebody does not loot but allow others to loot, which is a bigger crime is to be decided. This is not a bad agenda for someone who has proved at every stage in his life that he can get things done with integrity.

There must be a corruption-free society. For this each member of the society will have to introspect themselves and try to improve from today and grow economically. Economic growth helps to reduce poverty. Growth-oriented policies seek to increase gross national product (GNP), not to ameliorate poverty and that redistribution is the key to poverty reduction. Since the 1950s, developmental economists have understood that growth in GNP is not synonymous with increased welfare. But, even prior to Independence, India's leaders saw growth as essential for reducing poverty and increasing social welfare. In economic terms, growth was an instrument, not a target, that means by which true targets, like poverty reduction and the social advancement of the masses, would be achieved.

Two distinct ways in which economic growth would have this effect. First, growth would pull the poor into gainful employment, thereby helping to lift them out of poverty. Higher incomes would enable them to increase their personal spending on education and health (as seems to have been happening in India during its recent period of accelerated growth). Secondly, growth increases state revenues, which means that the government can potentially spend more on health and education for the poor. Of course, a country does not necessarily spend more on such items simply because it has increased revenue, and, even if it does, the programmes it chooses to fund may not be effective. In almost willful ignorance of the fact that the growth centred model has proved itself time and again, sceptics advocate, an alternative 'redistributive' developmental model, which they believe will have a greater impact on reducing poverty. Critics of the growth model argue that, it is imperative to redistribute income and wealth as soon as possible. They claim that the Indian state of Kerala and the country of Bangladesh are examples where redistribution, rather than growth, has led to better outcomes for the poor than in the rest of India. In impoverished countries where the poor exceed the rich by a huge margin, redistribution would increase the consumption of the poor only minimally and the increase would not be sustainable in a context of low income and high population growth. In short, for most developing countries, growth is the principal strategy for inclusive development, i.e., development that consciously includes the marginal and poorest members of a society. But the political sustainability of the growth—first model requires both symbolic and material efforts. While growth does benefit the poor, the rich often benefit disproportionately. So, to keep the poor committed to the system as their economic aspirations are aroused, the wealthy would be well advised to indulge less in conspicuous consumption. At the same time—and more importantly - the poor need greater access to education in order to increase their economic opportunities and social mobility. 'Less excess and more access' must become the principle that guides development policy.

Former President of India APJ Abdul Kalam has said the challenges of the world are poverty, illiteracy, drinking water, clean and green energy, equitable distribution of resources, quality education with values for all, overcoming societal imbalances, curing diseases, quality healthcare for all and good living conditions. Individual nations are working to find a solution to these challenges. However, there are many international dimensions for the cause and solutions. Hence, working for solutions is a collective responsibility of the global community.

Ideas and innovations are no longer geographically or politically confirmed. An invention made today somewhere takes no time to find its market thousands of miles away. Seamless flow of information and people also means that local or regional issues will invariably gain global prominence and unaddressed problems including poverty can mutate rapidly into global terrorism. This flow of ideas has also led to increasing importance of global human rights and propagation of the idea of democracy. There should be a world of nations where the divide between rural and urban, rich and the poor, developed and developing has narrowed down, where there is an equitable distribution of energy and quality water, where core competencies of each nation are identified. Missions synergizing the core competencies of nations lead to economic advantage and faster development of societies, where all students of all societies are imparted education with value system, where affordable quality healthcare is available to all. Here, governance will be responsive, transparent and corruption-free where crimes against women and children are absent and none in the society feels alienated. A world in which every nation is able to give a clean, green environment to all citizens, is prosperous, healthy, secure, devoid of terrorism, peaceful and happy. A world of nations with creative leadership is to ensure mechanisms to resolve conflicts between nations and societies keeping peace and prosperity of the world as a goal.

One of the goals is to reduce the rural-urban divide across the world. More than three billion people live in rural regions and empowerment of these three billion is important from the perspective of inclusive development, sustained peace and shared prosperity. Bridging of the rural-urban divide is closely linked with the mission of overcoming poverty and inequity. About 70% of the world's extreme poor live in villages. Driven by the need for education, healthcare and income, the rural population is migrating to urban areas for better opportunities, often meeting with despair. This further contributes to urban poverty as well leading to stresses and societal turbulence. The rural areas of the world have unharnessed resources, potential, youth and traditional skills. They have to be encouraged to add value. We would need to evolve sustainable development systems and deliver in an entrepreneurial manner. The need of the hour is the evolution of sustainable systems that act as enablers and bring inclusive growth and integrated development to nations of the world.

One such sustainable development system is the mission of provision of urban amenities in rural areas by creating three connectivities—physical, electronic and knowledge, leading to economic connectivity. The villages must be connected to themselves and to towns by good roads and, wherever needed, by railway lines. They must have other infrastructures like schools, colleges and hospitals. This is physical connectivity. Native knowledge has to be preserved and enhanced with latest tools of technology, training and research. The villages have to have access to good education from good teachers, must have good medical treatment, and new information on pursuits such as agriculture, fishery, horticulture and food processing. That means they have to have electronic connectivity. Once physical and electronic connectivity are enabled, the knowledge connectivity is enabled. That can facilitate productivity, knowledge, healthcare transparency and access to markets. Once the three connectivities are ensured, they facilitate earning capacity, leading to economic connectivity. When we provide urban amenities to rural areas, we can uplift rural areas, we can attract investors, we can introduce effectively useful systems like rural BPOs and micro-finance. The number of Pura for the whole of India is estimated to be 7,000 covering 6,00,000 villages where 750 million people live. Similarly, about 30,000 complexes would be required to convert the three billion rural population of the world into a vibrant economic zone and bringing sustainable development to rural areas.

The rural area has two kinds of entrepreneurs. Resource entrepreneurs will focus on the economic realization of the natural, traditional and human resources with the help of customized technology and modern management to enhance income of every household. They will play the critical role of moving resources up the value chain, with best practices and matching product to market. Their performance will be reflected in the overall growth of the GDP of the rural complex. Social entrepreneurs will work closely with resource entrepreneurs. They would focus on improving the human development index, in terms of education, healthcare and improvement of standards of living by provision of amenities and equity across various diversities. These entrepreneurs will promote purchasing power into better lives and higher skills. The entrepreneurs of rural area would work in close synchronization with local Pura champions who may be institutions or organizations of repute. They will be partners with the government, local administration and panchayatiraj institutions.

Enterprises from different parts of the world can be partners with activated norms by acting as equity investors, exploring and facilitating market linkages and providing a technological platform, best practices and innovative solutions to production challenges. Such collaborative platforms for 6,00,000 villages covering 750 million citizens in India alone will have an over—$200 billion market in the country, which can harness an agrarian economy leading to mutual benefits. This can be expanded to all countries.

As Mahatma Gandhi said it so appropriately 70 years ago, The world has enough to meet everyone's need but not everyone's greed."

A fundamental problem facing the world is rising inequality; joblessness and ultimately a lack of demand, causing deep recession. This is not a cyclical problem that will be addressed by stimulus packages but a more structural problem, inherent in the current growth process. Some argue why worry if inequality is rising as long as poverty is declining and Asia catches up with the West. In the long run, inequality will come down, while in the short run, poverty will be addressed. But such a model, especially in South Asia where poverty still remains deep and where exclusion could be socially explosive, would be unsustainable. Far-sighted Asian leaders recognize the danger and want both fast and more inclusive growth.

First, growth has been increasingly jobless, and the employment growth has declined for the same level of economic growth. Secondly, growth has been uneven across sectors and locations. For instance, agriculture has been left behind and in countries such as India and China, some regions have advanced faster than others. Policies too have relatively neglected the agriculture sector. Thirdly, globalization factors such as trade competitiveness, foreign direct investment and new technologies have favoured demand for skilled labour. In some cases, labour laws also often discriminate against formal employment and encourage 'casualization' of labour. Lack of access to credit for agriculture and small and medium enterprises and lack of social protection have all contributed to the exclusion of disadvantaged groups from the growth story.

Rather than trying to compensate those left out of the growth process, inclusive growth is about social and economic policies that focus on ensuring that the growth process better targets the inclusion of citizens into the delivery of growth as workers, entrepreneurs and consumers of public and private goods.

To complement national policies that target the inclusion of excluded citizens, there is also the need to ensure that the poor and vulnerable are able to tide over difficult periods. Within the inclusive growth approach, countries have successfully used instruments like conditional and unconditional cash transfers to make basic goods and services more affordable for the poor and vulnerable instead of using subsidies and tax concessions. Social protection measures that induce institutional and structural change increase participation of an even wider cross-section of society in the growth process. Many Asian countries are now trying to widen and deepen their social-protection programmes. China has rolled out an ambitious rural health insurance and India's Mahatma Gandhi National Employment Guarantee Act is an attempt to enhance livelihood security of rural households.

Many Asian countries have remarkable successes to share. Vietnam achieved 8% growth for a decade or so until 2008, with very little increase in inequality. Rural incomes rose as rapidly as urban incomes, as a result of efforts to increase connectivity to rural areas through all-weather roads and rural electrification, and a heavy focus on agriculture, both in food and cash crops.

China's remarkable success in poverty reduction during the initial years after systematic land reforms in 1979 was largely because of a sharp improvement in the terms of trade for agricultural products and an increase in public expenditure for the rural economy. Similarly, when India's green revolution resulted in fast agricultural growth in the 1970s and the first half of the 1980s, poverty declined despite a relatively low rate of economic growth.

For inclusive growth, we need to have a growth pattern that creates employment and the agriculture sector using the rural poor's unskilled labour is clearly the priority. Also, given that the centre of economic gravity is moving towards non-farm sectors and urban areas providing decent employment opportunities to all, particularly enhancing women's equality and empowerment would boost progress. Twenty-first century globalization is technology-biased and improvements in social and physical infrastructure would leapfrog modern economic development. Financial inclusion and social protection policies to protect the poor from economic and environmental vulnerabilities are an absolute necessity for stability and sustainable economic growth.

Growth will not be inclusive if some groups are discriminated against, overtly or covertly. Empirical evidence across the world indicates that group discrimination is largely on the basis of caste, ethnicity, gender and religion.

Leaving behind a large section of the population while some go ahead is not sustainable in today's world. Leaving behind a destroyed environment as you hurtle forward with rapid growth is also unsustainable. As we gobble up the world's resources, rising food and fuel prices are estimated to have caused a drop in purchasing power of the bottom 20% of the population by a quarter. Inclusiveness and sustainability are interconnected.

Growth at any Cost

The global economy is on the verge of a precipice. The IMF recently revised the global growth projections downward and commented that the world economy is in a 'dangerous new phase'. The US Federal Reserve observed that there are 'significant downside risks to the economic outlook' on the prospects for the US economy. Capital is gradually lowering to safe-haven assets with the value of US Treasury bonds, widely considered as a 'safe' investment, rising by over 3 per cent with their yield hitting a 70-year low of 1.77 per cent. By all measures, financial stress in key markets is running at the highest level since June 2009, and the sustainability of Greece's government debt is perilously low. What started as a Greek crisis about 2 years ago has become a problem for the global financial system. The fact that the value of German bank shares has more than halved in the last 2 years is indicative of the contagious nature of the crisis.

A comparison with the policy interventions that followed the Lehman shutdown and the options that are available now paint a very grim future for the global economy in the months to come. The aftermath of the Lehman crisis took the form of aggressive rate cuts, quantitative easing, injections of capital, bank rescues and provision of liquidity. However, these options are now largely unavailable or improbable in light of the huge fiscal deficits that have resulted largely due to the policies that were in place since 2008. Designing a politically-viable rescue plan for a group of 17 sovereign members of the euro zone is likely to prove an even more complex and difficult task.

In India, our policymakers have been staring hard at the time bound trade off between inflation and growth over the past 10 months. Inflation continues to be close to 10% and all attempts by the Reserve Bank of India to contain the spiralling prices by increasing interest rates with 11 successive rate increases have had little effect so far on overall price levels. Latest data on industrial production shows weak activity in most sectors or industrial activity. Analysts and economists have already revised downwards their growth forecasts for the current fiscal year, with some estimates putting the year-end number at 7 per cent! This is a sharp revision from a year ago when growth was expected to reach the 9 per cent mark. And, this still does not fully reflect the impact of the successive interest rate increases announced by the RBI that is expected to eat into the long term growth rates by at least another couple of percentage points. The ground reality, amidst a worsening economic climate, is stark. India has to either take the battle of inflation head on and sacrifice growth in the short run else, it needs to start refocusing its policies to stimulate growth so that it positions itself in a less vulnerable state should the rest of the world catapult itself over the precipice. Therefore, it is important for the policy makers to take note of the impending global gloom and recalibrate its focus on government spending. The government should move away from its explicit goal of deficit reduction and start increasing its spending on productive investments. The multiplier effect of a higher interest rate environment reducing domestic investment and a further pull out of global investment from India once the global economic activity nosedives—will result in a gravely dismal situation when it will be too late to reinvigorate the economy.

Moreover, the focus on increasing tax revenues (both direct and indirect) at this juncture is a bad economic policy and should be seriously reconsidered. Admittedly, India has one of the lowest tax GDP ratios in the world and the focus on increasing this number would be relevant in an environment when the growth outlook is positive and broadly optimistic. Clearly, that is not the case today as the advance tax estimates announced by several corporates confirm fears of an impending slowdown. It is, therefore, imperative that we start adopting policies that will not cause our economic growth to slow down further. In this context, it will be worthwhile for the government to evaluate the following options, which can be adopted in the short run, to position India to tackle the economic uncertainty that is about to unfold:

- Announce a roadmap for bigger government spending on infrastructure and other priority sectors and move away from its targeted deficit-reduction plan.
- Use part of the foreign exchange reserves for domestic high-return investment projects.
- Chart an immediate roadmap to push investment in the manufacturing sector.
- Improve the tax policy environment and dilute the aggressiveness on increasing ta.. revenues that is clearly having a detrimental effect on inbound FDI.

The new manufacturing policy, in proposing large-scale coagulation of funds and resources basically via government fiat to form industry clusters termed National Investment and Manufacturing Zones, is headed by a senior Central/state government official. It is stressed, would very likely lead to a high-cost industrial economy and much rent-seeking. The point is that given the lack of transparency and panoply of anomalies in a capital-intensive sector like real estate, which only add to the cost the proposed investment zones would almost certainly misallocate resources and fund, and provide thoroughly suboptimal results. It is a sheer waste of resources to aim to incentivize growth, including industrial growth, at high cost. It is duly noted that the game plan is to have in place extensive governmental oversight 'without being intrusive and giving rise to complaints of corruption'.

The 19th-century idea that supply would create its own demand or the readymade investment zones would find ready takers among manufacturers appears questionable, given that flexibility, openness and connectivity are at a premium in this day and age. Besides, the notion: that lumpy upfront investment that runs the real risk of being suboptimal, even inadequate—would necessarily step-up output substantially, needs to be comprehensively reviewed. After all, in a very fundamental sense, there are only two ways to boost output in the economy. One is to rev up the number of inputs that go into the productive process. The other is to innovate and get more output from the same number of inputs. And the latter course of action seems much preferable in a low-income, capital-scarce economy that has experienced less than a decade of a high growth. Hence the vital need to improvise, be frugal and keep tab on costs, in the process of boosting output. Infrastructure development in the manufacturing zones would require 'large investments', and that public funding alone would not suffice which is why the need for viability gap funding, long-term soft loans from multilateral financial institutions and external commercial borrowings. There is certainly an infrastructure deficit here and now, and it does make sense to mitigate the rigidities in the availability of physical and social overhead capital. Yet, any large-scale investment programme needs to take into account the strength of the business cycle, the length of the payback period and umpteen other sectoral peculiarities. Hence the need for cautious optimism, modular thinking and sustained incremental effort, particularly on commitment and investment decisions so as to better cope with the plethora of uncertainties in the business environment. Instead, the intention of the national manufacturing plan appears very much to lobby, tweak and change trade policy, duty structures and tariffs to 'ensure that changes therein do not adversely affect the manufacturing sector'. The real danger that value addition behind convenient tariff walls would be at huge national cost, has clearly been lost sight of. Certain aspects of the policy plan are unexceptionable, including that calling for 'concerted thrust on skill development', the objective to rationalize employment laws and stop floor practices, and the move to incentivize higher severance pay. Also, the plan to revisit and simplify, the nearly 70 laws and regulations that a manufacturing unit needs to comply with, and file as many as 100 returns annually, needs to be expedited. The case can be made for speedy deployment of capital assets, easier provisions on capital gains, even limited subvention for technology upgradation for small and medium enterprises. After all, the reason in the main for continuing underinvestment in manufacturing is due to the high cost of capital. And the latter state of affairs is due to the high fiscal deficit of the government and consequent crowding out of industry. And routine opacity in real estate, land acquisition and warped governance generally all add to costs and stultify output in engaging with the policy process.

De-Control of Fuel Prices

Freeing up prices of all petrofuels will encourage competition in the sector and lower retail prices. Oil marketing companies (OMCs) have raised petrol prices since June 26, 2010 continuously, the start of petrol price deregulation, India imports more than 75 per cent of its crude needs and imports can go up to 90 per cent by 2031-32, according to the Integrated Energy Policy, 2006. However there is decline in petrol prices during 2014.Crude oil, like many other primary commodities, is a major input in the production process of an economy. Till recently, government isolated domestic consumers from international oil price volatility by forcing OMCs to sell their products at prices below the cost of procurement at the refinery gate. This resulted in a huge fiscal burden for government and financial problems for public sector OMCs. Finally, in part adherence to the recommendations of Kirit Parikh Committee, government decided to deregulate petrol price for two reasons.

First, the inflationary impact of a hike in petrol prices is marginal as petrol has an insignificant weightage in the wholesale price index (WPI) and, secondly, the market-determined price of petrol would not affect the poor as it is consumed by two and four wheelers owned by middle and upper classes. But other petroleum products such as diesel, kerosene and LPG are still under administrative price regime. OMCs are still suffering from high under-recoveries by selling those subsidized products.

One of the objectives of deregulation was to encourage competition in the petroleum sector. A competitive price-discovery process empowers companies to follow their own judgments of market conditions, supply chain management and technology upgradation that would benefit the consumer through superior services and cheaper product prices. Unfortunately, we haven't experienced such competition so far. In contrast OMCs have formed a cartel: recent price hikes have been simultaneous and there was hardly a difference in prices. This is bad for the economy and may have to be addressed by the Competition Commission of India. According to OMCs, price hikes were due to depreciation of the rupee and hardening of global crude prices. That's fair enough as in both cases, import costs would go up. But there have been phases when the rupee appreciated and international crude prices were lower than the benchmark price. OMCs did not lower it as they sought to recuperate under-recoveries from selling subsidized petro products. Such measures kill the benefits of deregulation. Also, 'select deregulation' hurts petrol consumers. Data on retail petrol prices in countries across the world shows that Indian prices are among the highest in the world 'at current exchange rates. And, in terms of purchasing-power parity, Indian consumer pays the highest price on petrol barring some tiny, remote countries like Malawi, Eritrea and Timor-Leste. A closer look of price structure shows that huge amount of tax has been imposed on petrol price at the consumer end. State governments across the political spectrum have imposed high sales tax/VAT on petrol up to 25 per cent. This is on top of Centre's excise duty of 14.35 per litre and 7.5 per cent customs duty. Such irrational taxation should be minimised.

An equally-important concern is the price differential between petrol and diesel that has seriously distorted the fuel market. Government is reluctant to decontrol diesel price as it is wary of a political backlash, besides its impact on inflation that is already in double digits. However, there is no justification to supply subsidized diesel for power generation in shopping malls, commercial complexes, housing societies and as a fuel for diesel driven personal vehicles. Sales of such vehicles, that include fuel-guzzling sports utility vehicles (SUV), have risen significantly after petrol deregulation. So, one of the beneficiaries of this distortion is automobile companies. It defeats both the objectives of deregulated petrol price and regulated diesel price. This further justifies the recommendations of the Kirit Parikh Committee. There needs to be a complete deregulation of petroleum products to get the true benefit of deregulation.

The Government must get out of the messy business of fixing fuel prices. The government's decision to hike the price of petrol, and its likely rollback under pressure from the political parties was a great political blunder. The government claims that it had nothing to do with the pricing decision, which is preposterous because it owns all three major fuel retailers. These oil companies look to the government to sign off on every decision big or small, and it is inconceivable that they took the pricing call on their own, at this time. Yet, real decontrol of fuel prices is precisely what this government should do in order to get rid of the millstone of determining fuel prices off its neck.

Fuel pricing and marketing need to be freed up completely. Companies should be free to adjust prices up or down at the pump whenever they want without state interference. Instead of subsidizing fuels, the poor, who use kerosene for lighting or LPG to cook, should be compensated with cash or tradeable coupons. About half of the retail price of fuel is pocketed by Central and state governments as various taxes. New Delhi should scrap its special excise duty on petrol, and instead charge a low import duty on crude oil to make up the difference. State taxes vary from a low of 25 per cent in Chhattisgarh, Himachal Pradesh and Uttarakhand to a high of 33 per cent in Andhra Pradesh. These should be merged into a single, moderate rate. With freedom in pricing, will oil companies collude to jack them up? They might be tempted to, but allowing non-oil companies to sell fuel, from pumps in shopping centres and markets, will bring competition and hold down rates. After all, in the US, WalMart is one of the largest sellers of fuel.

Daniel Yergin, global oil guru, has written a new book, *The Quest*. Here he says, oil moved mainly East-West. That is, oil from the Middle East and Africa travelled east or west to the US and Japan. However new discoveries mean that by 2020, most oil transport will be north-south, from Canada and Latin America to the US.

This is simply another way of saving that traditional US dependence on the Gulf is going to disappear. Three major developments are driving this new phenomenon. The first is the steady rise in production of oil from Canada's tar sands, which hold more oil than all Saudi Arabia's reserves. Extracting oil from tar sands is environmentally messy and has attracted much green resistance. Yet, Canadian oil sand production has risen from nothing to 1.5 million barrels per day (mbd), and could double by 2020. The second development is the discovery of massive 'presalt' oilfields offshore in Brazil, making it a major exporter. Brazilian output will in a decade rise to at least 5 mbd, of half today's Saudi output. The third development is a new technology, fracking, which breaks up tight rock in shale formations and makes it economic to extract oil and gas from enormous US shale deposits historically regarded as uneconomic. The biggest shale oil development is in the Bakken shale in North Dakota, where production has touched 0.5 mbd and should double soon. This has given North Dakota the lowest unemployment rate in the US, just 3.8 per cent. Similar shale oil development is taking place in the Eagle Ford and Permian basins in Texas, and the giant Utica shale oil in Ohio and Pennsylvania. Total shale oil production should reach 3 mbd by 2020.

An analysis by Ed Crooks in the Financial Times points out that US oil consumption peaked at 20.7 mbd in 2007 and has since fallen because of recession and mixing ethanol in petrol. Falling consumption may continue because of tighter fuel economy standards and the rise of electric and hybrid cars. Large truck and bus fleets could conceivably switch to using cheap, abundant gas instead of liquid fuels. Ed Morse, a former US energy diplomat, estimates that US oil imports will fall from 10 mbd today to just 3 mbd by the 2020s, a quantity the US can get from just Canada and Mexico, without even tapping Brazil or Venezuela. Oil from neighbours will be much cheaper than Gulf oil because of lower transport costs. Most defence strategists have exaggerated notions of US dependence on Gulf oil. This year, of US imports of 10 mbd, just 1.3 mbd will come from Saudi Arabia. Other suppliers are Canada (2.6 mbd), Mexico (1.2 mbd), Venezuela (0.9 mbd), Nigeria (0.9 mbd) and minor suppliers.

US psyche was shocked as never before when the Arab oil embargo of 1973-74 led to terrible shortages, queues and fist-fights at petrol pumps, and politicians decided this could never be repeated. A second reason is that NATO partners, above all Japan, will continue to need Gulf oil. Thirdly, any interruption of Gulf supplies will send oil prices spiralling, whether the US imports oil from Canada or Saudi Arabia. The US will retain some interest in smooth oil flows from the Gulf even if its own imports from the region fall to little or nothing. However, the US budget deficit is a political hot potato. Rather than cut welfare entitlements, politicians rather cut military spending, especially in areas of falling strategic importance. Defence experts, have questioned NATO'S value to the US, other members spend so little that they do not materially assist the US security. The US wants to cut its won spending, placing a higher burden on NATO allies. The US will also want major oil importers to bear a larger share of the cost of policing the waters in and out of the Gulf. Japan is currently the largest importer from the Gulf, but will soon be replaced by China, with India a distant third. Japan's constitution limits its own defence spending.

The reported decision of the trio of public sector Oil companies to revise petrol prices fortnightly and peg domestic rates to the Singapore index for petrol is a welcome 'step'. The move would make the pricing of petrol more predictable and the price mechanism less opaque. In tandem, the government needs to walk the talk and duly implement its in-principle decision last year to decontrol prices of diesel, by far the most used petroleum product. We are increasingly and overwhelmingly dependent on oil imports and domestic prices of petro-products do need to reflect international scarcity value. The idea that raising prices of diesel—the fuel of transport and haulage – would amount to feeding inflation is misplaced and lacks empirical basis. Trucking rates are now highly competitive and transporters cannot simply pass on every cost increase to end-users. Besides, realigning retail prices of diesel with global rates would arrest inflationary expectations and stem unscheduled borrowings of oil marketers, which they resort to, when their revenue goes below costs, causing under-recoveries. Allowing diesel prices to rise to reflect costs is crucial, for keeping the budgeted fiscal deficit in check. Repressed diesel prices lead to excessive consumption and a larger fiscal deficit, which itself is a source of inflation.

However, the pricing of petro-products remains riddled with anomalies made worse by unreformed market design. Indirect taxes make up about half the retail price of petrol or aviation fuel (in most states), and are clearly inefficient. It makes better policy sense to purposefully widen the indirect tax base rather than steeply tax petro-goods. In sharp contrast, in the more progressive tax regimes abroad petro-products are taxed on a value-added basis, with no cascading of the levies along the value chain. It leads to better allocation of resources, improved efficiency, etc., for haulage and logistics. In parallel, we need to incentivize independent retailers of fuel with proactive policy, because protecting retail sales for oil companies from competition can well mean non-transparent, padded costs in storage and supply.

Reforms in Taxation

A debate is raging in the US over whether taxing the rich mere constitutes class warfare or tax fairness. President Barack Obama backs a "Buffett tax" aimed at Americans with high incomes, the name arising from iconic investor Warren Buffett complaining that the rich often have to pay taxes at rates which are lower than those paid by middle-class households. The difference in tax rates arises from the fact that non-salary sources of income such as investments and capital gains are usually taxed at a lower rate. The ostensible purpose of the Buffett tax is to help the US government trim its deficit - although in real life revenues realized through the tax will be only a minuscule proportion of the deficit. It's more of a political gesture on Obama's part, since presidential elections are due next year. Is there a lesson for India? It's been suggested that we should tax uniformly all income, irrespective of source. This is a very bad idea. Further, the former Finance Minister of India has recently said, " we must raise the revenue to defend the expected decline of resources?"

Investors need incentives, whether to put funds in property, stocks, inventories or business ventures. If income from investment gains is taxed lower, a risk-reward balance is struck and capital both circulates and is used productively. Business can't thrive, nor can money be generated from fixed resources without risk-taking, the fuel of investment spending decisions. Taxation must be innovatively geared to spur private investment and risk-taking. That means stimulating entrepreneurs' 'animal spirits', which Keynes described as "a spontaneous urge to action rather than inaction". Returns on the gambles investors take to create new goods and services benefit the economy as a whole. Stocks and mutual funds, for example, may be the middleclass investor's only hope for beating runaway inflation. They have already been taxed at source, and shouldn't be doubly taxed in his hands.

Due to the current global economic crisis and up-side down in the stock market, a Frenchman, Rene-Thierry Magon de la Villehuchet was believed to have lost around $1 billion and have committed suicide which made headlines of newspaper, but he was not only the investor to be devastated by Bernard Madoff's audacious fraud. It was only the fraction of the $50 billion that Madoff himself estimates to be the losses from the largest Ponzi scheme ever run. Coming on the heels of the subprime crisis, it highlighted the alarming trend of the lack of due scrutiny and enforcement of regulation. The idea of self regulation as watchdog has been shown to be a chimera. This is where regulatory bodies should come in. However, in foreign countries this has not worked. The Securities and Exchange Commission (SEC) in the US fell down on the job. There were ample signs that Madoff's investment advisory business and brokerage firm were operating on an unsound base. Returns were consistently high even in turbulent markets without any evidence of a legitimate strategy to sustain them. Despite this, the SEC cleared him after an investigation in 1992 and thereafter refused to intervene. Further, a committee was formed to advise the agency on new stock market rules.

It is a lesson for the Indian regulators to take note of it. The financial sector in the country may be more regulated than its US counterpart but that has not made it immune to con job. The 1992 securities scam is a case in point, as is the Anubhav Plantation scam. The chit funds continue to be an endemic problem, a large number of them are Ponzi schemes that collapse every year. Legislation barring them is not a solution given that the organized funds need a legitimate credit. Regulation is the only way out. Steps have been taken in this regard with the central Chit Funds Act of 1982. Furthermore, the legislation depends on the state government extending it to their respective jurisdictions. A fairly large number for reasons known only to them, have resisted. This state of affairs can no longer continue. The Indian market has been hit hard by the global slowdown. A fraud even a fraction as pernicious as Madoff's would destroy what little investor confidence remains. It is time for the recalcitrant states to swallow the pill. And as importantly, regulatory bodies such as the RBI and SEBI must continue to exercise full vigilance.

Poverty must decline rapidly and at a higher rate than the current 1 per cent, if the country has to achieve inclusive growth in the future. The concept of inclusive growth is very much the primary focus of India's 12th Five Year Plan. Indian economy has witnessed steady growth in the last few years. However, the country's agricultural sector is yet to grow at a swift pace and the benefits of the poverty alleviation have not reached to the beneficiaries. People do not have access to health facilities and financial and social infrastructure is yet to be developed. "The lower incidence of poverty and the rate of decline in poverty is an important indicator of inclusive growth. While the orientation of India's current government towards faster and more inclusive growth is visibly manifested in the theme of the 11th as well as the 12th Five Year Plan, the need to find a sustainable balance between growth and inclusion has become far more important than ever before. In fact, several states have shown a remarkable improvement in the 11th Five Year plan." In fact, some of them have demonstrated a higher growth rate than even the so-called advanced states.

Tax Evasion

Tax evasion cannot be abolished but certainly it can be reduced to a great extent. No one wants to evade taxes and every one desires to lead a respectful and peaceful life. Prestige has got greater value for everybody. Sometimes situations and circumstances lead them to adopt malpractices. How to reduce tax evasion is a burning question of the day. Readers must be aware of the first rule of administration of "Broken Window Syndrome," according to which when a passer-by sees a window of a house broken and on his second visit again he sees it is not repaired or replaced, he is under impression that there is no one to take care of the house. Next day another window of the house is also broken. An efficient and good management immediately repairs the broken window and message goes on. Similarly when a minor violation of rule is adequately and justifiably punished the message goes on and it forbids others from violation of rule.

There is a common excuse from tax evaders that it was his first instance of violation and have committed it due to ignorance of law. That is no excuse. If at the very first instance proper treatment under law is given, they would definitely feel that evasion of tax is not easy and punishable also. It is not good and can be severely punished if caught.

Sincerely acting on the following, tax evasion may be reduced:

- Strengthening the tax administration
- Proper acknowledgement of honest tax payers.
- And honest tax payers should be suitably rewarded. Even in jail in the USA, tax payers are separately kept. They receive better treatment.
- Low rate of duty. It is tested truth that lower rate of duty increases the total revenue collection.
- Provision for incentive for voluntary tax compliance and payment.

Tackling Fraud through Technology

A fraud is an act of deliberate deception with the intention of securing something by taking unfair advantage of another. It is a deception in order to gain from another's loss. It is a cheating intended to get an advantage. The Hon'ble Supreme Court in the case of CC Vis Essar Oil Ltd (2004 (172) EL T 433 SC) has observed that "by fraud" is meant an intention to deceive, whether it is from any expectation of advantage to party itself or from the ill-will towards other is immaterial. Fraud involves two elements, deceit and injury to the person deceived. Injury will include any harm whatever can to any person in body, mind, reputation or such others. The word `fraud' has not been defined under Central Excise Act. Basic element of fraud is deceit. Section 17 of the Contract Act states that fraud means making a suggestion, as a fact which the person does not believe to be true. Fraud also means active concealment of facts.

A plethora of frauds are taking place in different industries. Advancement of technology and reach of the companies to global and rural market is putting Indian industries as well as department at higher risk of fraud. We face various fraud risks. Tentacles of the counterfeit market are spreading across the world. Boundaries are no barriers to those who fake it. For instance, in inventory management, fraud may arise while dealing with vendors. Collusion of vendors and employees can put a great loss to the company and the department. First, disgruntled employees are dealing with vendors independently gives an opportunity to fraud, secondly vendors who create duplicate business addresses in order to reduce their tax liability. Apparently company employees would like to select one time vendor instead of looking up for special and regular vendor in the system. So, sometimes the entire list of transaction has no identifying information for vendors.

In Telecom, there are many opportunities of frauds. There are huge numbers of subscribers, number of transaction or calls and the revenue throughout is huge. In Telecom Industry 'Psheudo -churn' is a very common type of fraud. Defaulting individuals come back to the network with different names. Most frauds take place at the subscribers end. Due to advent of mobile device more contents move to mobile TV, contests, gaming, etc., and it is very difficult to capture revenue. Technology driven products like credit cards are more susceptible to frauds. Data on the credit cards can be stolen, when a payment is made through a credit card, the card is away from sight for few minutes and it is taken by a low paid employee like waiters in restaurants etc. A data copying device smaller than pager can be clipped in belt under the waiter's apron. When the card is swiped, data is copied on the device and within no time duplicate card is prepared. There is a plethora of data storing devices today which are leveraged by people with malicious intent. Confidential data may be stolen and copied on to several devices like pen drives, CD etc., and e-mailed to others. An investigator has to apply his mind and search for evidence. Sometimes, the evidence may even be a paper. In one instance, a document was found with scribbling 'store it in the safe' and the safe was located in the CEO's cabin.

Data is the basic tool of any investigation. A large chunk of data is available on the IT System of a company which can be extracted and analyized to probe and detect frauds. Sometimes solutions that enable key word analysis of data can help detect anomalies in uncovering frauds. In another instance during investigation, a key word in native language was coming up repeatedly—in English it meant 'free'. So simple data analysis revealed a significant fraud that company was supplying free material to the customers in the form of kick bags.

The practice of pre-authentication of the invoices/gate passes has now been abolished and we always find computer generated invoice. Number of copies of similar invoice can be generated. One copy is sent while transporting the goods which can be destroyed at the destination if not checked in the route and again the same invoice may be used to accompany another goods. Central Excise Duty is debited on the 5th of the next month. To check and prevent this there should be a checking *naka* on the National Highways at specified distance similar to Toll Tax *Naka* where every goods transport vehicle would produce the accompanying documents which will be entered in the computer through photo device within no time. And then it will be automatically transferred to concerned department for cross tallying. Technology can help in detection of duplication of data. This system shall definitely check and prevent the movement of goods on parallel set of invoices and also availability of Cenvat credit on forged invoice.

The first battle against the fraud is won when the company top management believes in good governance. Organizations need to go beyond the traditional thoughts on corporate governance and layout a complete risk management framework. Government will have to put robust mechanism, comprising IT solution and processes to prevent fraud. There should be a quick remedial action like punishment, etc., so there is no recurrence. Fraud is a reputation risk, regulatory risk and a confidence risk.

In a technologically advanced age, companies need to be more proactive towards preventing and combating frauds.

Amid mounting pressure from the Supreme Court, the government is set to accept tip-offs from foreign informers and whistleblowers for fishing out information on tax evaders who have parked money in Swiss banks and tax havens.

There are clear guidelines to pay informants and the same can be extended to cover foreign informers. While rules allow tapping such sources, it's an option that has never been explored by Indian authorities. India has been pushing for co-operation among countries in sharing information on tax evaders. At the G20 session in Paris over the weekend, the Finance Minister renewed the pitch for securing old banking information, without explicitly naming Switzerland. Over the past few years, some governments in Europe have used stolen data accessed from whistleblowers to investigate and pass on information to other countries. A few months ago, France shared with New Delhi a list of more than 600 bank accounts of Indians in HSBC, Geneva. The list was stolen by a former HSBC employee. Germany, too, bought stolen data on scores of bank account holders of LGT, a bank in Liechtenstein. The decision to use foreign unofficial sources comes at a time the income-tax department is carrying out raids at residences of individuals whose names figure on the list of HSBC account holders.

According to sources, there are indications that the department has also received details of several bank account of Indians with two other Swiss banks—Julius Baer and Credit Suisse. Residents who parked undisclosed wealth abroad either operated direct numbered accounts or used a discretionary trust to hold the money. In such structures, an NRI member of the family functions as settler of the trust and a tax professional—in most cases a chartered accountant—is appointed as the protector who looks after the interest of the settler, while other members of the family, most of whom may be resident Indians, are the beneficiaries of the trust. During recent raids, tax officials have landed up at residences of some of the trust beneficiaries.

There is a panic. There are many who are willing to give self-declaration of their wealth and pay penalty despite the fact that in many cases there have been no transactions in these accounts for past 6-7 years... They want to avoid prosecution. According to him, members of certain trades such as diamond exports have come under the glare of the tax department, which has also used passport numbers of residents to make enquiries on bank accounts with authorities in tax havens. Banks worldwide use passport numbers for customer verification.

Tax officials are hoping to secure information on Indian tax evaders through various channels, including whistleblowers and other informants, especially since foreign banks, most often, do not disclose client details.

However, taxmen will check the veracity of the information provided by informants before acting on it. In many cases, Indians hold legitimate money in foreign bank accounts and surely they cannot be subjected to any harassment, the official said. As per rules, the government is to pay informers only after tax evaders settle their dues. The term `informer' in the tax rule is generic. It does not say that the informer has to be a person of Indian nationality. So, there is no problem in covering foreigners or paying them. Usually, an informer is paid 10 per cent of the amount collected as tax from the evader. Investigation on account holders of HSBC, Geneva, is on and the department is set to launch prosecution proceedings in cases where criminality is proven. In some cases, the tax department had also found corroborative evidence to nail the evader.

Global Financial Integrity, a Washington-based think tank, has estimated the size of India's underground economy at 50 per cent of the country's GDP, or around $640 billion at end-2008. Of this, about 72 per cent of the illicit assets are held abroad.

There has been a gradual and structural shift in stance taken by courts. Indian courts, like western courts, now recognize criminal liability of a corporate. Former Prime Minister Manmohan Singh referred about trying corporates indulging in criminal activities. A company has a distinct legal personality. It can sue or be sued, can own and sell assets, or commit an offence that is of civil or criminal in nature. The old school of thought was that the corporate acts through its directors and officers, and should not attract criminal liability. It has been argued that punishment for criminal offences such as imprisonment cannot be conferred on companies and, hence, there cannot be criminal liability on companies. Major hurdles that faced the attribution of criminal liability on corporates were artificial juristic personality and absence of men's reason the part of the corporate. In India, there is uncertainty whether a company can be convicted for an offence where the punishment prescribed by the statute is imprisonment and fine. This controversy was first addressed in MV Javali vs Mahajan Borewell & Co and Others in 1997 where the Supreme Court had held that mandatory sentence of imprisonment and fine is to be imposed where it can be imposed, but where it cannot be imposed - namely; on a company - fine will be the only punishment. In the Velliappa Textiles case in 2003, the Supreme Court held that since company is an artificial person, it could not be physically punished to a term of imprisonment The court opined that where the statute provides for imprisonment or fine, it is not a problem, but where the statute provides for imprisonment and fine, the court is not given the discretion to impose fine in lieu of imprisonment. And, therefore, the company cannot be prosecuted as the custodial sentence cannot be imposed upon it. A couple of years after this decision, the apex court by majority overruled its own judgment in Standard Chartered Bank vs directorate of enforcement. It held that there is no immunity to companies from prosecution merely because the prosecution is in respect of offences for which punishment prescribed is mandatory imprisonment. In Iridium

India Telecom Ltd vs Motorola Incorporated & Others in October 2010, the Supreme Court held that a corporation is virtually in the same position as any individual and may be convicted of common law as well as statutory offences. The criminal liability of a corporation would arise when an offence is committed in relation to the business of the corporation—by a person or body of persons in control of its affairs and relied on the ratio in Standard Chartered Bank Case.

The apex court held that corporations can no longer claim immunity from criminal prosecution on the grounds that they are incapable of possessing the necessary men's rea for the commission of criminal offences. The notion that a corporation cannot be held liable for the commission of a crime had been rejected, by adopting the doctrine of attribution and imputation. The criminal intent of the 'alter ego' of the corporation, i.e., the persons or the group of the persons that guide the business of the corporation, would be imputed to the corporation.

In another judgment in July 2011 of CBI vs M/s Blue-Sky Tie-up Ltd and Others, the Supreme Court reiterated the position of law held that companies are liable for prosecution of criminal offences and fines maybe imposed on the companies. In the US and the UK, it has been a settled principle that corporates can be held criminally liable. Way back in 1909, in New York Central and Hudson River Rail Road Co vs UN, Supreme Court in the US had held that a corporation is liable for crimes of intent and stated: "We see no good reason why corporations may not be held responsible for and charged with the knowledge and purposes of their agents, acting within the authority conferred upon them. If it were not so, many offences might go unpunished and acts be committed in violation of law where, as in the present case, the statute requires all persons, corporate or private, to refrain from certain practices, forbidden in the interest of public policy." In HL Bolton (Engg) Co Ltd vs T J Graham & Sons, it was said, "The state of mind of these managers is state of mind of company, and it treated by law as such. So, you will find that in case where the law requires personal fault as a condition of liability in tort, the fault of the manager will be the personal fault of company." The recent judgments in India settle the doubt that corporations are liable to be prosecuted for offences under Indian Penal Code. With this, India now is in line with other jurisdictions such as the US and the UK when it comes to law in relation to criminal liability on corporates.

Bringing back unaccounted money slashed overseas

Higher tax regime and stringent foreign exchange restrictions in the past encouraged many Indian residents to park a part of their wealth abroad. For bringing this money back, India has entered into Tax Information Exchange Agreements (TIEAs) with a number of tax havens. Let's examine their efficacy in bringing back the existing money abroad, particularly from Switzerland where a majority of the Indian money is believed to be hidden.

Under the new UK-Swiss tax treaty, the UK will get from the Swiss authority tax on the Swiss assets of the UK residents, and, that too for the past years. The USA and Germany also got a good deal from Switzerland. India, however, got a raw deal—Switzerland will only provide information on black money, that too if it relates to a period after 1.4.2011. Further, India has to provide the name of the alleged Indian offender and the Swiss person who will have the information - it cannot ask for the details of all the Indian tax payers' bank accounts in Switzerland. It is a no-brainer that such a provision will not be very effective. Hence, despite the TIEAs, looking at our long drawn out administrative and legal processes and a large number of countries involved, the regular channels will not be effective.

Let's assume that a resident Indian has unaccounted monetary assets of ₹10 crore abroad which he earned 10 years back. Further, on that amount, he has earned, say, ₹15 crore in the past 6 years. Under the Indian Income Tax Act, income tax, interest and penalty on the income of only the past six assessment years can be recovered. Hence, in this case, the total incidence of income tax, interest and penalty levied on him comes out to ₹1.18 crores to ₹ 2.18 crores. Any unaccounted income earned prior to 1.4.2004 will not be taxable. Further, the person can be prosecuted in India for filing false returns of his income for all the past years. If the unaccounted wealth and income are held through a complex structure of trusts and companies, the tax implications may be different and lower.

On 01.06.2000, Foreign Exchange Regulation Act (FERA) was abolished and Foreign Exchange Management Act (FEMA) was enacted. Any violation under FERA cannot be punished now. However, if a resident Indian continues to hold any unaccounted foreign asset without the RBI's permission after the introduction of FEMA, he can be charged with a monetary penalty of up to three times the amount involved. It is very unlikely that compounding provision under FEMA would be invoked. Tax evasion is not an offence under the Prevention of Money Laundering Act. Thus, the combined outflow for a person under the income tax law and FEMA is likely to exceed 100 per cent of the total unaccounted money abroad.

Unaccounted Indian money lies in several countries. To motivate resident Indians to voluntarily bring back this money to India, the government should ensure that a person is not required to pay more than 100 per cent of his foreign unaccounted wealth under all the laws and is not prosecuted. This will enable India to get back billions of dollars lying abroad which will help bridge India's deficit.

In the past, the Supreme Court up-held the validity of the 1997 amnesty scheme (see 231 ITR 24(SC)). The Indian Parliament, with a simple majority, can take pragmatic steps to bring the foreign unaccounted money to India. Thereafter, strictly deal with those who do not voluntarily comply.

Goods and Services Tax (GST)

Services occupy an important place in the overall GDP of the Country. Nearly 57 per cent of the country GDP comes from services. Its contribution to GDP would be over 63 per cent if construction services are also included. Taxation of services under the proposed GST is crucial from the point of fairness, equity in taxation and tax buoyancy. The finance ministry initiated a public debate on how to include services under GST in concept paper services (CPS) released recently. The paper proposed a negative list of services that would be exempt from tax in eight sectors and 27 sub-groups of services, besides some conditional exemptions related to supplier or turnover.

Based on the feedback, the ministry issued a revised concept paper on services (RCPS). The negative list now included seven sectors (with eighth being a residual group) and 22 sub group of services. Some services had been removed from the negative list. For example, services of individuals to government in relation to their representation on anybody set up by government under the positive list. Agriculture and animal husbandry had also been kept out of the negative list. Services related to transport of goods to a destination outside India and supply of goods to a person engaged in transportation of goods are also taxable. Construction, works contract, etc, are also not in the negative list. Similarly, homeless shelters, orphanages, dead diction centres, child day care homes and places of worship have also been deleted from the negative list.

But the RCPS has also added a few new services to the negative list. These include services by specified persons (except a few notified), financial sector, transport, advertisements other than advertisements published in TV, radio, newspapers or displayed in electronic media. In its attempt to have a comprehensive service tax with a small negative list, first, RCPS does not seem to be a factor in GST. It presupposes continuance of Cenvat. This is obvious from the definition of service provided in RCPS. It is, therefore, important that the RCPS should be so revised. The best approach would be to bring out the list with the introduction of GST wherein one list of services and another for goods could be introduced.

Secondly, a review of the revised negative list of services under RCPS shows that it includes some services that comprise specified persons or sectors. For example, it excludes business, promotion, construction, insurance services, ports, postal services, security, transport of goods, etc. Thirdly, the negative list under RCPS is to be an extension of the existing service tax provisions. The list is already lengthy and runs the risk of securing additions at regular intervals. There is no justification for allowing this exemption without any pecuniary limit on the value of service provided. Presently, service tax is fraught with ambiguities on the definition of taxable services. This will inevitably lead to numerous classification disputes and complexities. These disputes can be avoided to a large extent under the 'negative-list' approach. But this list should be very small.

Fourthly, the cannon of fairness entails that the tax has to be progressive to help minimize the disproportionate burden on lower-income households. However, the exemptions fail to alter the overall distribution of a consumption tax. This is because an exemption benefits all consumers, regardless of their income status. Moreover, it benefits upper-income households even more. Given their higher purchasing power, their spending on exempted items is more than that of the poor. Lower-income families depend on public health services that are already subsidized or provided free of charge. Administratively also, given the diverse nature of services offered, exemption to health and education services would lead to definitional issues and classification complexities.

Finally, inclusion of many services in the negative list would mean that no credit would be available for the tax charged on their inputs. Given the value-added structure of the tax, this would cause 'tax cascading' through blockage of tax credits on inputs that go in the production of exempted services. At the same time, this would result in blocked input tax that would be embedded in the cost of the services provided, and this would lead to a regressive outcome. If relief is to be provided, it should be in the form of zero rating (i.e., no tax on output and full credit for input taxes), and not through tax exemption. A low rate of tax on the services in the nature of merit goods with a very small list of exempted items and zero-rating of basic health and educational services could be considered in the revised list.

Goods and Services Tax (GST) or VAT is a consumption tax levied on any value that is added to a product. In contrast to sales tax, GST is neutral with respect to the number of passages that these are between the producer and the final consumer; where sales tax is levied on total value at each stage, the result is a cascade (downstream taxes levied on upstream taxes). A GST is an indirect tax, in the sense that the tax is collected from someone who does not bear the entire cost of the tax.

Maurice Laure, Joint Director of the French Tax Authority, the Direction generale des impots, was first to introduce VAT on April 10, 1954. Initially directed at large businesses, it was extended over time to include all business sectors. In France, it is the most important source of state finance, accounting for 52 per cent of state revenues.

Personal end-consumers of products and services cannot recover VAT on purchases, but businesses are able to recover VAT on the materials and services that they buy to make further supplies or services directly or indirectly sold to end-users. In this way, the total tax levied at each stage in the economic chain of supply is a constant fraction of the value added by a business to its products, and most of the cost of collecting the tax is borne by business, rather than by the state. VAT was invented because very high sales taxes and tariffs encourage cheating and smuggling. It has been criticized on the grounds that (like other consumption taxes) it is a regressive tax.

Decontrol of Diesel

Government calls for pragmatism and flexibility. The focus needs to be on bettering life for the common citizen, not on fulfilling some theoretical shibboleth.

We have to ask ourselves why petrol prices have risen in India. To say it is a global phenomenon is lazy a analysis. In the West, there is a concern about a double-dip recession. Demand is slackening and world oil prices are softening. If oil prices have gone up in India, it is because the rupee has lost value vis-a-vis the dollar: Why has the rupee lost value vis-a-vis the dollar? It is because government and RBI have raised interest rates. Why have they raised interest rates? To fight inflation they say. Consider: raising petrol and diesel prices will only fuel inflation, leading the RBI to raise interest rates even higher. The rupee will depreciate even further. We are entering a spiral situation. We cannot 'fix' inflation by such short-term mechanisms that only end up making life more expensive for the poor. Actually, the criticism being made by corporate India that inflation cannot be fought by simply driving up interest rates indefinitely - looks at the same issue from another prism. It is important not to be ideological about the word 'control'. The value of the rupee and its convertibility is controlled. Administered prices for agriculture are, in a sense, controlled. If a similar cushioning is provided to the poor and the genuine middle class by safeguarding them against rampant oil price surges for reasons they are not responsible for and don't comprehend, it makes for good politics, sensitive economics and, broadly, wise government. Of course, those who buy subsidized diesel for their fuel-guzzling SUVs be asked to pay more. For the uninitiated, consumption figures available on the website of the Petroleum Planning and Analysis Cell (PPAC) show that diesel, kerosene and LPG make up for almost 60 per cent of the petro products consumed in the country. And they all happen to be subsidized. Petrol forms a mere 10 per cent of the product basket. Hence, the deregulation of petrol was always a case of some tokenist reformers pretending that the tail could wag the dog. Fact is, diesel accounts for a whopping 43 per cent of the entire basket. And as the differential between petrol and diesel mounts, every rational consumer can be expected to try every trick in the book to switch any other substitutable non-subsidized fuel for diesel. Little wonder that diesel is currently seeing a growth of 8.7 per cent, leading to the inexorable dieselization of the economy. While it does not need a bleeding heart to make a case for fuel subsidies, the point is that the administration of subsidies cannot be a game of passing the parcel. After all, with a provision of barely ₹ 85 per litre for marketing costs and margin, what is the scope for marketing companies to bear diesel under-recoveries as high as ₹ 8.57 per litre at current prices? With subsidized products making up 60 per cent of the basket, any attempt to pass such a weighty parcel will surely end up in one or the other player tipping over. A more rational way may be to segment the diesel market through product differentiation: farm or railway grade diesels, that at least would obviate the need to subsidize the private car segment. But more importantly, either the government should have the courage of its reformist convictions and decontrol diesel, or do away with the current sham reform over petrol pricing that is so angering the nation.

Reforms in Judiciary

Soli Sorabjee, the former Attorney General of India, has stated that in recent times, the Indian public has often seen the judiciary taking the Executive to task, even taking over some of its functions. It is seen that judges are overstepping the limits of their power? When the nation's founding fathers distributed powers between the three arms—Executive, Legislature and the Judiciary—they had, in foresight, built in checks and balances to maintain a power equilibrium. It appears that this equilibrium is threatened.

The hallmark of a great nation is its institutions. The stronger the ability of these institutions to uphold and preserve fundamental values, the greater the nation would be. When India's founding fathers wrote the Constitution, they created three arms-Parliament, Executive and the Judiciary—of the state that together were to be the keepers of the ideals of the nation as enshrined in the Constitution. Over the past several months, however the Parliament has become dysfunctional, the Executive has abdicated its duties and the Judiciary is cracking the whip. Many people think that it is cracking the whip a bit too much. But it is not like that. An active judiciary is one that takes its task of defending the fundamental rights of the people and their liberties against the onslaught of the state, earnestly. As far as judges are concerned, it is a matter of mindset. One judge could say, policy formulation is the job of the Executive and Judiciary does not need to intervene while another could believe that even in policy formulation, the Judiciary would need to step in to guard fundamental rights.

The occasion for this often arises when the Executive fails to discharge its statutory, constitutional obligations. As a result of this failure, the fundamental rights of the people are violated. For instance, there are laws to prevent children from working in hazardous occupations. Now there are parents who willingly let their children work because of economic necessities. The factory owners fix the inspectors and the laws that are supposed to protect the children are not implemented. In such cases, a court hearing a complaint from a bona fide NGO can order the state to enforce the laws because by not implementing them it is violating the children's fundamental right to a healthy life. That is activism in the right sense.

To give another example, a case came up before the Supreme Court regarding a care home for women in Patna. The home had very poor sanitation, leaky roofs and the living conditions of the inmates were horrible. The court immediately asked the government to look into it. Then the court went further. It asked the government to appoint a manager and fixed his salary. That appears to be overstepping. Such orders have fiscal implications and are really in the realm of the Executive.

The government recently accused the Supreme Court of trespassing into its territory when it ordered it to set up a special investigation team headed by a retired Supreme Court judge to probe black money cases. The government said it was judicial overreach into Executive functions and was against the principle of 'separation of powers'. What the court has done is to merely ensure that the investigation was done properly and everything was in order. The power of the Judiciary to review what the state does flows from the Constitution itself. In the Constitutional scheme Parliament is not supreme. It is subject to a major limitation - that legislation does not violate any fundamental rights or constitutional values. Who is to be the arbiter of that? It has to be an impartial umpire. And that is the task entrusted to the Judiciary; to ensure that fundamental rights are not breached and basic constitutional values are preserved. In other words, the chapter on fundamental rights acts as a limitation on Parliament's powers. And the court checks whether the Parliament has transgressed that limitation or not. The Indian Constitution anyway does not have any rigid separation of powers.

Every fundamental right is not spelt out comprehensively in the Constitution. For instance, the right to shelter, right to privacy, right to go abroad and right to education have all been deduced through creative interpretation by judges over the years of Article 21 which merely guarantees "protection of life and personal liberty".

Similarly, though not mentioned expressly in the Constitution, the Supreme Court has deduced the freedom of the Press from the guarantee of free speech and thus Press freedom has been given a constitutional status by creative judicial interpretation. That is certainly not overreach.

Judicial interpretations are based on the realities of the situation. Every country has to work out its Constitution according to its problems, needs and demands. As Justice Krishna Iyer once said: "Every new decision, on every new situation, is a development of the law. Law does not stand still. It moves continually. Once this is recognized, then the task of the judge is put on a higher plane." The courts cannot remain mute spectators when laws are not enforced and consequently, fundamentally rights are violated. If the Judiciary does not intervene, it would be an inactive Judiciary. It would be called as judicial abstention and not judicial restraint. Of course, the courts should not get into road-building and beautification of government buildings, but they should actively intervene whenever rights are violated and currently, the Executive's inertia is so pervasive that rights are routinely breached.

It is as fundamental to be able to breathe good air and live in a pollution-free environment as the right to live. In fact, it is the right to live with dignity. That is why the court was right in ordering Delhi buses to ply only on CNG. If that is considered judicial overreach, so be it. It is necessary and salutary. Judges should, however, be careful about one thing. Judicial activism should not become judicial adventurism. They should not get into areas in which they do not have any expertise. The court for instance, can order the government to prepare a welfare scheme. But not undertake the task of framing itself. And in PILs, the Judiciary should refrain from the temptation of getting media headlines.

Manufacturing Policy

In the last four decades, many emerging countries adopted development strategies that focused primarily on promoting the manufacturing sector. As a result, countries such as China, Taiwan and South Korea succeeded in accelerating the growth of output and employment in this sector. So, the robust growth in these countries can be mainly attributed to their strong and vibrant manufacturing sector. India has, for various reasons, failed to expand its manufacturing base and capitalize on employment creation in the manufacturing sector. Several earlier attempts have not yielded the desired result of promoting growth in the sector. The new manufacturing policy broadly addresses issues pertaining to flexibility in labour rules, reducing the burden of compliance by simplifying business regulations, providing faster clearances by proposing single-window system for clearances, simpler and expeditious exit mechanisms for closure of units while protecting the interests of labour. The policy also aims at capturing benefits arising out of clustering manufacturing activities by proposing National Investment and Manufacturing Zones (NIMZ). It acknowledges the fact that technology up-gradation is the only and fastest way to be able to compete globally and ensure sustainable growth in the sector. The policy proposes to establish Technology Acquisition and Development Fund that will address the concerns across industries. It provides part-reimbursement for technology acquisition and eliminates traditional barriers of cost problems, faced especially by SMEs. Thus, it intends to promote use of cleaner energy sources, renewable energy resources and energy conservation technologies in the manufacturing sector.

But the key to success will be policy implementation, but there are several challenges. First, contiguous land required for setting up NIMZ will not be available due to the size of the requirement. Moreover, acquiring land of this scale will be a major challenge in India. Limitation to acquire newer land parcels for industrial development has pushed up the industrial establishment cost and to prohibitive levels. The proposed special purpose vehicle (SPV) model for governing the NIMZ should take care of this aspect and adopt measures such as deferred payment towards land cost to ease the burden of entry cost for new units. Also, the policy relies excessively on creating few green field clusters, or NIMZs, only along the Delhi-Mumbai Industrial Corridor (DMIC) to catalyze growth in manufacturing. Thus, it appears that the NIMZs have been conceptualized on the basis of DMIC. This is exactly the reverse of what the policy should ultimately aim to achieve. In fact, policies such as NMP should lead to spinoffs, resulting in the creation of projects like DMIC—that aim to develop the entire region by providing superior infrastructure and promoting industrial activities. DMIC itself has not reached full-scale implementation stage and would take another 3-4 years to be operationalized. This, in turn, means that the proposed seven NIMZs will also take at least 3-5 years to start yielding desired results.

A more appropriate approach would be to focus on creating opportunity for incremental growth in such existing clusters or brown field regions, identifying existing clusters and extending benefits of NIMZ to these regions. Interventions in the brown field regions will have far-reaching consequences in terms of growth and employment creation and, thus, will lead to overall development of the region. The other key challenge for the Centre will be to obtain consensus from the states to be able to implement the policy efficiently and in a time-bound manner, so the coordination required for implementing such large zones will be tough as there will be multiple agencies to deal with, from *gram panchayats* to Central ministries.

In this context, the Noida model of Uttar Pradesh under UP Industrial Township Development Authority under Article 243 (Q) of the Constitution does hold a lot of promise, but action will largely rest with the state. There will be other instances where the local or state-level laws will conflict with the provisions of the policy. A case in point is state environmental laws. The challenge then will also be to resolve multi-jurisdiction conflicts that could arise during implementation.

Fiscal incentives proposed for private sector participation in skill training is welcome. But there are several existing schemes that also attempt to incentivize private sector participation. Around 17 government ministries and departments have various schemes for skill education and training. The challenge is to dovetail existing efforts of various other agencies. The policy and its regulation should address some of these challenges during the implementation stage. The degree of success of the policy will entirely depend on its ability to resolve these challenges and it will require huge efforts from all stakeholders of the manufacturing sector in drafting a coherent, well-detailed policy and a set of regulations.

Gen. Petraeus, Director of the CIA, says (*Time*, September 2011), "Policy is not always made—policy accumulates, the result of many decisions as a country moves forward, collectively". India will not increase the rate of growth of its manufacturing sector to 12per cent or 14 per cent by one policy announcement. Policy changes must accumulate in many areas. The NMP mentions these industrial relations, trade policies and business regulations which are necessary to induce the increase in investment and improvement in competitiveness of Indian industries required for it to create 100 million productive jobs in the next few years. Even good and comprehensive policies will not be sufficient. They must be implemented to produce results. Many analysts including Brinkerhoff and Crosby (Managing Policy Reform, 2002), say that the process of implementation must be integrated into an ongoing process of policy reform. They say, "Instead of identifying ideal solutions up front and top down, policy implementors need to iteratively develop "second-or-third best answers that collaborating agencies and stakeholders can agree upon." Therefore, the process required for the 'accumulation of policy' and many decisions that have yet to be taken as we 'move forward collectively'. This is what the Planning Commission has set about while developing a Manufacturing Plan. The parameters of the Plan are coherent with the NMP because the Dipp, the Planning Commission and NMCC have worked together, to develop the overall agenda for growing India's manufacturing sector. Whereas the NMP has described in detail the structures of the National Manufacturing Investment Zones, which is one component of the overall NMP, the Manufacturing Plan is advancing the development of policies required in other critical areas too and their implementation. The constraints on the country's manufacturing sector that policymakers must address now are fundamentally different to the constraints that were addressed in the policy reforms of the early 1990s. Then the constraint, was mainly government's restrictive licensing policies. Bold stroke of pen reforms could relieve industry of those constraints. The challenges to be overcome now, land acquisition, industrial relations, environmental clearances and so on, involve masses of other stake holders. They must be heard and satisfied that their interests will be served by the reforms, or they will block them. 'Changes must take place in how all sectors of society interact to coordinate the aggregation of diverging interests and thus promote policy that can credibly be taken to represent the public interest', Leila Frischtak says in Governance Capacity and Economic Reform in Developing Countries, a World Bank paper. The quality of the interaction amongs the stakeholders during policy formulation and implementation is the key.

The contrast between the development of China and India's manufacturing sectors is often made. Either to argue that India's democracy can come in the way of economic growth. Or to suggest that centralized industrial policy of a Chinese type, which India's economists abandoned, swayed by US ideologies to leave it to the market should return. But India is a democracy and cannot now be otherwise. Therefore, as a judo master would, rather than resist democracy, reformers must leverage democracy's strengths to achieve their goals. India's reforms will be accelerated by engaging citizens more fully and effectively in politics and policy making and also by modifying how public agencies operate infusing them with democratic principles. Consultation is the essence of democratic governance, more than simply government.

Even the US has realized that its government must have policies to revive manufacturing and hike employment. The President's Council of Advisors has submitted a report in June 2011 to ensure US leadership in manufacturing. It recommends many areas for action: training and education of the workforce, improving infrastructure, investing to overcome market failures to ensure new technologies are developed in the US, and promoting public-private partnerships and clusters. It also suggests some industrial sectors as future opportunities. However, the Council of Advisors says its recommendations should not be called industrial policy. That would be an admission of error, in the face of evidence of the decline of US manufacturing, in contrast to China, Germany, and Japan. Its recommendations should be called innovation policy.

Labour Reforms

Labour problem in India has been a constant decelerator in its economic growths. Both labour and management have to think for their mutual benefit, only then the problem can be sorted out. The management have to think for better wages, better facilities and creating a good working condition, at the same time labours have to think for more production, minimum wastage, etc., so that there is no loss to the management. In some areas like Bhind and Morena District of Madhya Pradesh, Kerala, West Bengal, no factory owner likes to establish their factory only due to arrogance of labour in those areas. The labourers do not like to work, when they are unemployed they promise for hard work but after their employment they feel secure but do not work honestly. When they are asked to work they threaten for strike through their labour union. This tendency of workers forbids the manufacturer to establish their factory in those areas. The factory owner contention is that they have invested their capital to earn something not to incur loss. There may be some other reasons also for none-establishment of factory like unavailability of power etc., but labour problem is one of the main problems. Management wants to exploit the labourer whereas the labourer wants minimum work and higher wages. Some balance is required to be made for better economic growth of the nation.

In agriculture also there is labour problem. First due to the government scheme like NREGA, etc., now labours do not want to work. If they work in NREGA scheme they receive their wages in cash whereas farmers pay the wages in grains. There is no accountability of work. Labourers demand wages as per the government rate but government has not fixed the minimum work to be completed, hence there is no accountability. If wages be fixed on the basis of performance of a labourer it will be beneficial to both farmers and the labour. The yield in farming is dependent on various factors like good monsoon, availability of fertilizers, better quality of seed, etc. A farmer has to think for all these factors. Labour is not the only consideration. Considering all these factors nowadays, there is no much profit in agriculture.

It appears that greed is the only reason for both exploitation by management and none-performance of the labourers. To avoid this, we will have to go in depth and correct the mentality of both management and labourers. We will have to find out a mutually acceptable solution which is beneficial to the management as well as labourers also. Ensure the management that there will not be any loss to them and also the labourers that they will be provided with higher wages with good working condition. For this performance-based wages be introduced and accountability with discipline be fixed.

We have seen during last period some high-profile cases of industrial unrest across India. In November 2010, an industrial dispute at auto components manufacturer Allied-Nippon in Ghaziabad led an irate mob of workers to lynch an assistant general manager. In September 2010, employees of Foxconn, a mobile phone accessories manufacturing company in Sriperumbudur, Tamil Nadu, went on strike demanding recognition of a second union. In June 2010, workers at a Hyundai factory in Chennai went on strike over a dispute with the management about sacked workers. Dismissed workers were eventually reinstated. There is much more than politics to the recent rise in labour unrest in India. It's a structural issue. Several years of rapid growth have created a skill shortage and skill mismatch. Workers in the organized sector believe their value is higher than the wages they are getting. In this scenario, labour problems may become more persistent. We need a supply response. It hasn't come in terms of better education so far. Also, there is an evidence though that NREGA has led to a rise in rural wages, it is in fact creating inertia in the rural workforce. So there may be a continued shortage of labourer, unskilled and skilled, for industrial employment.

There are other problems, notably in laws that govern trade unions and the employment of labour. Says economist Bibek Debroy, "The Trade Unions Act allows a multiplicity of unions and agreement reached by management with any one union is not binding on another." That could explain why some workers at Maruti Suzuki, like their peers at Foxconn in Chennai, want more than one union. It increases their bargaining power. Then there is the obstacle of labour laws, most importantly Chapter V-B of the Industrial Disputes Act, 1947, which requires any factory with over 100 workers to get permission from the Government before retrenchment, layoffs and shutdown. Governments rarely grant such permission for populist reasons. An amendment to this chapter in a Budget speech in 2001 created a mighty political storm.

A decade later, the status quo stands. Says Haryana Labour Commissioner Satwanti Ahalwat who was involved in the negotiations with the striking Maruti workers, "For social security of the working class, retrenchment cannot be allowed." Such laws create an entrenched labour aristocracy and stronger unions. Such labour laws also mean that organized sector employment covers only 10 per cent of the country's workforce. It is necessary to separate retrenchment from closure and layoffs in Section V-B, the former is not as controversial as the latter. "Apart from the Industrial Disputes Act, there are at least 50 other labour laws which can be changed by the states. "Even the Industrial Disputes Act can be amended by the states as labour falls in the Concurrent List of the Constitution." The Government of Haryana continues to insist that the Maruti strike was nothing more than a political conspiracy by the Left parties to incite industrial unrest in the state. "There is a move to politicize labour unions in Haryana by political elements that have lost their bastion in Bengal and Kerala," The Haryana Government may have some reason to sense politics. MSEU was seeking affiliation with the All India Trade Union Congress, affiliated to the Communist Party of India. "But the Haryana Government needs to recognize that the Maruti strike fits into a new pattern of industrial unrest which is not confined to any one state or any one political formation. It is time for both the states and the Centre to address the serious and fundamental problems in India's labour market and labour laws.

Managing Inflation

The global economy has entered a dangerous new phase. Growth in the West has slowed while downside risks to the global economic outlook have increased further. Financial market volatility has surged as private demand in the US failed to pick up sufficiently and sovereign debt and banking sector problems in Europe proved more tenacious than expected. International efforts are being made, including by the Group of Twenty (G20), to coordinate policies so as to avoid a major global disruption like the one we experienced in 2008-09.

India's inflation remains stubbornly high, registering at 9.7 per cent in September, 11 (WPI—year-on-year), while growth is slowing from 8.5 per cent in 2010-11 to 7.6 per cent this year by our current estimation. This confluence has led to understandable public debates about the efficacy of the RBI's actions. We are clearly of the view that the RBI's monetary tightening has been necessary and is bearing fruit on the inflation front, and is not the dominant factor in the growth slowdown that is already showing the early effects of the global slowdown. Thus, although some further monetary tightening is likely necessary under our baseline scenario to quell the entrenched, inflationary momentum, the RBI certainly has the room to act quickly if major risks materialize. Indeed, as in 2008-09, the RBI's ability and readiness to supply liquidity will play a critical role if a major external financial shock materializes. Fiscal policy has an important role to play in the balancing act as the authorities have emphasized. Restraining expenditure to the level of Budget FY2012 would help recreate the fiscal space to counter external shocks. It will also assist the RBI in combating inflation by moderating domestic demand pressures. A shift in government spending from consumption towards infrastructure, health and education, would help increase the economy's capacity to grow strongly overtime, while also making the growth process more inclusive.

The government also has a role to play outside of fiscal policy. There is a sense that a reinvigorated pursuit of the outstanding structural reform agenda, such as the introduction of the goods and services tax, further liberalization of the FDI regime passage of long-pending financial sector legislation, and measures to improve the business environment would attract investment currently being held back. This reinvigoration would help bring growth back to potential in the short run while relieving supply bottlenecks that could, otherwise, continue to stoke inflation. India has felt the repercussions of the current global uncertainties in its currency and equity markets. This is a natural outcome of India's increasing integration with the global economy and reflects the sharp increase in global risk aversion in recent weeks and months. Nevertheless, India's vulnerability to external shocks is relatively low at present. This is due, in substantial part, to the fact that banks are well regulated and have strong balance sheets, exports are surprisingly buoyant, and external debts are limited. And India has demonstrated its resilience by navigating the global financial crisis in 2008-09 relatively unscathed. Nevertheless, a high level of vigilance is needed in the coming months, and calls for continued efforts to create policy buffers. Joseph E Stiglitz, a world-renowned economist and Nobel laureate, believes that India should adopt more innovative ways, such as tightening reserve requirements, to tackle inflation instead of resorting to frequent rate hikes, which can prove to be counterproductive. He also emphasizes that the BRICS nations should refrain from extending support to the European Union unless adequate returns are guaranteed.

The further status that if the money is spent on education, technology and infrastructure then the nations balance sheet looks stronger and they're able to payback what they borrow. This may not be true for Greece, but in the US, the interest rates are so low that it makes sense. So we should cut back on wasteful spending like war and increase spending on investment. If we don't invest, we'll go down the Greece route where the economy grows weaker and the revenues go down and we're stuck in a downward spiral.

The major reason India is tightening is inflation, but the deeper question is whether raising interest rates is a very cost-effective way of dealing with inflation. We know the inflation targeting framework has been totally discredited by the crisis. So one has to be very careful about the use of inflation targeting as the basis of monetary policy. Turkey, for instance, lowered interest rates and tightened reserve requirements to curb inflation. This provided more flexibility, because if it looked like the economy was getting weaker, reserve requirement could be eased to increase lending and it worked better than controlling interest rates. India should also use reserve requirements or other instruments to tackle inflation. China has used exchange rate policy very effectively in promoting exports whereas India hasn't been able to do that. India's central bank should consider using the exchange rate policy as a broader way of responding to the flood of imports. I think the imposition of tariffs on Chinese imports would threaten a trade war. Exchange rate policy will be better as it has same broad based effects and will help exporters as well. India's financial sector has been asking for the same kind of deregulation as in the US and it would be a mistake to give in to that. India has fortunately had more regulation and that has protected you from some of the excesses. If you go down the same deregulatory route as America, you're bound to end up in a similar mess.

Investment should be given a big push to ease inflationary pressures and Speer growth.

- RBI signalling a pause in rate hikes from fourth quarter of 2011-12.
- FDI inflows have registered high growth over the last eight months.
- Mounting subsidies could push inflation and strain government finances.
- Inflationary pressures and slackening of investment will hurt growth.

Whatever the reason, there is as a sense that the run of negativism is touching the trough. Optimism and pessimism are relative terms, and what these really mean for growth?

We know that industry, in general, has been in doldrums with manufacturing and mining at low points. Construction has, of course, dipped. Yet, with the second and third quarters of this year 2011 expected to turn in 7.6-7.7 per cent growth, this spark does have the potential to translate into a better-than-expected fourth quarter. The strong underlying growth momentum has been hit on account of both relentless rate hikes and lack of support from government on policy moves. There has been some movement now on both these fronts. The RBI signalling the possibility of a pause comes as a big positive. It has, of course, made it clear that the pause hinges on inflation heading downwards, but more importantly, the RBI has moved beyond the headline number to measure the trajectory. On all accounts, inflation is heading down-wards slowly, though small spikes will remain. A pause, therefore, is imminent by the fourth quarter. So, will the rates begin to go down next year? If they do, how fast will the rate cuts be? All these questions will be better answered once we know how the fix plans to cooperate next year. The problem with the fix is that it is going to get even more strained, with the focus on subsidies growing in every dimension. What's worse, these subsidies push the possibility of a 4 per cent inflation level even further away, we are looking at 6.7 per cent inflation levels through the next year if growth is to be maintained at 7-8 per cent levels. That is the best we can do with a lazy government that appears to be resigned to such mediocre aims. It appears that the RBI has factored this into its policy now.

The other point of a new manufacturing policy, however, is not such an optimistic story. The policy says all the right things: simplification of regulations and procedures, exit mechanism, tax incentives, skill initiatives, green audits and so on. But the central focus is on National Investment and Manufacturing Zones (NIMZs). The simple question that begs to be answered is that even if these NIMZs work out as envisaged, what happens to the rest of the country? If laws can be avoided for some areas, why can't all industries and industrial areas be declared NIMZs? Why shouldn't there be a shift in business regulations and procedures across the country? Why shouldn't there be exit mechanisms for all units? Not every state can set up NIMZs, and more importantly, not every entrepreneur has the capacity to locate in these areas; effectively creating islands of excellence, without even trying to bring the others up to par with the basics, may push growth up a few points for a few years, but why go this route? Why will NIMZs work when SEZs did not? The government has wasted its and everyone's time. The issue is that the policy focus is not on the long term at all. If we have to resolve the pressing problem today that impacts the long term potential of the country, it's the need to kick start investment in a sustainable fashion. Getting the investment story right would also reduce inflationary pressures. If that is really so difficult, we should reconcile ourselves to a 7-8 per cent growth maximum being the best that India can do and focus on construction and services.

If inflation does not come down quickly, the government should try something else. It is suggested that the government should try a plan other than monetary tightening. Pulses, for example, had been a major source of inflation last year. This year, prices of pulses have dropped, thanks, in part, to some deft Planning Commission initiatives that saw the production of pulses nearly double. Vegetables stoke inflation at present. Stepping up the production of pulses is easier than stepping up the production of vegetables, thanks to the latter's perishable nature. This calls for a quantum leap in logistics: a cold chain and swift transport from production centres in villages to consumption centres in towns. And that will not come about on its own. Nimble trucks must procure vegetables from farms and accumulate them at climate-controlled collection centres to bring up volumes. From here, veggies must be moved in climate controlled containers to markets in towns. For this to happen, the Agricultural Produce Marketing Committee Act must be scrapped or modified to exempt perishables from its ambit in both the originating state and the consuming centre. The Act is meant to protect the farmer but ends up as a tool of entrenched middlemen to control prices and corner the bulk of the rise in price from farm-gate to retail. The rural roads project has been quite a success in states like Assam, many of them highly fertile. If refrigerated cars can be added to freight trains, and these run to a schedule rather than meander desultorily as goods trains run, veggies grown by Assamese farmers can beat down prices in Delhi. Bengal, Bihar and UP can join this vegetable train, with some key investment and coordinated efforts at the level of the producing states, the Railways and the consuming states.

Reforms in Eduction

A holistic education system helps people become discerning individuals. It helps them even during those dark and stormy times when anyone risks straying from the straight and narrow. Value-based education is the key to create a society that rises above materialistic goals. Those who criticize the focus on values must understand that materialism alone cannot be the purpose of life. A harmonizing balance of the material with the spiritual will help both society and individual to evolve. Let's not forget that education is that training which holds us in good stead when everything else seems to fail.

All normal human beings are born with powerful urge to learn. Almost all of them lose this urge, even before they have reached maturity. It is only the few who are so constituted that lack of learning becomes a nuisance. This is perhaps the most insidious of human tragedies. Children are wonders at learning their knowledge because of their powerful urge to learn. A child continuously asks 'why'. The why is the child's method of finding out. How many adults go about asking and thinking 'why'? How often they do it. The adults who lose this urge, stop learning. They stop growing intellectually, they stop changing.

Let's look at admission tests for engineering programmes, perhaps the largest one conducted in India. For decades, it has been implicitly assumed that physics, chemistry, maths (PCM) are good subjects to test after class XII for admission into engineering. But is this assumption valid, and do these tests form a good entrance test? Few, if any; studies have been done to examine this question. Other countries do not follow this approach. In the US, for example, the entrance test SAT is a general aptitude and thinking ability test, and many universities take admission in all programmes, including engineering, based on SAT scores. The insistence on PCM for entrance is more anomalous for information technology (IT) or computer science (CS) programmes, which form the bulk of the seats in engineering institutions, as the nature of computer sciences is such that it does not require proficiency in physics or chemistry for someone to do well. Studying the correlation of scores in major all-India entrance exams and class XII marks, with performance of students in the first semester in their CS/IT programme. In other words, how strongly performance in the entrance exams or class XII predicts performance in the first semester of a CS/IT programme. The rank correlation of a major all-India test for engineering with performance in these institutes was very weak, the performance in this entrance exam had no predictive value for performance in the institute. In other words, among the students admitted, those ranked in the bottom 10 per cent had about the same chances of doing well (or poorly) as students with a rank in the top 10 per cent. However, a reasonably strong correlation of class XII marks is associated with performance in all these institutes. That is, class XII performance is a reasonable predictor of how well a student does in these institutes. And a good correlation was found between performance in the aptitude test that was conducted for entrance and performance in the institute.

It seems clear that common "one size fits all" engineering tests which provide an ordered ranking of students are not suitable for selection into programmes like CS/IT, and can end up selecting students who may not have proper aptitude for such programmes. It is believed that research will find that similar situation exists with some other disciplines also. If we want to have a test that helps in selecting candidates who are most suitable for different programmes, it is best to have an entrance test which tests for aptitude as well as for a few subjects, and then gives the scores for different sections separately, rather than giving a ranking of candidates based on the sum of scores of all sections. With such scores, it will be up to the institutes to decide what weight they assign to different components for deciding the ranking for selecting candidates for different programmes. This will allow flexibility that different disciplines need for selecting appropriate candidates.

Such a test will also provide the ability to give weight to class XII performance, which will become just another component to be included. (Including class XII marks that will require normalization across different boards—a difficult, but doable exercise.) Overall, a test which has components to test for multiple orthogonal capabilities, and gives scores for each one separately, can open up possibilities of more rigorous and better suited selection criteria for different disciplines—that too, without requiring different exams for different disciplines or institutes.

There is a crying need for research in this area, and we need good research groups and centres which will study the effectiveness of exams on an ongoing basis, and conduct experiments, etc., to improve the tests. This research capability can then also be used to help reduce exam-related stress, and other such issues that need urgent attention in the country.

Let us do more to spread computer literacy. The 'world's cheapest computer' will finally see light of day. The ₹1,500 computing-cum-access device - a rejoinder to the $100 laptop used in the UNDP-backed global One Laptop per child programme has been over seven years in the making. Those years haven't treated India kindly as far as computer literacy goes. The direct correlation between a computer literate workforce and economic productivity has been proved time and again. In India's case, the IT sector accounts for about $78 billion worth of exports. But it employs only around 11 million people - a minuscule portion of our labour force. Factor in the increasing necessity of computer literacy in both classrooms and industries across the board and the demand is huge. But supply is minimum.

Government initiatives to spread computer literacy have fared poorly. In semi-urban and rural areas especially, there's often lack of basic educational infrastructure even when computers are provided. Lack of electricity, absence of computer literate teachers, inadequate security for equipment—have all these been problems. The new tablet-form in question can sidestep some of those issues for instance, with availability of solar power, its supply shouldn't be an issue. But there are several hurdles to overcome if we're to bridge the digital divide in this country. Internet access is increasingly a crucial part of computer literacy. We're faced with just a 6.9 per cent internet penetration rate as of 2010 and a serious lack of the infrastructure necessary to increase the user base. Much more needs to be done in these areas. Putting affordable computers in the market as a gateway device is an important step. But it's only the first one.

Three years ago, in 2008, 8,253 students scored an aggregate of 90 per cent and above in the Class XII Central Board of Secondary Education (CBSE) examinations. In 2011, that number has gone up to two and a half times, i.e., to 21,665. The rise in the number of students who have scored more than 95 per cent in aggregate in the CBSE class XII exams is even sharper, growing five and a half times from 384 in 2008 to 2,097 this year. Is the graduating CBSE class of 2011 simply much brighter than their peers three years earlier? Almost certainly not by that scale at any rate. What we are witnessing is an extraordinary degree of grade inflation where students of comparable ability to those say three years ago, or even 10 years ago, get a much higher grade for a similar performance. Far from helping students, grade inflation actually leads to serious distortions, often compromising standards. At the top end of the spectrum it becomes difficult to distinguish the truly exceptional students from those a rung below. At the lower end of the spectrum, it gives students with more limited abilities a false sense of academic worth. In 2011, a 90 per cent aggregate mark is of less value than it was in 2008. But at the school leaving age of 18, students tend not to analyze things in this comparative perspective. This leads to confusion, disappointment and hysteria, all of which have been witnessed in abundance this admission season as students from across the country line try to get into one of the premier colleges of India's most reputed university, the Delhi University.

Prima facie, cut-off marks which hover between 95 and 100 per cent, seem absurd. But that is the reality of getting admission into a B.Com Honours or Economics Honours course in the top five or six colleges of Delhi University. Colleges only have a limited number of seats and if more than 2,000 students in the CBSE alone have got over 95 per cent, upward pressure on cut-offs is understandable. There seems to be some evidence that the CBSE, which was once criticized for its subjective and error-prone examination system, has made an over-correction by making exams and evaluation completely objective. For example, students are now awarded full marks in English for an answer which may have poor grammar and sloppy language as long as it contains the right "key word." There has to be something terribly wrong in an examination system where just one word in an entire answer can get a student full marks. While grade inflation is a problem that needs to be addressed, policymakers also need to turn their attention to the fact that there simply aren't enough quality avenues for higher education in India. The number of students aspiring for higher education is growing rapidly. The number of good colleges remains stagnant. Many colleges and universities, particularly in provincial centres, have in fact declined over the years, putting more pressure on a select few in the major metros. This needs to change. The mushrooming of new, high quality colleges may eventually be the best antidote to grade inflation too.

Notes

Index

2 G,
- 92
- Auctions, 109
- Case, 118
- Controversy, 37, 38
- Engendered Judicial Interventions, 37
- Losses, 116
- Scam, 37, 108, 109, 116, 224
- Spectrum, 108, 110, 111, 113, 114, 116
  - Auctions, 118
  - Scam, 162
  - Scandal, 116
- Telecom Policy, 37
- Telecom Spectrum, 28

3 G,
- Auction, 114
- Spectrum, 111, 114

Aam Aadmi's 'Halla Bol', 107
Above Poverty Line, 34
Access to Education, 248
Accountability, 30
- And Competition, 132
- And Transparency, 156

Acharya Shantideva, 211
Ad Bustors, Art Magazine, 61
Adam, 24
Adhyatma Vidya, 211
Adivasis, 92
Administration Laws, 83
Administrative
- Challenge, 143
- Reform Commission, 88

Advancement of Technology, 268
African
- Development Bank, 121
- Nations, 157

Agartala's Bamboo Industry, 26
Agarwal, Rajeev, Vegetable Promoters, 117
Agarwal, Vijay,117-118
Agitation and Non-Violence, 155
Agricultural
- Growth, 253
- Produce Marketing Committee (APMC), 297

Ahalwat, Satwanti, Haryana Labour Commissioner, 292
Ahimsa, 155, 156

And Satyagraha, 154
And Swaraj, 58
Ahuja, Shiney, Actor, 173
Aid
Agencies, 129
Dependency, 132
Funded Projects and Programmes, 131
Industry, 124, 132
Related Corruptions, 128
Transparency, 129
Aid-Funded Projects, 123
AIMS Indian Project, 86
Akbar, 201
Alcoholism, 227
Allotment Terms, 45
Ambani, Anil, 117
Reliance Commercial, 117
Ambedkar, BR, 136
Speech in Constituent Assembly, 136
Ambit Capital, 53
America, 127
America's
Bill Gates, 64
Occupy Wall Street Agitation, 62
American
Dream, In Disastrous Money Chase, 62
Fall, 62
Recovery and Reinvestment Act, 158
Ancient
Monuments, 68
Ram or Egypt, 196
Techniques of Meditation, 226
Andhras, 198
Anglo-Hindu School, 200
Anil Dhirubhai Ambani Group, 54
Anna Hazare, 108, 154
Army, 154
Bill, 153
Brigade, 92
Is India, 107
Hazare's Crusade Against Corruption, 67
Movement, 153
Ramlila-Ground Marching Song, 107
Supporters, 107
see also Hazare, Anna
Anti-
Anna bias, 138
Corruption
Agencies, 119
Framework, 87, 88
Laws, 88
Measures, 125
Movement, 27, 39
Policies, 120
Protest, 159
Score, 100, 101, 103
Graft Watchdog, 134, 140
Antiochos, Greek King, 198, 199
Anti-Poverty
Crusaders, 36
Program, 32, 33, 35
Schemes, 36
Anubhav Plantation Scam, 266
Aplysia, 8
Arab Spring, 62
Archaic Laws, 84
Arjuna, 209
Armed Forces Special Right Act, Abolition of-, 168
Armies, 165
Art
Forms, 21
Of Living, 230
Ashoka, 196, 199
As Dhammashoka, 197
Conquest of Kalinga, 195
Imperial Rule, 198
Pillar at Sarnath, 198
Reign, 195, 197
Ashram Life, 218
Asian
Countries, 253

Leaders, 252
Assamese Farmers, 298
Atman, 209
Aurangzeb, 201
Authoritarianism, 62
Autogenic Training in Western Countries, 233
Ayodhya, 195

Baba Ramdev, 144, 145
Bahamas, 162
Balwa, Shahid, 116, 117, 118
Ban on Formation of Trusts, 95
Bangladesh, 28, 248
War, 31
Bankers and Brokers, 62, 64
Banking System, 105, 106
Barak Obama Mooring, 30
Basu, Kaushik, Economist, 142
Bedi, Kiran, 144
Behavioural Disorder, 14
Behura, Siddarth, Secretary Telecom, 116
And Chandolia, 119
Bell, Griffin, 103
Belly Movement, 243
Beloved-of-Gods, 198, 199
Below Poverty Line, 34, 35
Benami Property, 76
Bengal
And Kerala, 292
Presidency, 202
Bentham, Jeremy, Philosopher, 142
Bentinck, Lord William, Governor, 202
Bhagavad Gita, 190, 191, 208, 212, 213, 220
Bhalla, Surjit, Economist, 70
Bharadwaja, Valmiki Disciple, 194
Bhasmasur, 192
Bhojas, 198
Bidding Process, 162
Big Brother Govt., 63
Bigotry, 14
Bihar,
Chief Minister, 176
State Mineral Corporation, 47
Bilateral Donor, 124
Biochemical Studies, 233
Birth of Samuel, 222
Black Money, 104
Blair, Tony, UK PM, 157
Boddh Dharma, 224
Bomb Blast in South and Central Mumbai, 178
Bombay High Court, 148
Bradley, Omar, Army General, 180
Brahma Sabha, 199, 200
Brain
Power, 75
Wave Pattern, 232
Breathing Exercises, 240
Bribe, 39, 74,86,87,96,108,118,162
Givers, 159
Bribe/Illegal Money, 97
Bribery, 129
BRICKS Nations, 294
Britain,
Murder Rate in-, 188
Police System, 167
British
Citizen Charter, 85
East India Company, 202
Exchequer, 105
Laws, 203
Raj, 172
Rule, 199
Soldiers, 31
Taxman, 105
Broadband Network, 26
Broken Window Syndrome, 267
Buckingham Palace, 107
Buddha, Gautama, 198, 225, 226, 239
Teachings, 195
Buddhacarita, 193
Buddhism, 196, 198, 199, 225
In Ceylon, 196
Buddhist
Meditation, 225, 226

Morality, 197
Policy, 196
Sutras, 211
Buffet Tax, 264
Bureaucracy, 28, 75
Bureaucrats, 30

Cairo to Manhattan, 62
Calorie Fundamentals, 32
Campaign Against Sati, 202
Canada, 165, 261
Capital Budgets, 122
Capitalism, 61, 65
In US, 65
Captive Mining, 47
Care Home For Women in Patna, 283
Carey, Williams, 202
Cayman Islands, 105
CBI
Investigation, 37, 54
Vs Blue Sky, 274
CBS Reality, 14
Central
Board of Secondary Education (CBSE), 301, 302
Bureau of Investigation (CBI), 37, 54, 113, 116, 117, 118, 141, 224, 274
Investigation Agency (CIA) (US), 287
Vigilance Commission (CVC), 92
Chanakya, Famous Economist, 208
Chandolia, RK, A Raja's Former Secretary, 118
Chandrasekhar, R, Secretary Telecom, 115
Charitable Trust, 93
Charter Mark Award Scheme, 86
Chavez, Hugo, 93
Chawla, Ashok, 163
Cheap Excavations, 146
Cheating, 9, 50
Worst Crime, 7
Chhatisgarh, 46, 261
Chief Election Commissioner, 91
Child Marriage, 200
Children Fundamental Rights, 283
China, 80, 97, 146, 253, 295
And India's Manufacturing Sectors, 288
Population, 172
China's Success in Poverty Reduction, 253
Chinese
Imports, 295
Martial Arts, 16
Nationals (Mafia) Operation in-, 172
Hong Kong—China, 172
Philosophy, 18
Chit Funds Act, 1982, 266
Cholas, 198, 199
Chota Rajan, 173
Chromosomes, 22
Churchill, Winston, 31, 103, 107
Chyavana, Great Seer, 193
Cineyug Films, 118
Citizen's Charter, 85, 86
Citizens Interest Group (CIG), 78
Charter, 78
Civil
Administration, 197
Disobedience, 136
Disorder, 119
Rights, 189
Service Rules, 108
Society, 84, 107, 125, 130, 133, 153, 160
Society Activists, 36
Society Movements Against Corruption, 39
Society Organization (CSO), 77, 130, 159, 160, 161
Classical Chinese Philosophy, 16
Coal
Block Allotment, 45
Block Corruption in Allotment, 45
Mines, 47

Nationalization,
Act, 46
Policy, 46
Coalgate, 45
Coalition
Government, 116
Politics, 40
Code of Discipline, 229
Colleges and Universities, 303
Colonial
India, 107
Rule, 58
Commonwealth Games, 134, 163
Communal Divide, 179
Communication Skills, 57
Community Policing, 180
Company's Act, 1956, 84
Competition Commission of India, 259
Comptroller and Auditor General (CAG), 41, 45, 90, 111-115, 117, 122, 141
Report, 46
Sources, 115
Compulsory Voting, 42
Computer Literate Teachers, Absence of-, 301
Concept of Vegetarian, 197
Concessions to Miners Given by Portuguese, 148
Confucianism, 17
Congress Leadership, 154
Connecticut General Assembly, 19
Construction Services, 277
Consultancy Industries, 129
Control Autonomic Nervous System, 231
Corporate Governance and Ethics, 159
Correa, Charles, Well known Architect, 149
Corrupt
Business Politics Nexus, 52
Countries, 80
India Amongst -, 80
Politicians, 88
Practices, 82
System, 82
Corruption
Act, 1947, 84
Among Aid Recipients, 121
Amongst Public Servants, 84
Among Conflicts, 157
And Crime, 12
Can be Uprooted by Social Awakening, 8
Combating, 73-163
Defined, 96
Defined by Transparency International, 96
Economies of-, 98
Free India, 75
Free Society, 75, 247
In Aid, 120, 129
In Allotment of Coal Blocks, 454
In Bilateral Aid, 120
In India, 76, 101
In Ten Sectors, (CTS), 76
Administration, 76
Education, 76
Health, 76
Judiciary, 76
Land and Building, 76
Police, 76
Power, 76
Railways, 76
Ration (Public Distribution System), 76
Telephones, 76
Political, 120
Rampant in-, 79
Angola, 79
Bangladesh, 79
Indonesia, 79
Kenya, 79
Madagaskar, 79
Nigeria, 79
Paraguay, 79
Ranking Data, 79
Scams, 26

Scandal, 38
Types, 82
Counter-
Insurgency Plan, 176
Terrorism Centres, 180
Crash of 2008, 62
Creativity and Dishonesty, 51
Credit and Employment Scheme, 69
Crime (s), 12, 14, 15, 19, 134, 171, 172, 187, 247
Control, 164
Organized, 171
Rate, 224
Syndicate, 173
Crime—Prevention Mechanism, 17
Criminal
Aggression, 181
Conspiracy, 116, 117
Group, 172
Groups Organization, 172
Justice Administration, 168
Justice System (CJS), 167, 169
Mind, 181
Organisations in Pre-industrialized Japan and Italy, 171
Tendencies, 184
Trial, 174
Criminals, 8, 11, 13, 14, 16, 19-21, 135, 142, 166-168, 171, 184, 186, 274
Criminalization of Politics, 134
Cronyism and Corruption, 121
Cross Border Investigation, 87
Crude Oil, 250
CS/IT Program, 299, 300
Cultural
Factors, 15
Pattern, 182

Danes, 202
Daoist
Metaphysics, 17
Philosophy, 17
Darul Uloom Deoband, Islamic Seminary, 171
Darwinian Natural Selection, 165
Dawood Ibrahim Kaskar, 173, 177
Day of Judgment, 221
DB Realty, 117, 118
DC Bono, 214
Death Penalty, 19
Debt
Crises in Europe, 26
Initiatives, 126, 127
Decentralized Governance, 75
Decontrol of
Diesel, 280
Fuel Prices, 258
Deep Meditation, 22
Defective Electoral System, 43
Deficit Reduction Plan, 256
Delhi
High Court, 114, 117, 180
Mumbai Industrial Corridor (DMIC), 286
Slums, 144
Delhi—Uttar Pradesh, 298
Democratization and Liberalization, 125
Demonic Forces, 13
Fear—Ambition, 13
Denmark, 98
Deregulation, 119, 258, 259, 260, 281
Deregulatory Route, 295
Deshmukh, Vilasrao, CM Maharashtra, 178
Destruction of Places of Worship, 137
Development
Assistance Committee, 129
Model, 247
Policy, 248
Projects, 177
Strategies, 285
Dhamma, 199
Disadvantaged Groups, 252
Distorted Economy, 65
Distric
Bhind and Morena (MP), 289
Mineral Foundation, 150

DMK in Tamil Nadu, 69
DNA teleportation, 23
Domestic
 Economy, 35
 Industrial Development, 28
 Violence, 13
Donor
 Corruption, 129
 Country, 120
Donors, 125, 126, 130, 132
Doshi, Gautam, 116
Dowry, 174
 Harassment, 175
Dualism, 18
Duke University, 49
Dumb Doll, 107
Durga Killing- (DK), 192
 Madhukaitava, 192
 Mahishasur, 192
 Shumb-Nishumbh, 192
Dutch, 201
Dyfunction Family, 14

Eagle Ford and Permian Basins Texas, 262
Economic
 Governance, 38
 Growth, 36, 79, 97, 111, 124, 247, 252, 253, 256
 Reform in Developing Countries, 288
 Reforms, 125
 System, 64
Economies, 65
Economy, 26, 46, 103, 105, 149, 157, 167, 257, 294, 295
 And Poverty, 131
 Capabilities, 28
 System, 64
Educating and Empowering, 81
Education, 14, 62
 And Health, 247
 And Health Care, 251
 And Skills, 36
 And Technology and Infrastructure, 294
 Development Fund, 121
 Health Care and Income, 249
 Moral and Ethical, 78
Educational
 Infrastructure, 301
 Levels, 16
 Political and Economic System, 12
 Recreational and Religious Characteristics, 15
 System, 32
Ego, 24
Election, 43
 Commission (EC), 44
 Reforms, 133
 Rules, 133
Electoral
 Reforms, 42, 44, 76, 132, 133, 135
 Rules, 75
Electricity Tariffs, 45
Electromagnetic (EM), 21
Electronic
 Media, 278
 Voting Machine (EVM), 42, 43
Elmer, Rudolf, 106
Embezzlement of Public Funds, 79
Employment Guarantee, 35, 36
Endogamy, 201
Energy Sources, 34
Enforced
 Authority, 172
 Widowhood, 201
Entrepreneurs and Researches, 27
Entrepreneurship, 28
Eradicating Poverty, 35
Eradication of *Sati*, 202
Eritrea, 260
Ernst Stavro Blofeld, 49
European
 Central Banking, (ECB), 68
  Frankfurt, 68
  Germany, 68
  Sydney—Latin America, 68

Commission, 121
Powers, 201
Union, 120
Evanglical Church in Britain, 202
Evil Genius, 49
Extortion, 175
Extractive Industries Technology Initiative (EITI), 157
Extremist and Militant Forces, 169
Extremists, 170

Fair Winged Birds, 25
Faltering Economy of US, 26
Family Structures, 16
Farming and Handicrafts, 27
Fatwa Against Terrorism, 171
Federal Bureau of Investigation (FBI), 15
FEMA (Foreign Exchange Management Act), 276
Feuds, 30
Fields, WC, American Comedian and Writer, 132
Fifth Pillar, 87
Fight Against Corruption, 103
Finance
Ministry, 111
Research, 27
Financial
Inclusion, 253
Institutions, 257
Meltdown, 64
Projects, 135
Sector, 266
Legislation, 293
System, 63, 70, 79
Transparent and Accountable, 63
Finland – Sweden, 79
Fiscal
Finland – Sweden, 79
Fitzgerald, Scott, 64
Great Gatsby Book, 64
Five Year Plan
(2nd), 47
(5th), 47
(12th), 267
Flagship Schemes, 177
Flow of Fresh Water from Mandovi Zuari, 148
Food and Agriculture Organization (FAO), 32
Foreign
Direct Investment (FDI), 256
Inflows, 295
Regime, 293
Donations, 160
Exchange Regulatory Authority (FERA), 276
Exchange Resource, 256
Informers and Whistleblowers, 271
Forests and Minerals, 91
Formation of Interest Group of Citizens, 77
Formula I Grand Prix in India, 27
Fraud and Corruption, 8
Frauds, 9, 268-271
And Land Grabs, 135
Fraudulent Practices, 125
Free
Market, 65
Software Market, 66
Software Movement, 66
Software Movement, Founding Guru, Richard Stellmen, 66
Will, 19
Freedom
Movement, 58
Led by Gandhi, 141
Of Representative and Speech, 7
Of Speech and Expression, 62
French, 201
Tax Authority, 278
Fuel
Inflation, 280
Pricing, 261
Retailers, 260
Fundamental

Dualism, 40
Rights, 282, 283

Gambling Dens, 173
Gandhi (Gandhiji), 107, 153, 220
Gandhi,
And Non-Violence, 218
Mahatma, 12, 207, 216, 251
Mohandas Karamchand, 103, 217, 218
Gandhi's (Mahatma)
Ashram, 219
Belief in Pooran Swaraj, 59
Leadership, 58
Satyagraha, 155
Gandhian Idealism, 107
Gandhi, Shailesh, 144
Gandhigiri to Annagiri, 107
Gaurav Mehta of Ambit Capital, 53, 54
Gautama Buddha, 226
General Excise Act, 268
Genocide, 188, 189
George Saros Funded Institute for New Economic Thinking (INET), 65
Ghana, 157
Global
Anti-Capitalism Protest, 61
Coalitions from Africa, 128
Competition Bidding, 45
Economy, 254
Financial Integrity, 272
Financial System, 254
Human Rights, 249
Recession 35
Slowdown, 266, 293
Terrorism, 248
Warming, 15
Globalization, 253
Goa, 146, 147
Goa, Daman and Mining Concessions Act, 148
Goenka, Vinod, DB Realty MD, 116, 117
Goethe's Faust, 49
Good
Capital and Bad Capital, 64
Governance, 73
Governance System, 91
Govt. Aid and Corruption, 119
Graft
Crusade, 26
In Coal Mining, 46
Gram Panchayat, 286
Graphic Designs, 50
Greed, 73, 91
Greek
Buddhist Monks, 199
Crisis, 254
Kings, 198
Alexander, 198
Antiochos, 198
Antigonos, 198
Magas, 198
Ptolemy, 198
Greeks in India, 199
Group
C-Staff, 108
Discrimination, 254
Of 20 (G-20), 271, 293
Of 20 Industrialized Nations, 72
Growth
Oriented Policies, 247
Sector, 161
GST (Goods and Services Tax), 277-279
Guarantee of Free Speech, 284
Guha, Ramachandra, 153
Guilt, 215, 216
And Frustration, 215
Guilty Feeling, 215
Gulf Oil, 263
Gungi Gudiya, 107
Guru Nanak, 201

Haiti, 98
Haji Mastan, 173
Half Naked Fakir, Winston

Churchill, 103, 107
Harassment Corruption, 142
Harris, Sam, Neuroscientist, 19
Harvard
Business School, 49
University Study, 22
Haves and Haves Not, 27
Hazare, Anna, 26, 44, 88, 90-92, 135, 136, 137, 138, 140, 141, 143, 144
Anti Corruption Movement, 134
Socialist Activists, 133
see also Anna Hazare
Headley, David, 179
Healing, 231
Health
And Education Institutions, 85
And Education Sectors, 76
Corruption in-, 76
And Education Services, 279
Education, 27
Hegde, Santosh, 52, 147
Former Lokayukta of Karnataka, 52, 54
Hellenic Countries, 198
Herbal Medicine, 199
Hero-Worship, 136, 137
Hewart, Justice Gordon, 103
High
Beat Music, 21
Court, Bombay, 148
Court, Delhi, 180
Speed Fibre Optic, 26
Higher Education, 303
Himachal Pradesh, 261
Hindu
Funeral Practices, 199
Religion, 200
Traditions, 200
Hinduism, 201
Hirankshpu, 192
Hiranyaksh, 192
Honesty Score, 100
HSBC Geneva, 271
Human Rights, 125
Framework, 33
Humayun, 201
Hunter-Gatherer, 181, 182
Societies, 188
Hydrotherapy, 218
Hypertension—Insomnia, 233
Hypertension—Rheumatic Disorder, 234
Hyundai Factory Chennai, 291

ICICI Bank, 51
Illegal
Graftification, 142
Mining, 134, 152
Scam, 224
Scandals, 152
Properties, Sealing of-, 90
Import Markets, 35
Inclusive
Growth, 252, 253, 266, 267
Trade Agenda, 29
Income
Disparity, 63
Tax Act, 82, 152
Incredible India, 107
Indebted Poor Countries, 126
India
Against Corruption, 143
A Developing Nation, 7
A Soft State, 166
And China, 252
Inclusive Innovation Fund (IIIF), 26, 27
Most Regulated Economy, 82
Regulators, 266
India's
9/11, 178
Coal Sector, 46
Democracy, 90
Domestic Laws, 88
Financial Capital, 178
Financial Sector, 295
Fight Against Corruption, 101
85th Among 180 Countries, 101

Foreign Debt, 105
Inflation, 293
Leadership, 158
Market Potential, 26
National Manufacturing Policy, 28
Panchayats, 26
Population, 89
Reforms, 289
Unique Development Pattern, 28
Vulnerability and External Shocks, 294
Youth, 11

Indian
12th Five Year Plan, 266
Courts, 273
Economic Role, 110
Economy, 26, 51, 266
Governance, 40, 157
Income Tax Act, 276
Industries, 268, 287
Jugaad, 225
Law, 166
Nationality, 272
Penal Code, 81, 84, 173, 174, 275
Political Economy, 40
Price—Highest in World, 260
Tax Authority, 106
Tax Evaders, 272
Telecom Vs Motorola, 274

Indira
Awas Yojana, 158
Is India, 107

Indonesian Island of Bali, 203

Industrial
Development, 111
Dispute Act, 291, 292
Economy, 256
Growth, 26, 256
Relations, 288
Unrest, 291, 292

Industries And Industrial Areas, 297

Industry, 40

Infant Mortality Rate (IMR), 32

Inflammatory Speech, 21

Inflation, 294-297, 302

Informal Economy, 28

Information Technology, 76, 78, 88
System, 158, 270

Infrastructure, 35
And Industry, 134
Development, 257

Inheritance Rights of Women, 200

Inner Training, 225

Innovators And Finance, 26

Inscriptions, 197
(13th), 196

Institute for New Economic Thinking, 65

Institutional
And Legal Framework, 33
Corruption, 134
Mechanism, 59
Reforms, 58, 77

Integrated Emergency Policy, 258

Integrity Workshop, 131

Intelligence
Agencies, 169, 178
Training of Personnel, 180
Gathering, 179, 180

Internal Security Reform, 178

International
Agencies and NGO, 157
Finance, 122
Monetary Fund, 126, 254
Oil Prices, 259
Tax Evaders, 106
Trade Agenda, 28

Internet Rates, 294

Inter-State Wars, 165

Intra-Party Wars, 30

Investigative Journalism, 131

Iraq or Myanmar, 98

Iraq-Daifur, 188

Irish American Street Gangs, 172

Iron Ore, 149, 150

Islam, 23

Island of Integrity, 128

Israel, 97

Italian Mafia, 172
Italian-American Mafia, 172
J&K Minerals, 47
Jacob, Jack, General, 31
Jainism, 155
Jan
    Lok Bill, 137
    Lokpal Bill, (JLB), 143, 144
        Campaigns, 144
        Second Freedom Struggle, 143
    Sanghatan, 144, 145
    Sunvai Success, 144
Japan, 172, 263
    Constitution, 263
Jayaprakash Narayana, 143
Jewish Religious Year, 221
Jews, 220, 222
Jharia Belt in Jharkhand, 46
Jihadi Theocrat, 135
Job Generation, 75
Joint Parliamentary Committee (JPC), 114-116
    Constitution of -, 116
Jokepal, 108
Joseph, Warioba, Chairman, President, Commission of Enquiry against Corruption, 124
JP Movement, 141
Judgments of Courts of Law, 187
Judicial
    Interpretation, 284
    Reforms, 119
Judiciary, 51, 75, 84, 93-95, 160, 167, 168, 281-284
Jurisdiction, 87

Kabutarkhana in Dadar, 178
Kadekodi, Gopal K, Environmentalist, 148
Kahu, Dominique Strauss, IMF Chief, 173
Kakodkar, Rajendra, 146, 147
Kalaignar TV, Director, 117, 118
Kalidas, 198
Kalinga, 195, 196
    War, 197, 224
Kalle Lasn, 61
Kambojas, 198
Kanimozhi, K
    Bail Application, 118
    DMK MP, 117
    MP Rajya Sabha, 116, 117
Kargil, 180
Karim Lala, 172
Karim Moran, Film Director, 117
Karma, 213
Karunanidhi, K, DMK Chief, 116
Kasturba, Mahatma Gandhi's Wife, 217
Kejriwal, Arvind, 143
Kenya, 126
Kerala, 248
Keralaputras, 199
Khadigram, 59
Khap Justice, 137
Kick Backs, 79
Killing – Intoxicants, 229
King Ashoka, Transformation to Boddh Bhikshu, 8
King Piyadasi, 199
King's Law Against Sport Hunting and Branding, 197
Kirit Parikh Committee, 259, 260
Kol Nidre Prayer, 222
Krishna, 190, 191, 208, 209 *see also under* Shri Krishna
    Incarnation, 195
Kundalini Meditation, 233
Kusa and Lava, 195

Labour
    Laws, 291
    Reforms, 289
    Unrest in India, 291
Lal Batti, 91
Land
    Acquisition Rules, 134
    And Housing for Bribes, 134

Grafts, 91
Records, 135
Latin America, 261
Laure, Maurice, Joint Dir French Tax Auth., 279
Law
And Order, 168
Commission, 174, 175
Enforcement Agencies, 15
Makers and Policy Framers, 134
Of Ahimsa, 217
Laws Against Corruption, 143
Leadership, 28, 37, 57, 100, 169
Dark Side of -, 57
Economic and Political, 29
Leases, 48
Least Corrupt Countries, 101
Left Wing Extremism (LWE), 179
Legal
Mechanism, 82
Terrorism, 173, 174
Legislation, 59, 90
Legislative Deterrence, 140
Lehman Shutdown, 254
LGT Bank, 271
Liberalization, 119
And Globalization, 83
Liberation, 206, 231
From Personhood, 204
License Permit Quota Regime, 82
Licensed Technology, 111
Limbic System, 205, 206
Linus Torvalds, 66
Little Tennessee River, 103
Loan Funded Projects, 131
Local Anti-Corruption Allies, 132
Lojong, 211
Lok Pal Movement, 90
Lokayukta Report, 141
Lokpal, 75, 88, 108
And Lokayukta Bill, 90
Bill, 76, 135, 137, 140, 141, 143, 144, 156
Issue, 133
Legislation, 106
Movement, 133
Long Term Growth and Economic Success, 157
Lord
Brahma, 194
Buddha, 232, 233
Denning, 103
Lower Manhattan, 71
Lutyen's Delhi, 31

Mafias, 135
Mahabharata, 195
Maharashtrawadi Gomantak Party, 152
Mahatma Gandhi National Rural Employment Guarantee Act, 253
Mahendra, King Ashoka's Son, 196
Mahesh Yogi, 232
Malawi, 260
Malcolm, Governor, 202
Male Criminal, 186
Malnutrition, 32
Malpractices, 134
Mamta, 107
Managing Policy Reforms, 287
Mandovi and Zuari, 148
Manmohan Singh, former Indian PM, 273
Manufacturing
And Mining, 296
Policy, 285
Manufacturing Zones, 257
Maoist, 177
Leaders, 175
Political Philosophy, 176
Rebellion, 176
Threat, 175, 176
Maoists, 92, 176
Maran Brothers, 54
Member, Ruling Coalition, 54
Marine Snail, 8
Market
Capitalism, 64
Economy, 65, 119

Structures, 143
Marx, 63
And Mammon, 107
Mass Slaughter, 21
Material Nature, 213
Materialism, 9, 14, 164
Matka, 173
Matrimonial Litigation, 174
Mauryan Empire, 198
Maya, 107
Mazdoor Kisan Shakti Sanghatan (MKSS), 144
Media, 75
Medical Research Centre of Bombay Hospital, 242
Meditation, 208, 212, 217, 225, 227, 229, 231
And Spiritual Practices, 8
Course, 240
Methods of-, 232
Of Yoga, 233
On DNA, 22
Meditation—Techniques, 225
Mental
Impulses, 231
Impurity (ies), 241, 224-245
Peace and Energy, 215
Metals and Mining, 53, 54
Micath White, 61
Micro Finance, 250
Middle
Class America, 63
East, 261
Migration to Cities, 89
Migratory Birds, 29
V-Shaped Flight Formation, 29
Militancy in Jammu and Kashmir, 168
Military Intelligence (MI), 180
Mill, John Stuart, 136
Mind Therapy (Spirituality), 18, 20
Mine
Economy, 146
Operations, 147
Chowgules, 147
Salgaocars, 147
Sesa Goa, 147
Timblos, 147
Owners, 149
Miners, 148
Mines and Mineral Development and Regulation Act 1957 (MMDR ACT), 48
Mining
Barons, 52
Reddy Brothers Karnataka, 52
Bill, 149, 151
Leases, 146, 148
Legislation, 149
Minerals and Metals, 149
Sector, 150
Ministries- Finance and Home, 30
Ministry of
Coal, 45, 49
Environment and Forest, 148
Power, 49
Miscarriage of Justice, 15
Mobile
Licences, 117
Revolution, 41
Technology, 157
Telephony, 111, 118
Telephony in India, 41
Modern
Children TV Program, 189
Technology, 47
Mohammad Athar, 179
Monarchial Parliamentary Democracy, 195
Monetary
Policy, 294
Rewards, 51
Money Laundering Act, 76
Monitoring Committees, 85
Montagnier, Luc, 21
French Scientist, 21
Nobel Prize Winner, 21
Movement of Reformist Bengalis, 200
MPs Local Area Development Fund, (MPLAD), 40

Mudaliar Varadarajan, 173
Mukherjea, Saurath, 53
Mulayam and Marxist, 106
Multi-
 Acre Palaces, 31
 Jurisdiction Conflict, 287
 Lateral Agencies, 120
 Party Parliamentary Democracy, 43
Mumbai
 Bomb Blasts, 1993, 173
 Serial Blasts (1993), 170
 Crime, 177
 Underworld, 173
Murder Rate in Britain, 188
Musashi Miyamoto, Samurai Warrior, 13
Muslim
 Community, 179
 Employees, 170
 Federalism, 171
 Psyche, 171
MV Javali Vs Mahajan Borewell and Co., 273

Nabhakas, 198
Nabhapamkits, 198
Nair, Hari, 116
Narada, 193
Narakas, 21
 Reserved for Murders, Rapists,--, 21
Nariman, Fali, 153
Nation's
 Iron and Magnesium Ore Deposits, 146
 Resources, 91
National
 Advisory Council, (NAC), 36, 75
 Alliance of Peoples Movement, 144
 Borders, 172
 Coal Development Corporation (NCDC), 47
 Collaboration, 47
  Former West Germany, 47
  France, 47
  Japan, 47
  Poland, 47
  Soviet Union, 47
 Commission Report, 180
 Counter Terrorism Centres, 180
 Institute of Oceanography, (NIO), 146, 148
 Integrity System, 130
 Investment And Manufacture Zone (NIMZ), 285, 286, 288, 296, 297
 Rural Employment Guarantee Work (NREG), 56
 Rural Employment Guarantee Act (NREGA), 36, 290, 291
 Security, 169
Nationalization of Coal Mines, 47
Native
 American Skeletons, 188
 Americans, 189
NATO
 Allies, 263
 Partners, 263
Natural
 Disaster, 119
 Dualities, 16
 Justice, 103
 Resources, 161
Navanirman Movement, 143
Naxalite Affected States, (NAS), 176
 Bihar, 176
 Chhatisgarh, 176
 Jharkhand, 176
 Maharashtra, 176
 Odisha, 176
 West Bengal, 176
Naxalites, 175
Negative
 Traits into Positive Qualities, 7
 Vote, 44
Nehru (Jawaharlal), 153
Nehru's

Quit Daughter, 107
Socialistic Rural Agenda, 89
Netherlands, 165
Netravati Wildlife Sanctuary at Colombo, 146
Neurological Scientists, 8
Neurosciences, 65
New
Economic Foundation in London, 65
Technologies, 252
Telecom Policy, 1999, 111
York Stock Exchange, (NYSE), 61
Zealand, 98, 165
No to Bribes, 86
No Vote Option, 133
Noble Peace Prize, 189
Noida Model of Uttar Pradesh, 286
Non-
Cooperation, 136
Governmental Organizations (NGO), 36, 78, 94, 124, 129, 143, 282
Workers, 68
Sectarian Techniques, 230
Violence, 156, 197, 217
Ahimsa, 197
Disobedience, 154
Movement, 141
Northern Ghats, 148
NRIs, 174
NSG Commanders, 178
Nuclear
Energy Projects, 137
Giants, 180
Power, 70

Obama, Barack, US President, 70, 107, 264
Occupy Phoenix Protest, 62
Odisha, 195
Offenders, 14, 21
Official Poverty Line, 32
Oil
Imports, 263
Industries in Africa, 157
Marketing Companies, 258, 259
OM Meditation, 242
Emmet Fox Exercises, 223
On-Line Voting, 42
OP Saini's Court (Special Judge), 116
Opposite Party, 37
Organization for Economic Cooperation and Development (OECD), 129
Organized
Crimes, 172
Group, 171
Original Ban in Bengal (Sati), 203
OWS (Occupy Wall Street) Movement, 62
Protest, 64, 65

Pakistan, 28
Pakistan's
ISI, 177
Macho Yahya Khan, 107
Pakistani Muslims, 170
Pali
Language, 226
Sources, 199
Panaji, 147
Panchayati Raj Institutions, 251
Pandyas, 198, 199
Paramilitary Forces, 176
Parekh, Deepak, Chairman HDFC, 51
Parliament And Assemblies, 76
Parliamentarians, 91
Parliamentary
Committee, 131
Constituencies, 89
Democracy, 90
Parsayat, Ajit, 168
Parshuram Killed Shahasrabahu, 192
Patanjali
Sage, 232
Yoga, 22, 217
Pensions, 142

Petri-dish, 8
Petro Products, 263, 264
Petroleum Planning and Analysis Cell (PPAC), 281
Philosophy of Dong Zhongshu, 17
Photo-Electric Plethysmograph, 241
Physics, Chemistry and Mathematics (PCM), 299
Pillars and Rocks, 197
Pink Chuddi Campaign, 89
Pinker, Steven, Harvard Psychology Professor, 164
Pipara, Surendra, 116
Pitinikas, 198
Planning, 47
Planning Commission, 30-32, 34, 288, 297
Plant Domestication, 182
Pluralism, 119
Policies and Planning, 77
Policy
- And Program Framework, 81
- Formulations, 282
- On Coal, 48

Political
- Agitation, 155
- Class, 40, 106
- Corruption, 70
- Donation, 151, 152
- Leaders, 62
- Leadership, 40
- Nexus, 51
- Parties, 40, 42, 43, 45, 76, 90, 106, 129, 151, 152, 161, 260
- Patronage, 132
- Reforms, 132

Politically Corrupt India's Democracy, 87
Pollution, 73
- Free Environment, 284

Polygamy, 200
Ponzi Schemes, 266
Population Density, 15
Portuguese, 201
Poverty
- And Corruption, 100
- Official Definition, 31

Power Plants, 46
PPP Projects, 159
Practising Vipassana, 227
Prajnaparamita, 211
Pranayama, 232
Prashant Bhushan, 143, 144
Presalt oil fields Offshore in Brazil, 262
Press Freedom, 284
Prevention Of
- Corruption Act (PCA), 1988, 77, 81, 84, 85
- Money Laundering Act, 276

Preventive Measures, 130
Print and Electronic Media, 78
Private
- Equity Players, 27
- Sector Bribery, 88
- Sector Governance, 124

Privatization, 119
- Of Water, 70
- Process, 124

Privy Council in London, 202
Procurement
- Contracts, 123
- Procedure, 180

Promissory Note, 87
Prophet Moses, 222
Prosperity Score, 100
Protesters, 62, 67, 70
Psychology of Criminal Mind, 180
Psychosomatic Changes, 232
Psych-Physical Structure, 240
Public
- Accountability, 134
- Delivery of-, 33
  - Education, 33
  - Food, 33
  - Health Care, 33
- Interest Litigation (PIL), 44, 52
- Service Reforms, 130

Punitive Measures, 13

PURA, 250, 251
Puranas, 21

Quit India, 59
Quran, 24

Racism, 13, 14
Radiation, 21, 23
Radical Innovation And Transformation, 66
Raghuram Rajan, 153
Raine, Adrian, Psychologist, 184
Raja, A, 109, 116, 117, 119
  Telecom Minister, 118
Rajdharma, Concept of-, 195
Ram
  Pradhan Committee, 178
  Sena, 89
Rama
  And Lakshmana, 192
  Of Ayodhya, 195
Rama's Incarnation, 195
Ramayana, 191, 193, 194, 198, 224
Ramlila Maidan Delhi, 91, 155
Raniganj
  Belt in West Bengal, 46
  Coal Quality, 46
  Jharia Belt, 47
Rape Victims, 8
Rapists, 14
Ravana, 192
  Demon King of Lanka, 195
Red Tapism, 86
Reform of Mining and Mineral Pricing, 151
Reforming Bureaucracy, Police and Judiciary, Electoral System, 88
Reforms In
  Education, 298
  Judiciary, 281
  Taxation, 75, 264
Reforms, 7, 12, 43
  Of Hinduism, 200
Regional
  Parties, 40
  Political Parties, 89
Reliance Telecom, 117
Religion And Spirituality, 156
Religious
  Fundamentalism, 179
  Organizations, 161
  Reforms, 200
  Teachers and Priests, 197
Renunciation, 208
Representation of People Act, 134
Research Organization, 129
Reserve Bank of India, 255, 266, 280, 293, 296
Reservoirs, 149
  Anjunem, 149
  Salaulim, 149
Residential Zone of India, 31
Resource Entrepreneurs, 250
Revolutionaries Discoveries, 22
Revolutionary Change, 41
Right of
  Property, 103
  Education, 283
  Information, 51, 82, 143, 144
    Applications, 162
    Law, 163
  Information Act, 2005, 75, 78, 87, 158, 159, 162
  Privacy, 283
  Recall Elected Representatives, 41, 44, 133
  Reject, 41, 43, 44, 133
  Vote, 42
Rights of Tribals, 177
Rigveda, 220
Rishi
  Narad, Great Poet, 8
  Valmiki, 8 *see under* Valmiki also
Risk Management, 66
River Ganga, 194
Role of
  CBI, 91
  Civil Society, 90

Rolland, Romain, 220
Rome, 67
Roosevelt, Theodore, 189
Rosh-ha-Shana, 221, 222
Roy, Aruna, 153
Roy, Raja Rammohun, 8, 199, 200, 202
  Bengal Reformer, 202
  Great Social Reformer, 8
  Indian Religious, Social, Educational Reformer, 199
  Social Reformer, 200
Royal Navy, 219
Ruling Party, 153, 168
Rural
  Consumer Goods, 70
  Economy, 253
  Electrification, 253
  Health Insurance, 253
Russia, 97

S Tel, 114
Saffron Shining, 107
Sahajananda Swami, 202
Saints And Villains, 62
Sam Pitroda Led National Innovation Council, 26
Samadhi, 22
Sanghamitra, King Ashoka's Daughter, 196
Sanjay Chandra Unitec Group, 116
Sanskrit Poetry, 193
Sanyam, 22
Sarameyasanam, 21
Sarkari Lokpal Draft, 92
Sarnath, 198
Satan, 23, 25
Sati, 200, 201, 203
  Pratha, 8
Satiyaputras, 199
Sattari And Sanguem Taluks, 148
Satyagraha, 59, 136
Sayana, Vedic Commentator, 25
Scams, 75
Scandals, 153
  And Scams, 91
Scheduled Caste Tribes, 32
SEBI, 266
Second World War, 31
Secret Ballot, 133
Sector
  Agriculture, 266
  Financial, 266, 293, 295
  Growth, 161
  Manufacturing, 256, 258, 285
  Mining, 150
  Telecom, 115
Securities and Exchange Commission (SEC), 265
Security Forces, 169, 177
Seglitz's Joseph, Nobel Laureate, 65
Self
  Cleaning, 216, 217
  Declaration, 272
  Purification, 216, 217, 218
  Purification by Self-Observation, 241
  Realization, 208
  Transformation, 216
Sen, Amartya, 153
Sense Organs, 231
Sensory Perceptions, 74
Serial Blast at Opera House, 178
Serotonin Levels, 183-185
Service
  Charter, 78
  Sector Led Growth, 35
Sesa Goa, 152
Sexual Misconduct, 240
Shah Jahan, 201
Shah, MB, Supreme Court Justice, 149
Shahla Masood, RTI Activist Killed in Bhopal, 141
Shakespeare or Kalidasa, 191
Shamatha And Vipashyana, 226, 229
Sharad Kumar, 117
Sharma, M, 168
Shiv Sena, 152
Shri Krishna, Killed Vanasura, 192
Sicilian Mafia, 172

Singarini Collieries Ltd., 47
Singapore and Hong Kong, 142
Singh, RP, Author—2G Report, 113
Sinners, 21
Sita, 195
Sivaji,
  Software Engineer, 86
  Turned Corruption Crusader, 86
Skill
  Clusters like Auto Components Belt at Faridabad, 26
  Development, 258
  Education, 287
  Training, 287
Skilled
  Jobs, 28
  Labour, 252
Slade, Madeleine, Mrs., 219, 220
  Devoted Disciple of MK Gandhi, 219, 220
  Later Mirabehn, 220
Slaughter or Mutilation of Animals, 197
Slowdown, Impact of-, 35
Smart Cards, 135
Smugglers, 8
Smuggling Syndicate, 172
Soares Bryan, Indian Inst. of Architect, Chennai, 149
Social
  And Economic Development, 111
  And Physical Infrastructure, 253
  Awakening, 8
  Development, 124
  Disorder, 12
  Entrepreneurs, 251
  Legislation, 174
  Media Role, 90
  Network, 8
  Order, 181
  Protection Programme, 253
  Reform, 200
  Safety Net, 36
  Structure, 182
  Welfare, 16
Socially Responsible Investing (SRI), 65
Societies Act, 160
Socio-Economic Level, 185
Sorabjee, Soli, 153
South African
  Facility, 126
  Jail, 217
  Policies, 125
South Korea and Taiwan, 36
Special
  Economic Zones (SEZs), 297
  Purpose Vehicle (SPV), 286
Speculative Misadventurism, 63
Spiritual
  Experience, 205
  Practices, 209
  Qualities- Samadhi, 211
  Rebirth, 218
  Techniques, 208
  Training, 156
Spirituality, 8, 192
Sports, 16
Sri Lanka, 28
Sri Sri Ravi Shankar, 144, 145
SRI, Industry, 66
Stages of Dhyan, Dharana and Samadhi, 217
Standard Chartered Bank, 273, 274
Stanford University, 157
State
  Environmental Laws, 287
  Of Enlightenment, 208
States of Commonwealth, 95
Steglitz, Joseph E, Nobel Laureate, 294
Stock Market, 26, 52, 65, 265
Stress Reduction Programme, 233
Structural
  Reforms, 134
  Regime, 293
Stupa of Sanchi, 196
Stupas and Viharas, 196
Subprime Mortgage Lenders, 63
Subramanian, Shriram, 53

Subsidies, 34, 35
Administration of-, 34
Sufism in Middle East, 233
Super Consciousness, 231
Superstitious Practices, 200
Supreme Spirit, 25
Suresh Tendulkar Committee, 34
Survival of the Fittest, 165
Sushil Kumar, Raja's Legal Counsel, 117
Sustainable
Development, 250
Society, 75
System, 250
Swadeshi, 59
Swaminarayan Sect, 202
Swan Telecom, 116, 117, 118, 119
Sweden, 98, 165
Swiss
Bank, 104
Bank Accounts, 105
Banking Association, 105
Banks, Tax Havens, 271
Switzerland, 104, 105, 275
SY Quraishi, Chief Election Commissioner, 44
Symbolism of Hanuman, 191
System of Reward and Punishment, 82
Systematic Land Reforms, 253

Tackling Frauds Through Technology, 268
Tagore, Rabindranath, 25, 199
Taijitu Symbol, 17
Taiwan And South Korea, 285
Taj Mahal Palace, 178
Tamrapani, 198, 199
Tamsa Stream, 194
Tax
Administration, 111
Evaders, 8
Evasion, 14, 267-268
Information Exchange Agreements, (TIEA), 275
Reforms, 135
Revenues, 256
The Rich, 64
Taxation, 265
Team Anna, 44, 90, 135, 141
Technical Assistance, 122
Technique of Self-Observation, 238, 240
Technique – Courses, 229
Technologically Advanced Age, 271
Technology, 26, 158, 159, 180
Acquisition and Development Fund, 285
In Electoral Matters, 42
Up-gradation, 259, 285
Telecom
And Media, 54
Commission, 110
Growth, 112
Industry, 269
Minister, 109, 110, 114, 116, 119
Policy, 41, 109
Regulator, 110
Sector, 115
Ten
Days of Repentance, 221
Least Corrupt Countries, 98
Tendulkar
Committee, 32
Formula, 32
Terrorism, 13, 60, 180
Causes, 179
Terrorist Blasts in Delhi, 170
Terrorists, 8, 171, 177, 178
Teshuva, 221
The Ramayana,
By Rishi Valmiki, 8
The Great Epic, 8
Therapy Program, 12
Thirty Years War, 188
Thug , 171
Organized Group of Criminals, 171
Tibetan Kadampa, 211

Tifila, 221
Tihar Jail, 52
Tilak, Lokmanya, 59
Times Square, 67, 71
Timor-Leste, 260
TM Meditation, 233
Tools of Technology, Training and Research, 250
Trade
  And Agriculture, 197
  Openness, 28
  Unions Act, 291
Traditional
  Chinese Medicine, 16
  Skills, 249
TRAI (Telecom Regulatory Authority of India), 110, 114, 118, 119
TRAI's Response to CBI, 116
Training
  Opportunities, 121
  Program in Paris, 220
  Schemes, 121
Transparency, 78, 121, 149, 156, 157, 159, 160, 250, 256
  And Accountability (T&A), 79, 82, 85, 88, 120, 128, 159
  And Methodology of Auctions, 110
  In Governance Laws, 75
  In Operations of Trusts and Societies, 95
  In Spectrum Allocation, 162
  International, 101, 128, 129
Tribal Hamlets, 65
Tribals, 175
Triple Action Formula for Crime, 12, 19
Truce, 30
Trust, 93-95
Tsunami of Corruption in India, 14
Turkey, 294
TV Channels-CNN-IBN, 152
Twin Birds Verse from Rigveda, 24
Tzedakah, 221
Uganda, 125
UK, 97, 275
  Public, 168
  US and Germany, 104
UN, 121
  Development Programmes, 300
  System, 120
Unemployment, 14
Unified Access Service (UAS) Licence, 113, 115
Unitech Wireless, 117, 118
United Republic of Tanzania, 124
Universities, 197
Unnatural Sex, 21,
Unscrupulous Netas, 11
UPA, 38, 56, 109
UPA-I, 38, 56
Urban Centres, 176
Urbanization, 15
  Of India, 89
US, 62, 73, 86, 95, 97, 103, 127, 178, 179, 261, 263-265, 274, 275, 289
  Advertising Agency, 50
  And Germany, 275
  And UK, 275
  And UK Police, Special Status, 167
  Budget Deficit, 263
  Congress, 103, 158
  Economy, 254
  Federal Reserve, 254
  Leadership, 289
  Oil Companies, 262
  Psyche, 262
  Security, 263
  Supreme Court, 103
  Treasury Bonds, 254
US-Swiss Tax Treaty, 275
Utica Shale Oil, Ohio, 262
Uttar
  Pradesh Industrial Township Development Authority, 286
  Ramayana, 193, 195
Uttarakhand, 261

Vaghul, N, 51
Vairagya, 209
Vaishnava, 155
Vaitarni, 21
Valmiki,
  Adi Kavi, 193
  Ant-Hill, 193
  Ramayana, 195
  Rishi, 224
  Teachings, 193
  The Great Poet, 192
Valmikism, Religious Movement, 193
Value Based Education, 298
Valya Koli, 193
Vedanta
  College, 200
  Resources, 151
Vedas, 21
Vedic
  Exercise, 231
  Mantras, 23
  Seer, 24
Vegetarianism, 217
Velliapa Textile, 273
Vietnam, 253
Vijay Anand, 86
Vinod Rai, CAG Chief, 113, 114
Vipassana, 226, 230, 231, 239, 241, 243, 246
  Benefits, 230
  Meditation, 226, 227, 230, 232, 240, 243
  Meditation Methods, 242
Virtue of Sacrifice, 219
Vivekananda, Swamy, 12, 74
Voluntary Disclosure by Ministers, 162

Wall Street
  Agitation, 61, 72
  Operation, 64
Walmart, US Largest Seller of Fuel, 261
War Veterans, 8
Washington Square Park, 71
Water
  And Belly, 242, 243
  Transit and Irrigation System, 197
Waves and Particles, 191
West Bengal, 127
Whistle Blower, 131
  Elmer, 106
White Collar
  Crime, 166
  Criminals, 166
Wikileaks, 106
Wilberforce, William, 202
Women Protection Against Harassment, 174
World
  Bank, 123, 125, 126, 131, 132
  Bank Sponsored Working Group (WBSWG), 131
    Anti-Corruption Activities, 131
    Investigative Journalism, 131
    National Integrity, 131
  Economy, 254
  Human Development Report, 81
  Trade Organization, 134
  War, 188
  War I, 164, 172

Yakuza (Mafia), 172
Yamadharma, 21
Yang, Energy, 18
Yang, Heated Energy, 18
Yergin, Daniel, Global Oil Guru, 261
Yin-Yang, 16-18
  Balance, 18
  Concept of-, 17
  Relationship, 18
Yoga, 74, 226, 233
  Of Meditation, 208
  Practice, 8
  Sutra, 207
Yogic
  Exercises, 234
  Postures, 232
  Vashistha, 193
Yogis, 209

Yom Kippur, 221, 222
    Day of Atonement, 221, 222
You Are My Sonia, 107
Young India, 220
Yusuf Patel, 173
    Specialist in Gold and Silver Smuggling, 173
Zaveri Bazar, 178
Zen Meditation Japan, 233
Zero
    Sum Game, 44
    Tolerance, 127
Zimbabwe, 138
Zola, Emile, 164
Zuccotti Park, 71